I'm Doing Fine.
Don't Forget to Write!

by
Maria R. Eckhoff

All rights reserved. No part of this book shall be reproduced or transmitted in any form or by any means, electronic, mechanical, magnetic, photographic including photocopying, recording or by any information storage and retrieval system, without prior written permission of the publisher. No patent liability is assumed with respect to the use of the information contained herein. Although every precaution has been taken in the preparation of this book, the publisher and author assume no responsibility for errors or omissions. Neither is any liability assumed for damages resulting from the use of the information contained herein.

Copyright © 2016 by Maria R. Eckhoff

ISBN 978-1-4958-1203-3

Printed in the United States of America

Published October 2016

INFINITY PUBLISHING
1094 New DeHaven Street, Suite 100
West Conshohocken, PA 19428-2713
Toll-free (877) BUY BOOK
Local Phone (610) 941-9999
Fax (610) 941-9959
Info@buybooksontheweb.com
www.buybooksontheweb.com

Dedicated to

the Class of 1943

and

all of the men and women who served in World War II

and

those who supported the war effort from home.

May their stories never be forgotten.

Foreword

The word "Jap" seen in the World War II-era headlines, news stories, letters, and other publications is now considered derogatory, as noted in most dictionaries. In quoted material, the term is retained to ensure historical accuracy. Words and images reflect the time and should be received in that context.

All images are property of the author unless otherwise noted.

Table of Contents

Chapter 1 – The Train 1
Chapter 2 – Before the War 9
Chapter 3 – At War—Now What? 17
Chapter 4 – Great Lakes Naval Training Center 25
Chapter 5 – Class of 1943 41
    Victory Corps 42
    Meet the Class of 1943 42
    Graduation Week 59
Chapter 6 – Clinton 67
Chapter 7 – Whidbey 115
Chapter 8 – Port Hueneme: ACORNs and CASUs 135
Chapter 9 – Finally Left Port 141
Chapter 10 – Destination Unknown: South Pacific 149
Chapter 11 – Saipan, Mariana Islands 155
Chapter 12 – NAB Kobler 163
Chapter 13 – Going Home 191
Afterward 205

Chapter 1 – The Train

Larry had barely settled into the well worn seat when the train lurched forward. *Now I've done it. There's no turning back.* In the distance, an insistent horn bellowed a staccato rhythm not unlike that of Morse Code—Long...Long...short Long—the telltale signal of a train saying "See you later."

Outside the somewhat grimy windows on both sides of the Pullman car, the view was limited to dozens of other cars on adjacent tracks—one pulling into the huge terminal, others at rest. The passengers all looked the same—soldiers, sailors, merchant marines—all in uniform—interspersed with civilian boys, not quite men, probably on a train for the first time. Some were headed to uncertain destinations, others passing through or perhaps making a welcome—but all too brief—visit home.

The dark haired, fresh faced young man barely noticed any of it, his mind awash with conflicting images of his family and thoughts of patriotism and the future and duty...but where did his duty really lie? Had he done the right thing signing up for service in the Navy? Mom did sign her approval on his enlistment papers. Maybe he rationalized, "Well, if I hadn't enlisted, I would have been drafted—I could have ended up anywhere. Not sure I would have fit in with the Army." Did he know that Air Force flight crews going to Europe had about 25 missions in their tour of duty? Did he know that only 1 in 3 of those crews survived the full tour with many lost before five missions? What was it like on a ship in the ocean? He'd never even seen the ocean except in pictures. It could be exciting to see other parts of the world but this isn't a vacation and why did the world have to be at war when he graduated from high school?

Minutes ago he was one of hundreds making their way through the massive Union Terminal with its art deco styling and rotunda resembling the shell of an enormous opera house. Inside, the dome was ringed by massive murals constructed of tiny colored tiles and featuring people of all walks of life who made Cincinnati great—an artistic metaphor mirroring the activity of the populace passing below. Standing in the long queue in front of the window, which looked like an oversize gilded bird cage, Larry shifted from one foot to the other while waiting his turn. He wondered whether his cousin Milton was selling train tickets today.

Chapter 1 – The Train

It was slightly more than 10 years ago when Union Terminal, the first unified rail station in Cincinnati, opened for business. In addition to trains coming and going, the facility offered plush men's and women's lounges with restrooms and bathtubs for passengers who desired a respite from a long journey. Travelers could purchase everything from clothing, toys, and books, to the latest newspapers and periodicals right off of the newsstand. After a light meal, an air conditioned movie in the newsreel theater was just the place to pass time while waiting for a train.

A postcard of Union Terminal in Cincinnati, Ohio circa 1940

When it was time to leave, passengers boarded from one of 16 gates in the 450 foot long concourse which straddled the tracks behind the rotunda. Luggage was taken by elevator to a room under the tracks where a tunnel and ramps led to the platforms for loading.

Neon sign on a corner wall at Union Terminal leading to the concourse

Chapter 1 – The Train

A mere three months ago, when Larry was probably more concerned about mid-term exams than what was going on at Cincinnati's train hub, he might have seen this article in one local paper and wondered about his future.

Buried on page 29 of the March 19, 1943 *Cincinnati Post*, an article by Alfred Segal mused about the "Poignant Realities of Conflict Seen in Railway Station." The author "went to Union Terminal to look for the war." It was the waning weeks of winter in the Ohio valley and by many accounts, the war seemed far away. Oh sure, there were updates in the three daily papers, the *Cincinnati Enquirer*, *The Cincinnati Post*, and *The Cincinnati Times-Star*, and radio provided daily commentary. Those who could afford it, caught the MovieTone newsreels at a local theater before the main feature. Still, it seemed like one day was just like the last—business as usual if you will.

> "Downtown you'd scarcely know there's a war on. The way things go on as usual. Women shopping for spring outfits. Men rushing around on their ordinary business. People in cocktail lounges."
>
> "'You've got to go to the railway station to see the war and to feel it,' we were told and that's where we went, and took a seat and watched the war march past. The thousands of soldiers and sailors marching to their mysterious destinies."
>
> "It was around 6 and every train was pouring them out singly and in companies. They were passing through, stopping off to change trains, marching double-file to dinner in the terminal's restaurant."
>
> "People hurrying to their trains stopped to look at them with the kind of reverence that takes its hat off. They looked like all America: The scholarly-looking soldier with the spectacles. The slender one who may have been a window trimmer at the Emporium of Four Corners, Wis. The 18 year-old who only a few days ago put his school books away. Negro boys. Chinese. An Indian. Two Filipinos."
>
> "An enormous poster hangs from the rainbow-like dome of the terminal: Three powerful bared arms stretch upward: The arm of a soldier with a rifle flanked by the arms of workmen, and over all the words: 'Strong in the strength of the Lord, we who fight the people's cause will never stop until the cause is won.'"
>
> "Yes, that's how interminable it looked: The march through the station never stopped. This seemed a cross-roads on the American way and never a moment without the tramp of footsteps marching."
>
> "A train had unloaded a company of boys in steel helmets. Until this moment the steel helmet had been seen here only in the pictures from North Africa and Guadalcanal. Now it was like something bringing poignant reality. People said these must be boys going to ships."
>
> "USO ladies were standing by not obtrusively but deferentially... 'Would you like to rest in the USO lounge? It's just at the left of the entrance.'"
>
> "'Thank you ma'am, ever so much.'"

United Service Organizations (USO) was created in 1940 before the United States entered World War II initially to provide Canteen services for the troops. President Franklin

Chapter 1 – The Train

Roosevelt contacted six private organizations—the National Catholic Community Service, National Jewish Welfare Board, Salvation Army, Traveler's Aid Association, YMCA, and YWCA—and asked them to find ways to meet on-leave recreation needs for the members of the Armed Forces, focusing on their spiritual, religious, educational, and welfare needs. The organizations formed a joint entity and the USO was incorporated February 4, 1941. They set up recreation and food facilities in railroad stations of larger towns. There were also community oriented and Red Cross canteens scattered across the country.

One of the first USO lounges in the country when it was opened in May, 1941, Union Terminal USO eventually served nearly 3 million service members.

Entrance to USO at Union Terminal, Cincinnati

Volunteers from various cultural and religious backgrounds baked pretzels, donuts, and cookies to serve their guests. The USO lounge and the rest of the terminal's public spaces were open to all regardless of color which was not always the case in some parts of town. As the war continued, the USO provided cots and bunk beds for traveling soldiers.

Back on the train, Larry loosened his shirt collar as the stagnant air on the barely moving train compounded with the heat and humidity prevalent this time of year in Cincinnati was making him sweat. At least there would be some air movement through the open windows of the coaches when the locomotive picked up speed.

As the train continued on its northward route, young men's hearts may have leapt briefly at the sight of Crosley Field, home of the Cincinnati Reds, near the C&O tracks. They could almost smell the fresh roasted peanuts from Jim Shelton's cart. The black man nattily clad in a top hat, bow tie, and tails with his ever present smile was a fixture with his cart just outside the ball park since 1932. *The Cincinnati Times-Star* reported that the Reds were in third place in the eight team National League, one game behind Leo Durocher's second place Brooklyn Dodgers with a record of 27-22. First place was held by the St. Louis

Chapter 1 – The Train

Cardinals at 31-18. Closing his eyes, a young man could almost taste beefy, sizzling hot dogs slathered in yellow mustard, his mouth watering at the thought, while the Redlegs—Lonnie Frey, Estel Crabtree, Gee Walker, Frank McCormick, Steve Mesner, Eric Tipton, Eddie Miller, Ray Mueller, and Ray Starr raced from the third base dugout onto the field. He dozed off to sleep listening to an imaginary play by play and echoes of the voices of former Yankee pitcher Waite Hoyt, Lee Allen, and Dick Bray.

What a difference six years makes. During the last two weeks of January 1937 when six to twelve inches of rain fell in Ohio, the Ohio River flooded communities from Pittsburgh, Pennsylvania to Cairo, Illinois and everywhere in between. For people still picking themselves up from the Dust Bowl era and trying to survive the Depression, the devastation was stunning. Parts of Cincinnati were under water for 19 days, with 10% of the city inundated. Electricity and fresh water were in short supply. More than 50,000 people were homeless. With the river finally cresting 28 feet above flood stage and nine feet over the record set in 1884, Cincinnati was reeling.

Streetcar service in the area was curtailed but Union Terminal and most of the tracks were an island barely reachable with most approaches under water. Even with 80 feet of flood water, and some flooding of lower levels, most of the terminal, including tracks and platforms, remained dry.

And Crosley Field? The center and left field walls were completely covered by water. Only the light standards and part of the grandstand roof protruded from the murky water as it engulfed the rest of the Mill Creek Valley. Undeterred, a couple of players took to a boat and rowed over home plate which was under 21 feet of water.

As the train meandered along, many young men tried to take their minds off of the trip by studying the lighter sections of *The Cincinnati Times-Star*. Larry might have noticed that the Evanston Theatre was showing "Meanest Man in the World" and "Mayor of 44th Street"; and on Sunday Gene Tierney and George Montgomery would be featured in "China Girl." He wondered when he would see Evanston again. Flipping to the comics, a smile could be persuaded by Moon Mullins, Dick Tracy, Joe Palooka, or Little Orphan Annie.

Reality reemerged at the sight of an article titled "Cigarettes Needed on Fighting Fronts." Yes, believe it or not, the greater Cincinnati area had a campaign to acquire 10,000,000 "Smokes for the Folks in our Fighting Forces." They had arrangements with cigarette companies to buy them at 5 cents a pack for overseas shipment. Persons or organizations who donated $50.00 or more could have their name placed on the package. At the height of the war, cigarettes sold for about 80 cents a pack in North Africa.

The public was also encouraged to buy War Bonds and stamps and the Red Cross held blood drives for soldiers. Larry's sister, Dorothy, donated blood one time but found out she was anemic and couldn't donate after that. However, their mother went by streetcar to give blood on more than one occasion during the war.

Though another article reported the first production B-29 bomber had rolled off the Wichita line this month and the allies in the Pacific battled for Guadalcanal, here in Ohio, as in most parts of the country, the biggest change to daily life was mandatory rationing. It included shoes and liquor—one quart (by package) or one quart by glass per ration period (two quarts in four weeks).

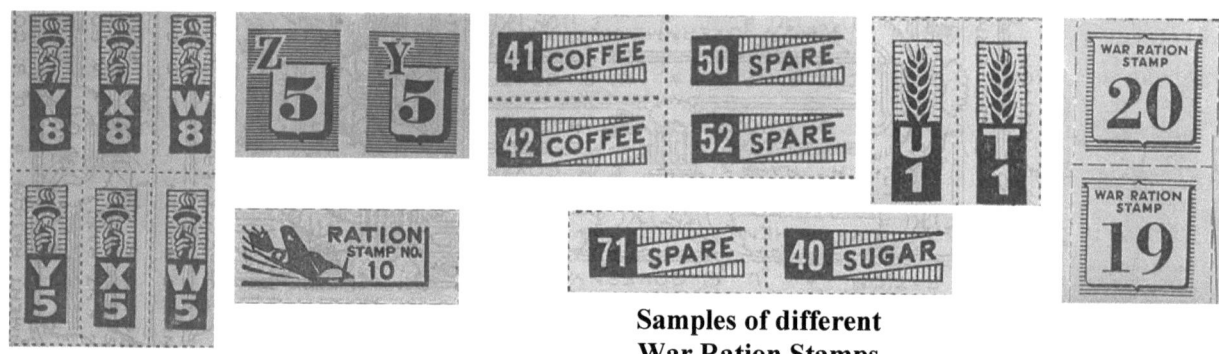

Samples of different War Ration Stamps

Christ and Good Samaritan hospitals in Cincinnati were designated as emergency base hospitals by the Office of Civilian Defense and a staff of physicians was to be organized at each one. Emergency staffs were organized to care for casualties from abroad should it become necessary. Arrangements were also made outside each city in case a hospital was bombed during an air raid.

Someone passed a copy of *The Cincinnati Post*, the second of the three local dailies to circulate through the car. No one wanted to read about the planned blackout that was held around town a week or so ago. The Civilian Defense Corps wanted to do a surprise blackout. Many people didn't realize that regulations required them to prepare to black out all lights in their homes, schools, or other establishments. Blackout violators were fined $25 each (a lot of money in those days).

Chapter 1 – The Train

Front and back covers of a Civilian Defense Index booklet distributed locally

The pocket size Civilian Defense Index provided detailed advice about a variety of topics that citizens needed to know about in the event the war reached the United States.

The first half covered topics such as Air Raid Precautions and Blackout Information, while the second half provided detailed first aid instructions.

Readers instead wanted to imagine being at Coney Island amusement park's 57th birthday celebration. A bonus was getting to hear clarinet player Jimmy James and his orchestra at

7

Moonlite Gardens with Betty Benson providing vocals. Oh to be on the Island Queen riverboat as it left the foot of Broadway downtown during one of its five times daily excursions up river to the park at the eastern edge of town. Though many just took the bus or streetcar into the city to board the Queen, round trip fare on the riverboat included parking if you or your friends were lucky enough to have a car and enough gasoline ration stamps to make the drive from your neighborhood. Saturday and Sunday admission to Coney was 50 cents for adults and 25 cents for children.

Passengers entering Coney Island from the Island Queen on the Ohio River

While the *Post* told how the Gilbert Islands in the south Pacific were pounded by Navy planes, Larry was outwardly relaxed as he stared out the window, southern Ohio slowly being left behind though his mind was still churning with a cyclone of thoughts. Then his mind focused on a single image—his dad. How he missed him. The 20th was Father's Day and now he was leaving home without any fanfare, only 17 years old, going to an uncertain future in the United States Navy while the world was at war.

Chapter 2 – Before the War

As the freshman class of 146 boys walked, bicycled, or took the streetcar to Purcell High School in September, 1939, it must have been with a sense of unease. Europe, politically and economically unstable since the end of World War I, was a powder keg. Adolf Hitler and his National Socialist (Nazi) party rearmed Germany and furthered his ambitions of world domination by signing strategic treaties with Japan and Italy. While the 13 and 14 year olds were adjusting to a new school, joining clubs, and doing all of the things teenage kids did in 1939, Hitler invaded Poland and drove France and Great Britain to declare war on Germany. In the lands across the mighty Atlantic ocean, World War II had begun.

It was in the newspapers. It was part of the suppertime conversations. Did America really have anything to worry about? After all, an ocean separated the United States from the conflicts abroad. So went the debates.

William and Anna Eckhoff on their wedding day circa 1921

It had already been an unsettling year for Larry. Exactly one month after he became a teenager, his dad, William, passed away of a brief illness (apparently meningitis) on a cold winter day in January, 1939, only weeks before his 48th birthday. Bill, as he was called, was the third youngest of ten children born to a German immigrant father, a tailor who had passed on in 1918, and a mother from Kentucky, herself the middle child of twelve. In addition to his mother and six surviving siblings, Bill left behind a wife, Anna, and seven children between the ages of sixteen and thirteen months. Larry was the eldest son, in the eighth grade, with two older sisters in high school, each born only a year apart.

Across America, kids were growing up in tight knit communities or on family farms. Before Pearl Harbor, the world was limited to their own neighborhood—some number of blocks of houses and storefronts or acres of fields along dirt roads. For some city kids, war was the biggest adventure of their lives. In 1940, only about half of American homes had "full" indoor plumbing—running water, private bath, flush toilet—and nearly 25% had no electricity.

Chapter 2 – Before the War

Many folks had ice boxes instead of refrigerators and back yard outhouses were still common in many areas. In the *Williams Cincinnati City Directory*, a bell symbol between the house number and the family name indicated the residence had a telephone.

The Cincinnati & Suburban Bell Telephone Company placed an ad in a September, 1940 issue of *The Cincinnati Post*:

"Weather Forecast for the Year: Always tough going for people without Telephones"
"Heat, cold, rain, snow—there's always something unpleasant for those who choose to run errands instead of telephoning them. The telephone is a splendid buy, if only for the speed and convenience it adds to your goings and comings, and for its prevention of damage and discomfort in all kinds of weather. The cost of this service is only a few pennies a day. Save yourself and save your money—order a telephone today."

A telephone? These were families trying to survive after the stock market crashed in 1929. There was much poverty as so many people lost everything when the banks collapsed. They worked hard and did the best they could with what they had. During the Depression, some older kids found work on farms and made a little money. That also meant their share of what little food there was could then go to their siblings at home. Joining the Army was a step up for many—at least they would be assured boots, clothing, and three meals a day.

Still, there were plenty of things for Cincinnati teenagers to do, if they could afford it.

September brought the first week of the 1940-1941 skating season at the Norwood Roller Rink with skate-dancers in abundance trying their "skate legs" for the first time since the rink closed the previous spring for complete remodeling. Among the new features were a dairy bar with booth service, new indirect lighting, and a supply of white skate shoes for the ladies. Skating was held nightly except Monday while bowling was the latest sport to win over the school crowd.

Many Cincinnati neighborhoods had their own movie house and the Evanston Theatre boasted a twin bill with Lon Chaney Jr. starring in "One Million B.C." and Wayne Morris featured in "Flight Angel."

The Back to School section of one local newspaper showed images of typical boy's high school attire being sold: "the popular wool sweater, tweed trousers, and school shoes."

The Cincinnati Times-Star headlines that same week both threatened and encouraged:

Chapter 2 – Before the War

"Will 'Erase' Cities of Britain, Hitler Warns"
"Three Air Raids are Beaten Off By Brits"
"U. S. Speeds Action to Take Over Bases"
"Hitler to Seek Revenge on U.S." – Churchill

"Biggest Attack of War on London"
"Huge Waves of German bombers in groups of 20, sweep in over capital" after 16 hours of surcease

Seemingly insignificant was President Franklin D. Roosevelt's trade with England: 50 old Navy destroyers went to England for their fight with Germany in exchange for a 99 year lease of naval and air bases in British territories in the Atlantic—two in Newfoundland, Bermuda, Antigua, St. Lucia, Trinidad, British Guiana, and the Bahamas. FDR said "they will keep the enemy from our front door." A year later he would find out his "back door" was far more vulnerable.

At the same time, a debate raged in Congress on the Burke-Wadsworth compulsory military training bill. Some members assailed conscription and accused FDR of trying to embroil the U.S. in the war. In some circles, this was no insignificant argument.

The threat of a draft was affecting major league baseball's ability to sign the players they scouted. Cardinal scout Jack Ryan said "We can't afford to invest the money of our clubs in the young fellows who will be first in line for conscription...of course, if a youngster performs with exceptional ability, we sign him up. However, there are many players we'd like to develop further in the farm clubs. The threat of conscription makes it inadvisable for us to offer them contracts." Semi-pro teams and sandlots produced more good talent than in many years.

The far away war news ran right next to an ad for a new 1941 Hudson Six DeLuxe sedan $846 (white wall tires, deluxe hub caps, and new deluxe running boards extra) by the Hudson and Terraplane Sales Corp, 1038 Gilbert Avenue, Distributor.

There were efforts afoot to include area state highways and bridges as part of the 80,000 mile network of "strategic military roads", which had to support tanks and heavy gun carriages, because the infrastructure was more likely to be maintained.

By December, tension with Japan was increasing. The Sunday morning *Cincinnati Enquirer* was printed December 7, 1941 before the bombing occurred. The page 1 headline "Roosevelt Protests to Mikado" was a direct message to Emperor Hirohito and was viewed as a possible "step of last resort" to avert an open break with Japan. At the time, there were roughly 125,000 Japanese troops with concentrations in French Indo-China and two heavily escorted Japanese convoys headed to the Gulf of Siam.

The page 2 headline "Increased Navy is Needed to Defend Seas, (Secretary) Knox Says" sharpened the focus a bit more. During the 12 months which ended June 30, 1940, 325 new ships were commissioned and 2059 new airplanes acquired. There was a net increase in personnel of 15,259 officers and 100,282 enlisted men. At year's end, there were 3926 aircraft, an increase of 82% over the previous year with an emphasis on dive bombers and fighter types "of greater hitting power." Pilot personnel increased 48%.

That same Sunday issue regaled the weary with possibility in the Travel Section.

"Transportation Attacks Huge Task; Citizens Seek Escape from Humdrum"
"Reserve Resources Used As Air, Rail Lines Unite In Winter Rush to South"

The transportation and travel business was also influenced by the defense priorities. Ocean-going vessels were requisitioned for defense traffic and two-thirds of the world removed from travel routes but many Americans were still ready for a journey and dozens of tourist destinations were enumerated in the long article. Railroads were confronted with the most difficult problems in years. Officials had to set up new schedules and requisition long-idle equipment to handle troop movements and heavy freight traffic to all parts of the country.

> "Riding trains in any direction one sees officers of the Army, Navy, and Marines traveling on defense errands. Nearly every train has a troop car coupled to the baggage cars immediately in the rear of the engines. Railway and bus terminals seem unusually busy with soldiers, marines, and sailors, traveling singly and in groups."

Few resort cities in the South who catered to winter vacationers were not situated near an Army or Marine base. Many of their local social and municipal organizations, along with the USO, provided entertainment for men in uniform in these areas. Beaches, skating rinks, and golf courses were open to them without charge. Even private homeowners were ready to share their hospitality and dining rooms with the men during Christmas week.

By lunchtime, everything changed.

***The Cincinnati Enquirer*, Monday, December 8, 1941, 6:00 a.m. Extra**
"American Battleship Reported Sunk, Another is Set Afire in Jap Attack"
[7:35 am PH/Honolulu time, 1:05 EST)

Hirohito announced Japan was at war with the U.S. at 6:00 a.m., 2 hrs 55 minutes after the White House heard reports of the Sunday morning raid on Hawaiian defenses. The Pan Am base on the Pacific island of Guam was also bombed.

Associated Press December 7 Washington

"Civil Aeronautics Authority issued orders grounding all private airplanes in the U.S. and its possessions, except commercial airliners."

The Cincinnati Enquirer, Monday, December 8, 1941, 6:00 a.m. Extra, page 1

"Heavy Losses Suffered By Army and Navy, Roosevelt Reveals", Washington, December 7

—(AP)—"President Roosevelt informed cabinet officers and congressional leaders of both parties tonight of 'doubtless heavy losses sustained by the navy and also large losses sustained by the army in Hawaii. The careful…phraseology hinted at blacker tidings to come."

"Japan attacked every main United States and British possession in the Central and Western Pacific and invaded Thailand today in a hasty but evidently shrewdly-planned prosecution of a war she began Sunday without warning."

"The Japanese formal declaration of war against both the United States and Britain came two hours and 55 minutes after Japanese planes spread death and terrific destruction in Honolulu and Pearl Harbor at 7:35 a.m., Hawaiian time (1:05 p.m. Eastern Standard Time) Sunday."

"The claimed successes for this fell swoop included sinking of the United States battleship West Virginia and setting afire of the battleship Oklahoma."

"…Compiled from official and unofficial accounts from all affected countries, the record ran like this:"

"Honolulu bombed a second time; Lumber-laden United States Army transport torpedoed 1300 miles west of San Francisco and another transport in distress; Shanghai's International Settlement seized; United States gunboat Wake captured there and British gunboat Peterel destroyed; Capture of the United States Island of Wake; Bombing of the United States Island of Guam; Bombing of many points throughout the Philippine Islands; Invasion of Northern Malaya and bombing of Singapore; Invasion of Thailand (Siam) and bombing of Bangkok; report 104 dead"

"Wave after wave of planes streaked over Oahu in an attack which the army said started at 8:10 a.m., Honolulu time, and which ended at around 9:25, an hour and 15 minutes later. Witnesses said they counted at least 50 planes in the initial attack."

"The attack seemed to center on Hickam Field, a huge army airport three miles northwest of Honolulu, and Honolulu, where the islands' heaviest fortifications are located.....Army officials said two Japanese planes had been shot down in the Honolulu area. Planes which did not bomb Pearl Harbor apparently headed for Hickam Field. But there the attackers apparently did not confine themselves to the heavily fortified areas. From Wahiawa, a town of 3,000 population about twenty miles northwest of Honolulu, came reports that 10 or more persons were injured when enemy planes sprayed bullets on the streets."

That same Extra edition outlined "war measures" being taken immediately within the United States following the "hostilities with Japan":

Chapter 2 – Before the War

- Censorship was imposed on all outgoing communications
- Amateur radio communications were halted except for those specifically authorized in connection with the emergency
- All army and navy officers were ordered to wear their uniforms instead of civilian clothes
- Suspicious aliens rounded up on Pacific Coast and in Alaska, Hawaii, and Panama Canal Zone
- Industrial plants were directed to guard against sabotage
- Departure of Japanese from the U.S. and financial transactions by Japanese were banned
- Armed guards were thrown around key buildings in the capital
- Securities Commission reported to be studying whether to close security exchanges tomorrow
- Mayor Angelo J. Rossi of San Francisco declared the city to be in a state of emergency
- The Police Chief of Norfolk, VA, ordered all Japanese to be arrested

The chairman of the Civil Aeronautics Authority, Robert H. Hinckley, announced that all American airlines, on domestic and foreign routes, were instructed to take no Japanese nationals on board. Yet the "danger of war hysteria" was also a hot topic.

The next day, *The Cincinnati Post* reported that the U.S. Navy was reducing the minimum term of enlistment from four years to two.

> "It was emphasized, however, that volunteers for both the Navy and the Navy Reserve must serve throughout the national emergency, or for the duration of any war in which this country might be involved."
>
> "Although the Navy's announcement of the new short-term enlistment did not state the reason for the changed policy, it was believed to be connected with the drop in enlistments for naval services which followed the torpedoing of the destroyers Kearney and Reuben James."
>
> "Regular enlistments in the Navy are for six-year terms."

To add insult to injury, it was reported that the bombs dropped on Honolulu were probably made from metals sent to Japan from the U.S. This included scrap iron, oil, ferro-alloys, autos and parts, metal working machinery, aircraft and parts.

> "This country has been supplying Japan with the raw materials of war for many years. Our exports of war goods to Japan actually increased after the invasion of China began.."
>
> "In 1937 this country supplied 54 percent of all strategic war materiels imported by Japan. In 1938 it supplied 56 percent."
>
> "In 1939 scrap exports from here to Japan were still going up. This country was furnishing almost all of Japan's aviation gasoline. There was some debate in Congress about an embargo, but no action."
>
> "In the first quarter of 1941...the United States sent Japan 8,341,000 pounds of lead, nearly three times the quantity sent in the same period of 1940...1,097,000 barrels of gasoline, nearly five times as much. It was not until mid-summer that trade with Japan was brought to a halt."

Across the Atlantic in London, England, Winston Churchill declared war on Japan fulfilling a pledge made in November that Britain would stand with the United States if war came to the Pacific. Canada and the Netherlands East Indies also formally declared war with Japan on the same day.

***The Cincinnati Post*, Monday, December 8, 1941, page 18**
"Cincinnatians Calm But Grim at News Of Japan's Attack"
"Street Crowds Eager For War News, Read Without Emotion"

"Cincinnatians took the news that Japan had declared war on the United States with a calmness typical of a people schooled in international surprises."

"But all were deeply interested, and a chill wind that whipped through Fountain Square failed to drive the men and women from the corner of Walnut and Fifth street, where scores grabbed newspaper extras as fast as they appeared and watched late war bulletins on an electric sign."

"Except for a larger crowd than that usually found at the square, there were few expressions concerning the move that has at last brought America into the new world conflict. Overcoats were tightly buttoned against the cold wind, and the features of men and women were set in grim determination."

"Newspaper boys screaming 'War Extra!' netted hundreds of sales, and while persons who searched the news columns for added information eagerly, they read without emotion."

"One man, standing among a dozen others before the window of WCPO on Walnut street, studied a bulletin carrying unconfirmed reports that a U.S. warship had been sunk in the engagement at Pearl Harbor. He clutched a cigar firmly in his teeth."

"'What fools we were,' he said, 'to sell them scrap iron. They're using it on us now.'"

"It was a day when Christmas shoppers went about their business with an undertone of gloom darkening faces that wanted to be cheery."

"It was a holy day too, for Catholics who heard priests at Masses request prayers for a 'speedy and honorable peace, especially on this feast day honoring the Blessed Virgin, patroness of our country …'"

"Then neighbors began calling friends. Tenants cried upstairs to as whether the Joneses had heard it right."

"'Did they say the Japs had bombed Hawaii?' 'Is it true, this broadcast about fighting against the United States?'"

"Mothers whose sons had been drafted, sisters whose brothers only recently wrote home about being with the folks for Christmas, sweethearts waiting for another love letter…these were the women whose heart strings fear clutched in a place even so distant from the smoky theater of war as Cincinnati. Then downtown radio stations picked up the dreaded news."

"WCPO's front windows magnetized crowds of spell-bound men, women, and children. WCKY's lighted bulletin board focused all eyes upward."

"Just a few squares away, the gradually filling streets bore scores of parents with children, downtown to see the Christmas sights. A huge Santa Claus in the Fair Store continued his raucous 'Ha! Ha! Ha! Merry Christmas.'"

Chapter 2 – Before the War

As a Junior in High School and just days from his 16th birthday, did Larry's view of the future change as President Roosevelt officially declared war on Japan? Did Larry and his family ever talk about him going to college? Sixteenth birthdays were supposed to be momentous occasions. The newspaper headlines read as follows:

The Cincinnati Enquirer, **Wednesday, December 10, 1941**
"Yanks Will Win! Roosevelt Says; Calls Nazis and Italians Enemies"
"Japanese Claim Sinking of Two British Warships"

The Cincinnati Post, **Wednesday, December 10, 1941**
"U.S. Army Battles Invasion in Philippines, Routs Japs"
"2 British Battleships Sunk by Japanese"
"Both Coasts Hear New Air Raid Alarms"
"Thousands on Way to Work in New York as Sirens Wail"
"Military Training in Schools Discussed"

Articles about the chance of initiating compulsory military training in Cincinnati high schools, as discussed by the Board of Education, and about dormitory girls at the College of Music forming a Knitting unit under the auspices of the Red Cross were overshadowed by the full page Christmas ads for Pogue's, Sears Roebuck and Co., Rollman's, and Shillito's department stores.

The Cincinnati Post, **Wednesday, December 10, 1941, page 13 and 15, by Richard C. Hottelet, United Press Staff Correspondent; Washington, Dec. 10**
"Report U.S., Britain, Dutch To Join Navies Against Japs"
"Officials Say Such Combination Gives Allies Preponderance of Sea Power; See Hard Fight Ahead"

"The sinking of the British battleship Prince of Wales and the battle cruiser Repulse today shocked American naval officials who still were awaiting details of a 'serious attack' to their own fleet at Hawaii."

"Prince of Wales, newest battleship of the British navy, was a sister ship of the King George V. The two ships were the first of a class of five 35,000 ton battleships which many naval experts held to be almost unsinkable."

Whatever possibilities Larry and his friends may have considered for their post-high school lives, barring a quick end to the war, would have to be put on hold. The only certainty this day was uncertainty and the greater likelihood that the future held military service in one form or another.

Chapter 3 – At War—Now What?

"They've bombed Pearl Harbor!" "Who's Pearl Harbor?"

That may have been the first reaction of many people unfamiliar with the geography of the U.S. territory of Hawaii. Couple that with the fact that most people were focused on events going on in Europe. Many Depression era Americans were only the first or second generation born in this country of European immigrants and a large percentage of Cincinnatians still had relatives living in places like Germany and Ireland, with still others in Italy, England, and Scotland. They didn't know much about issues in the Pacific.

Service to the country didn't seem like such a bad deal to men with families still reeling from the Crash. Work was still hard to find in the late 1930s leading up to the war. To some young men who had never strayed beyond their own neighborhoods, the prospect seemed like an exciting adventure, though patriotism loomed large. Some men most intrigued by the Navy had never seen a ship up close.

Soon after the declaration of war, posters appeared on every imaginable wall encouraging service in the military and at home. Civilian airplane spotters were particularly desired due to concerns about German attacks on the East coast. Spotters had to roughly determine a plane's altitude, direction, and distance then report to the appropriate authorities.

The Eckhoff family moved to their middle class Evanston neighborhood in 1934, leaving William and Anna's original little white house in College Hill, a suburb across town. Most of the houses were two story clapboards, many with a third floor attic, and a basement. Front porches were the norm but it was not unusual to also have a back porch. Most summers, the family had a garden, mainly tomato plants.

The older girls walked (a long walk, according to Dorothy) to Cincinnati's Commercial High School in East Walnut Hills, though they briefly attended St. Mary's, an all female school some miles away. Larry attended the all male Purcell High School, while his younger siblings old enough to attend school were close by at St. Francis DeSales elementary.

Beginning in his junior year at Purcell, Larry worked as a store clerk at Glicksberg Pharmacy located at the corner of 1901 Hewitt Avenue and Wold not far from his home. From September, 1941 to June, 1942, he somehow managed to work 35 hours per week, for 0.25 cents per hour, while also attending high school. The druggist who owned the store was Hyman E. Glicksberg. It is unknown whether anyone working there got a sense of Mr. Glicksberg's concern for European Jews or relatives he might have there. Larry's sister Dorothy, one year older than her brother, said they didn't hear much about what was happening with the Jewish people in Europe. During the last six months of Larry's senior year, January through June 10, 1943, he was a soda dispenser at Glicksberg's soda fountain. Preparing and serving soft drinks and ice cream dishes, working behind the counter, and selling merchandise in the drug store earned Larry $6.50 per week.

William Eckhoff and six children circa Spring 1936-Larry, age 10, on top step with his dad; middle from left Dorothy and Mary Jane (holding Billy), front: Donald and Lois

There were five Christmas seasons during which the United States was officially at war—from 1941 to 1945. People were coping with the uncertainty and learning about far flung places they'd never heard of. Not many high school students had cars, and in February, 1942 automobile production stopped in favor of war material production. Even getting to the train stations may have required using gasoline rations if people had access to a car. In Japan, they celebrated the anniversary of the succession of Emperor Hirohito on December 25. In Cincinnati, many tried to decorate for the season and get in the Christmas spirit while also supporting the war effort. Writing letters and sending packages to service

Chapter 3 – At War—Now What?

members was another way to show ones patriotism and people were encouraged to write even if they didn't personally know someone in the service.

At one point, Admiral Halsey made a plea to Admiral Nimitz: "Please stop the flow of Washington experts and sightseers to the war zones. Each expert means 200 less pounds of mail." Word from home was vital to the morale of service members who daily waited to hear their names called during Mail Call.

News was slow. Citizens depended mainly on radio and newspapers, and to a lesser degree, newsreels at theaters, for information.

The peace sign (which later became a symbol of the 1960s Vietnam War protest movement) arose in 1940 as a sign of Victory when "a Belgian refugee called for a V to be marked on walls in defiance of the Germans." On radio, they used the opening notes of Beethoven's 5th Symphony, which happen to be Morse code for V—dot dot dot dash—and Churchill used the V with his fingers for Victory.

In Cincinnati, "Glory Girls" held a Victory Book campaign collecting donated books for the troops. On February 10, 1942 the first 3000 books were loaded on a Green Line Steamboat headed for Louisville, Kentucky and then on to Fort Knox to be shipped to soldiers.

Sharonville USO girls by the piano circa 1944, L to R, (seated) Ruth Potthoff, (standing) Erma Dunlap, Florence Barkau, Pauline Lehrter, Abigail Mehaffie, Elaine Duermit, Ruth Mehaffie, Jeannette Haubner (with pearls), Mildred Sheldon, Jeanne Lehrter, (next to chair) Frances Even, Iona Glazer, Kathleen Jesse, Audrey Fenstermacher

Chapter 3 – At War—Now What?

It wasn't only the older students and adults dealing with the war. Around the city and in the northernmost part of the county, in the small town suburbs and semi-rural areas of Evendale and Sharonville, elementary students were actively engaged in the war effort. Both towns have their roots as farmer way stations and count many veterans of the Civil War. As the Big Four Railroad grew up along the stagecoach road, the towns saw many World War I doughboys pass through the depot, residents and non-residents alike. So it was not surprising that the towns did what they could during this latest conflict. Everyone knew someone in military service, supporting the Red Cross, or participating in the USO center at the Big Four YMCA, adjacent to Sharon Yard.

The pupils of Evendale Public School published a school paper called *The Spotlight*. Three consecutive holiday issues, published December 29, 1941, December 24, 1942, and December 24, 1943, included articles with their young perspectives on the war and the ways they were contributing. In addition, the January 28, 1942 issue of *The Engineer*, published by the students at Sharonville School a couple of miles further north, had insight by another young author. While considering war alongside their holiday celebrations, they learned about staying calm in the face of conflict, doing for others who were less fortunate, and conserving precious resources.

"WAR"

"Japan made a bad mistake by striking at Pearl Harbor without warning. It will make every true American angry, and make the soldiers fight harder. It was a bad thing for them to do. The Americans will realize that they must fight harder if we are to keep the small islands in the Pacific Ocean, off the coast of Japan."

"If an air raid alarm should come when your children are at school, the Organization for Civilian Defense says you should watch out for your safety, and the teacher will look out for your child. Do not use the telephone, for you might prevent an important call from the fire department or some other important place. Stay off the streets, and get under cover. This is hard advice, but if you obey the rules you will be helping yourself and our government. (Similar advice was published in *The Engineer*.)"

"County Having Scrap Metal Hunt"

"We can hunt scrap metal if we want to during Christmas vacation. The child in the county who finds the most scrap gets a 25 dollar war bond, and the one that comes second gets five dollars in war stamps. We have blanks from the County Scrap Committee on which to write down what we locate and tell what kind of scrap it is. We don't have to haul it in; we just have to tell where it is, and they will get it."

"American Junior Red Cross Badges"

"We gave out American Junior Red Cross Badges this month. Everybody got one. You were supposed to wear them on your coat. Last year they were tin, but this year they are cardboard. They gave them out because they wanted to show who was helping the soldiers and other needy children and people."

Chapter 3 – At War—Now What?

"Save for America"
"The Boy Scouts are making a weekly campaign to collect all the paper they can. This is one way that we are helping our country to defend itself from enemies. We would like you to help us by saving all your papers. The Boy Scouts of America want to help Uncle Sam in every way they can."

In December, 1942 as the first anniversary of the Pearl Harbor attack approached, Larry, like many high school seniors, was nearing his 17th birthday. How many of his classmates prepared college entrance applications? How many assumed they would patriotically enlist in the service, whether the war was still ongoing or not?

At Purcell High School, that spirit was evident in the dozen or so Cavaliers who enrolled in the National Youth Administration (NYA) workshop at 8th Street and Gilbert Avenue in downtown Cincinnati.

Purcell NYA students included Larry, far right, second from back smiling

Under government supervision, they learned the essentials of welding, radio, and machine shop techniques for four hours each day, except Sunday. Those graduating received a record card of their achievements, which when presented at their draft board, aided greatly in their classification. Larry achieved 320 Hours in Radio Technology, and according to his NYA supervisor, had a "splendid work record."

Chapter 3 – At War—Now What?

Larry's National Youth Administration Certificate of War Production Training

By Christmas season 1942, war time shortages caused citizens to change their eating and driving habits. For optimum mileage, the speed limit was set at 40 mph and only four gallons of gasoline per week was allowed.

People had a hard time getting their minds off of the war. It even permeated entertainment as the film "Casablanca" starring Humphrey Bogart and Ingrid Bergman premiered in New York City and comedian Bob Hope took his first tour starting at a military base in Alaska. More than 100,000 Japanese Americans were put in stateside prison camps—some staying for three years.

Country wide, young men were enlisting in the armed services—some before finishing high school. They had various reasons for enlisting. These men, like Larry, all chose the Navy.

> "Everybody wanted to get into the military service. Everybody did. There wasn't any talking about it or anything like that. We self-committed ourselves to it."

> "Well, there was something a little more interesting about the Navy and going on ships and traveling around the world and doing things like that and being an infantryman just did not appeal to me."

Chapter 3 – At War—Now What?

"Why did I join the Navy? So I would have three squares a day and a nice warm bunk at night and I'd always liked ships. Where was I living at the time? Hamilton, Ohio."

"We enlisted when we were seventeen because when you [enlisted] before your eighteenth birthday, you had the choice of service."

"So I picked the Navy. It took me about ten seconds to decide that because I figured as long as the ship was underneath me, I would have a clean place to sleep and clean meals."

[Why did I decide to enlist in the Navy?] "Keep out of the mud, I suppose. Well that's not true about everybody, you know. A lot of people enlisted in the Army too. But, I figured I'd sooner spend my life at sea."

It is unknown why Larry chose the Navy. On his June 17 application for enlistment, he noted "Patriotism" next to Reason for Enlistment. His sister Dorothy said there was no discussion about Larry entering the service, though the family was sad and anxious about it. She actually considered joining the Navy as a WAVE (**W**omen **A**ccepted for **V**olunteer **E**mergency **S**ervice)—she liked the uniforms—but thought she would get too homesick. Larry signed on for three years as an Apprentice Seaman in the U.S. Navy Reserve (USNR) at a pay rate of $50.00 per month, pay day being the last day of the month. He was described as having a ruddy complexion, brown hair, brown eyes, 20/20 vision, stood 67 1/2 inches tall, and weighed 129 pounds. His application required his mother's signed consent since Larry was only 17 years, 6 months old. What went through her mind as she enabled her oldest son to go off to war?

Larry Eckhoff in front of his house

He officially entered service June 22, 1943 at the Naval Reserve Center in Cincinnati, Ohio. Fingerprinted upon entry, he had to sign an affidavit attesting that he was not drawing, nor had a claim pending, for a pension, disability allowance, disability compensation, or retired pay from the Government of the United States (not including members of the Fleet Reserve or Honorary Retired List). He might have stifled a chuckle at the thought of receiving a pension for all of the hours worked after school at the drug store.

Like other servicemen, Larry also paid $6.50 per month, beginning July 6, 1943 for a $10,000 National Service Life Insurance policy which would be paid to his mother if he perished during service. A sobering thought for a teenager just days out of high school.

Chapter 4 – Great Lakes Naval Training Center

June 24, 1943

Dear Mom,

Arrived at Chicago about 8:25 and switched trains for an elevated for Great Lakes. We got here at about 10:30 Chicago time. After riding on the trains all day everybody was plenty dirty. When we came into camp we had to sign away $23.50 for a mattress, 2 blankets, and a pillow and then we went to bed in triple bunks. I got a middle bunk. There were 59 from Ohio and a couple thousand more from the rest of the country. This morning we had to get up at 5:30 but I didn't mind cause I woke up earlier. We had scrambled eggs, cereal, stewed apricots, and coffee for breakfast. Now we are back in the barracks waiting for the worst. Stomach is O.K.

Your son,

Larry

Like most of the young men his age, Larry found himself in a town he'd only read about. Chicago, Illinois didn't really look that different from Cincinnati but it *was* different. Most recruits likely arrived at a train station in Chicago. The elevated trains were designed to keep people moving even in times of deep snow and made a stop at, or very near, the base.

Great Lakes Naval Training Station, situated next to Lake Michigan on a site donated by the Commercial Club of Chicago, was established April 27, 1904 by an act of Congress that was ridiculed as "pork" spending. When it was finally opened by President Taft, October 28, 1911, it was used to develop and train officers and petty officers. By World War I, it had grown to be "the largest and most efficient" naval training station in the world receiving 125,000 men for training between April 6, 1917 and November 11, 1918, and transferring nearly 97,000 to sea duty. Less than a week after the United States entered the first World

Chapter 4 – Great Lakes Naval Training Center

War, trainloads of recruits began arriving at the facility designed to accommodate 1500 seamen. It was capable of quartering, feeding, and training 50,000 men at a time by 1918. By Armistice Day, Great Lakes had grown to over 12,000 acres and 775 buildings, nine of which were drill halls that held an entire regiment of 1726 men.

According to the Ninth Naval District War Diary for Great Lakes NTS, June 26, 1943, there were 134 officers and 562 chief petty officers assigned to Recruit Training. "The number of recruits in training is as follows: 37501 white recruits, 6853 negro recruits, 38220 total white billets, and 11060 total negro billets." The U.S. Naval Hospital also had 49 WAVES who reported for duty. Larry was assigned to Great Lakes for recruit training on June 23, 1943 as part of Company 855, 53rd Battalion. He may have planned on two months there but the center received a dispatch reducing the training period of white recruits to seven weeks, effective immediately. Recruits would be expected to learn it all in a lot less time.

After arriving at the main gate, Larry was probably taken to a receiving unit. The first full day at camp, he most likely found himself with dozens of other recruits in one of those large buildings where he was told to remove his civilian clothing and bathe. To young men who up until now had not strayed far from home, the experience could have been like herding cattle through a high school shower room. In the medical department, each man received a physical exam to ensure trainees were physically sound, and some shots (such as inoculation against smallpox and typhoid), while having their shirt, pants, and shoe sizes written right on their body. A dental officer examined their teeth, noting their condition. They were called back at a later time for any required dental work.

The men made their way to the supply department where the clothing sizes were checked and the recruits were issued everything they needed—shirts, pants, socks, shoes, and a large duffel bag to keep it all in. A Bag Layout card shows all of the issued clothing and other items and how they should be packed in a bag. The 784 page Navy Bluejackets' Manual, issued to all Naval recruits, recommended disposing of all civilian clothing since they could not be kept at the station or on board ship—uniforms were all that a sailor needed. It was considered "a suit of honor" to be proudly worn anywhere. It was reported that the sailors put their clothes in a ditty bag with a tag on it and sent them home.

The Bluejackets' Manual covers everything a sailor needed to know. Divided into seven parts, the book describes for a recruit the basics from clothing to rules and schools. Information for all enlisted men ranged from hygiene to characteristics of ships. There are sections about seamanship and gunnery, physical drills, landing forces, and gas-protective apparatus. One single chapter covered everything from hammocks and medical service to profanity and moral turpitude. The manual was "originally prepared in 1902 by Lieutenant Ridley McLean, U.S. Navy, and revised…to modernize the manual so that it agrees…with the latest training courses and includes such other information as would tend to make an able seaman and a thorough man-o'-war's man."

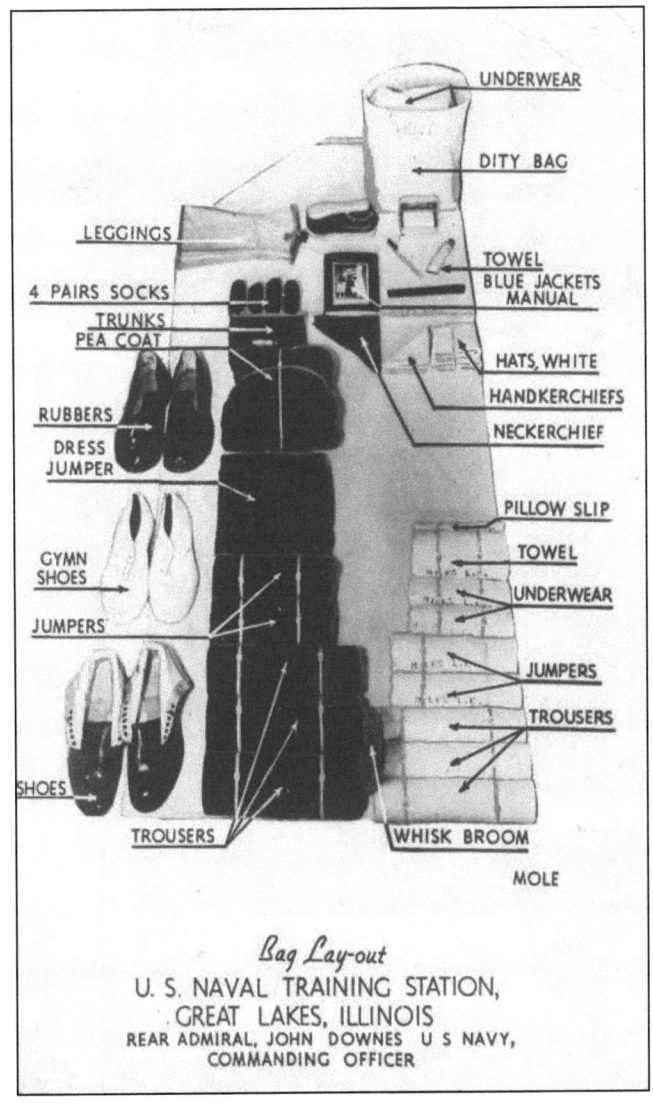

The first page a sailor would read, even before the table of contents, furnished the National Anthem—three verses of the Star-Spangled Banner—ironically, penned by Francis Scott Key while on a ship wondering whether the Americans at Fort McHenry survived the fierce land and sea battle of the previous night.

Sufficiently supplied, recruits were escorted to the barracks where they would live for their weeks in boot camp. Larry was assigned a bunk in the barracks (there were about 100 men in a company) and was introduced to his Company Commander, a chief petty officer. At least he got to go to sleep that first night. Some men started their first day in the Navy on guard duty from midnight until 4:00 in the morning.

Chapter 4 – Great Lakes Naval Training Center

Larry's scrapbook contained a set of 25 glossy captioned photo cards, slightly smaller than business cards, produced by the Navy and designed possibly to show family and friends what life was like for sailors in training. A sampling of the cards is reprinted here.

One former sailor remembered his experience, which may or may not have been colored by the years that had passed since his days at Great Lakes.

"In the boot camp, I got a lot of shots. Everybody lined up and went down through a line and they had medics putting shots in both arms at the same time. Half of the guys passed out from the double—it was a double typhoid shot. As soon as you got the shot, they took you out there on the what they call a grinder which is a drill field and work ship and down and around and around. The ones that wasn't sick from the shots got sick from that. It was an experience. They lined you up there and they run you down the line and give you clothes. One guy hand you some underwear and another one would hand you jumpers. I was tall and skinny and the Navy's clothes was square cut. If you was a 21 waist, you had a 21 length. If you was 36 waist, you got a 36 length. I didn't get any white clothes, which helped out because after about one week in boot camp you got what they call kitchen duty and mess duty. All the guys with the white clothes, they had to get up and wash their clothes every night and make sure

Chapter 4 – Great Lakes Naval Training Center

they was good and clean and go back down in the mess hole first thing in the morning and serve food. And the guys that didn't have whites…worked in the kitchen cleaning pots and pans. The cooks take good care of you in there because they feed you all kinds of goodies."

"They gave you shoes with leather soles and they put a black rubber sole on it. And then when you wore them in the barracks you saw your little scuff marks all over it and they give you a steel wool and you had to clean the scuff marks off about two times a day. They had a …chief petty officer in charge and he…met us on the first day. You got to know him for about one day and then we didn't see him again until we left, so he really had it made."

Lying awake in the pre-dawn hour, Larry's eyes adjusted to his surroundings only to find he wasn't in his bed on Bevis Avenue. His thoughts drifted to his room at home, or rather, the attic space shared with his brothers, Don, who was 13, and Billy, only 7. The usually messy attic was unfinished with one window in the front and two in back which allowed for plenty of ventilation but could be hot in the sultry Cincinnati summers and chilly in the snowy winters. The rest of his family, his mother and four sisters, took up the second floor bedrooms in the modest home.

Thoughts of the recent past were sharply replaced as he was startled completely awake by reveille—was it morning already? On a normal day, many seamen rolled out of their bunks at 5:30 a.m.—some as early as 4:00 a.m.—hastily dressed, did push-ups, calisthenics, and ran, then practiced marching in formation until 7:00 a.m., by which time, anything being served in the mess hall was a welcome sight. Before long, they would be marching again.

Many recruits never forgot their first breakfast in the Navy. One man recalled having black coffee, beans, cornbread, and an orange on Wednesday mornings.

> "This is not my idea of an ideal breakfast, but that's what they had the first morning I was in the Navy, and I decided I didn't want to eat this so I headed over to the GI can and am gonna dump it. Master Arms said, "What are you doing?" And I said "Well, I don't want this, I'm not gonna eat it" and he said, "You took it you're gonna eat it." That's something you learn when you get in the service, if you take the food, you eat it; if you're not gonna eat it, don't take it."

Some days the noon meal consisted of lunch meat and cheese—cold cuts. Some recruits thought this was great because they had never had that at home. Some of the city boys didn't like it because they ate it all the time at home.

As the days wore on, many of the recruits were homesick. Those first days after traveling on a train (or bus) to Chicago, to getting uniforms and equipment, and what seemed to be mass confusion and organized chaos was completely foreign from what they knew. For some

Chapter 4 – Great Lakes Naval Training Center

it was a radical change but it didn't take long to get into the routine away from civilian life. No longer were they answering to their parents each day but following the orders of superior officers. Expectations were high.

They learned how to dress and clean up barracks. All sailors were introduced to signaling, firefighting aboard ship, gunnery, including aircraft gunnery, and drilling with rifles. They learned how to stand watch on ships, use communication systems, and how to reply to the bridge of a ship. It wasn't unusual to get kitchen work, such as washing dishes, as well. If their mothers could only see them now.

The Bluejackets' manual provided this advice:

> "You may be homesick and lonesome for a while. We all were. You are starting a new life, with new surroundings and new friends. Grin and bear it like we all did. No man ever succeeded by hanging on to his mother's apron strings all his life. But right here, do this: Write home often and ask them to write to you often. A letter from home will buck you up more than anything else."

Photo: Larry Eckhoff as a recruit at Great Lakes Naval Training Center

Days in camp were physically demanding. Drills could be disorienting. The military required toughness, mental as well as physical, and a sense of duty to country and comrades. Sailors had no idea what they'd face in war and had to be ready for anything, though some of the horrors and dangers were more than could be taught. In the month of June, there were 16,158 recruits trained in gas warfare defense.

For some, the most difficult part of boot camp was carrying all of their belongings—sea bag, mattress, mattress cover, hammock, and such—from the barracks down to the train station. The lot weighed in at 80 pounds and it had to be carried on their backs. Surely some thought they might collapse under the load.

Most of Larry's personal experiences at Great Lakes are unknown but, based on the descriptions of others who were there around the same time, a lot was happening.

> "We learned [that] when you learned how to march you learned how to think, and you learned how to cooperate; it was just another day, and you learned how to keep your bunk clean, your bed made, and all your equipment clean...and—that's what boot camp is all about...teaching you discipline and teaching you how to think on your feet and everything. We did."

A boat crew in action during races held at Great Lakes Harbor, June, 1943
Photo courtesy of Ninth Naval District War Diary, June, 1943

Conditioning was rigorous. During the first days in camp, all recruits spent time exercising—sometimes until they could do no more. While just another form of workout for the former high school athletes and farm boys, the rest were sore in places they didn't even know had muscles. They did calisthenics, marching, rowing. and maneuvered through obstacle courses. In between, there were classes all about the Navy, ships, and first aid. There were requirements recruits had to meet before completing boot camp.

Of course, there were swimming pools and the lake. All Navy recruits had to learn to swim if they didn't already know how. With constantly changing conditions on board a ship, being able to swim and knowing how to save lives, if necessary, was a requirement. Some had to jump off a tower into the water, which is a pretty scary thing but it could save ones life if they ever had to abandon ship ten stories above the water. Without knowing how to jump properly it could kill a man when he hit the water.

The Ninth Naval District War Diary, June, 1943, included photos of recruits taking their swimming test in one of the many pools

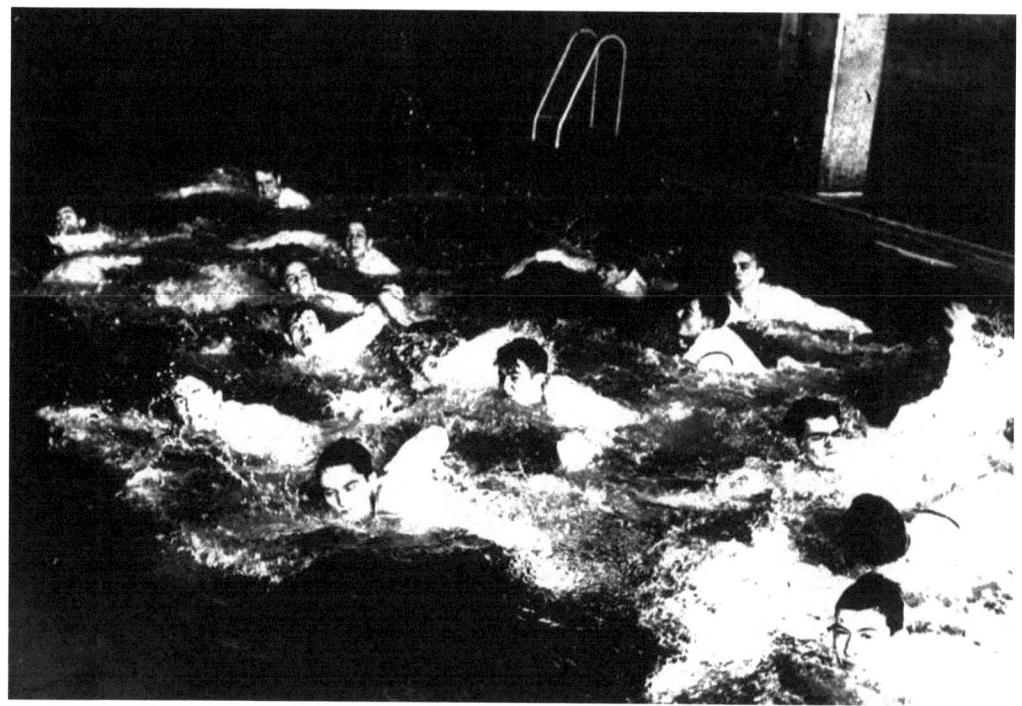

"Sailors adrift fully clothed…recruits learn to swim under conditions simulating an emergency"

After a march to Lake Michigan, recruits might board lifeboats and row, sometimes with 20 men in a boat at one time. They saw the planes flying and the carriers out on the lake. Recruits learned about lifeboats, antiaircraft guns, and firefighting. One man recalled it being "exciting" to shoot the 20mm and 40mm antiaircraft guns down on the lake.

Great Lakes Naval Training Station Cutter Drill

Some nights they had in house patrols, like fire patrol. Recruits walked around the whole compound and checked the boilers, making sure that the guys were firing everything and nothing was going wrong. Sailors also collected points for various good behaviors. If a guy got enough points, he might not have to go to muster for a lecture, or a drill—he might be able to skip certain activities.

With the war going on in Europe and in the Pacific, the men, boys actually, probably wondered where they would wind up when their training was complete but news from the outside world was scarce. There were no newspapers at the station. Someone usually had a little radio but the seamen were kept busy from the moment they got up until lights out—generally around 9:00 p.m. If there was time for anything at all, it was usually a nap. While one recruit recalled witnessing "a lot of poker games and dice, shooting craps," another said it felt like school where the classes were never over.

Chapter 4 – Great Lakes Naval Training Center

> "It was really strong because they were trying to get you in condition, physical condition, to be fit for service. We had drills, we had to take exercise, and then as a punishment if you did something wrong, they would have us do what is called the Great Lakes shuffle. You put a piece of steel wool under each foot and scrub the scuff marks off of the drill hall. So they had men in line all the way across and you would go the length of that building."

Another recruit described the Shuffle a different way.

> "They didn't allow any fighting to happen. When we did anything wrong, they had what they would call the Great Lakes shuffle. We would have to put steel wool under our feet and use floor wax to shine the floors. Everybody in the outfit had to pay for it. They didn't allow anything to happen to the floors. They had these what they call Johnson bars—heavy brushes that they would swing backwards and forward and actually shined the floor. That's another thing that we had to do for punishment."

> "If they caught people fighting, they wouldn't have their leave, you know, where they could go to town or…anywhere off the base, you know. You couldn't go off the base."

Much of the drilling took place between the barracks and Lake Michigan, rain or shine. In the summer, the breeze blowing off the lake was probably welcome. Fortunately, Larry wasn't there during the winter when the frigid air and snow could be almost unbearable.

Interestingly, there were two baseball teams at Great Lakes Naval Station during World War II. An all black team included Chuck Harmon, who in 1954 became the first black player to suit up for the Cincinnati Reds, and Larry Doby, who became the first black player in the American League with Cleveland in 1947. The white team included such greats as future Hall of Fame catcher Mickey Cochrane, 40 years old in 1943. He played and managed in the majors for 13 years but never went back after the war.

After major league seasons in 1940 and 1941 that finally were rebounding from the Great Depression, 500 major league players and 3500 minor leaguers were called into service. The loss of manpower affected attendance, and while given the go ahead by President Roosevelt to continue playing as a way of maintaining morale and providing recreation for war workers, teams also had to cope with equipment and accommodation shortages. Clubs recruited players from Latin America, draft rejects, and men who were too young or too old to serve. At least fifty Latin American players were in various lineups during the war but black players remained off limits. Major league owners, some financially strapped, won praise for supporting the war effort with bond sales, free admissions for servicemen, and donations of equipment and radio broadcasts of games to the armed forces.

Chapter 4 – Great Lakes Naval Training Center

Navy training was as much learning how to work with people as it was learning various skills. Larry and the rest of the young recruits learned how to adjust. Their furniture consisted of the bunk they slept in and a footlocker. Their roommates were complete strangers from various backgrounds. All branches of service brought together men who might never have met otherwise. People of different religions and ethnic backgrounds from all parts of the country were thrown together. They had to learn to live together and rely on each other. Their lives would depend on it. There was little privacy or peace and quiet. There were rules against swearing, though there was plenty. Shirt tails had to be tucked in. Discipline was paramount.

Former sailors recalled learning the proper way to take care of their clothes. Since they couldn't iron their uniforms, some had ways of rolling their garments so that when they unrolled them, they looked like they had been pressed. Another noted:

> "My uniform was a pair of blue pants and instead of the creases going out, the Navy prided themselves with the creases going in. The same way with the blouse or jumper, the top, all of the creases were in so that when you ...press your uniforms, you put them between your mattress and the springs and you lay on them and you turn them inside out...that's how you get the creases to go in."

On a typical day, when Larry was working, after getting out of boot camp and school, he wore blue jeans—they called them dungarees in the Navy—along with a chambray blue shirt and a white cap. That was the uniform of the day unless a sailor was going out on liberty or somebody official was visiting requiring them to get dressed up.

At the end of boot camp, and in the best shape of their lives, the graduates usually got a week's leave before being deployed. On August 12, 1943, Larry completed recruit training and advanced to Seaman Second Class (S2C). He was authorized nine days leave from August 12, 1943 to August 21, 1943 and was excited to spend a week at home before reporting for his next assignment.

Chapter 4 – Great Lakes Naval Training Center

Larry Eckhoff, August, 1943 graduating from Great Lakes Naval Training Center

Chief C. W. Hasson, Great Lakes Naval Training Center

Back home, if he picked up the Friday, August 13, 1943 edition of *The Cincinnati Post*, he read about the bombing of two major European cities, Rome and Berlin. As far away as that seemed, Larry probably wondered whether he might wind up on a ship crossing the Atlantic to join the fray. Turning the page he discovered even the Cincinnati Reds would not go untouched by the war. Ace pitcher, Johnny Vander Meer, best known for hurling back to back no hitters one week in June, 1938, received a draft notice. He would soon leave his wife and child, along with his major league teammates for a stint with his country's team.

Like all Cincinnatians, new recruits fresh out of boot camp didn't have to look far to be reminded of the war. On any day, a walk along the Public Landing provided a view of all manner of war craft floating on the Ohio River, including sub chasers and mine sweepers.

Chapter 4 – Great Lakes Naval Training Center

Larry and his mom, Anna while home on leave August, 1943

Larry near his front porch at home on Bevis Avenue on leave after training at Great Lakes NTS, August, 1943

A two part article in *The Cincinnati Post* in mid-August, 1943 highlighted the work of the Coast Guard in keeping war materiel moving along inland waterways along with a message about SPAR recruiting and the need for more Coast Guard members.

The Landing Ship Tanks (LSTs) were built up river from Cincinnati and floated south to the Mississippi. The Coast Guard was in constant communication from the time the LSTs launched until they passed the Cincinnati area.

LST 325 docked for tours in high water on the Ohio River at Covington, Kentucky (across the river from Cincinnati) during Cincinnati's Tall Stacks riverboat event, October 05, 2006

"The LST flashes word when it reaches the Cincinnati area. Messages might come through Station X—Cincinnati Police—or through the Coast Guard's own communications system. Once the boat enters the Port of Cincinnati, the Ensign (Ship Movement Officer) takes over. The Coast Guard assigns river pilots to ride the bridge with the LST commander. For sailing the Ohio isn't like going to sea."

"An escort vessel is provided the LST. This Coast Guard boat travels a mile or two ahead, warning that the big boat is coming down and guiding the LST around the bends."

"Perhaps there is mail—or cigarets—to be delivered to the LST. The giant can't stop—too much lost time, for a war is going on—so the Coast Guard assigns a boat to make the transfer. It is done while both are under way."

"The procedure is repeated at other ports downstream until—and it doesn't take long, for those LSTs really go—the tank ships have reached tidewater."

LST 325 docked on Ohio River at Aurora, Indiana, September 24, 2011

Chapter 4 – Great Lakes Naval Training Center

When Larry left for Great Lakes not quite two months ago, the gasoline ration was four gallons. Now, that was reduced to three gallons, and neighbors wondered whether their local filling station would have to close. For some it seemed that their only hope for survival would be an Office of Price Administration ruling allowing them to make up the difference in income by increasing the per gallon price of gas.

Basic Mileage Ration Stamps issued by the U.S. Office of Price Administration

There was a three cent profit margin on regular and 3.5 cents on premium. For most, a 25% reduction in sales could not be made up or offset by further reductions in operating costs so many could be forced to close unless higher profits were allowed. The worst sufferers were the stations dependent on gasoline sales alone. There was some relief for those who also did repair work as repairs were on the increase since no one could buy new vehicles.

Front of a Mileage Rationing Record to be presented with each gasoline ration application

Back of a Mileage Rationing Record to be presented with each gasoline ration application

Reading the August 17, 1943 *Cincinnati Post* before supper, Larry would discover that he clearly was not alone as a new Navy recruit.

"Frank Knox, Secretary of the Navy, reported today that the naval services—Navy, Marine Corps, and Coast Guard—now have a total of 2,666,500 officers and enlisted personnel and that by the end of the year the number will increase to 2,861,000—nearly three million in all. The figures include women reservist members of the WAVES, Women Marines, and SPARS but do not include Navy nurses."

The days on leave passed by too quickly. Some friends and classmates were also home on leave but others were scattered among bases or ships across the globe. It was one thing to be away from home for seven weeks at training camp but when his transfer orders arrived, to who knows where? It was impossible for Larry to guess when he might again see his neighborhood friends or when he would be sitting at the supper table with his family. As the food was passed around, he wondered whether his mom and six siblings would be ok without a man in the house.

Chapter 5 – Class of 1943

Cincinnati is located in Hamilton County, Ohio. Even in 1943 the student population was diverse—east side, west side, central, small-town rural, suburban, public-private-Catholic, college prep, co-ed or segregated by gender; neighborhood enrollment vs. drawing city wide; large, medium, and small schools—they could represent any town in America. Most teenagers weren't very mobile. Even kids from the larger city schools were mostly familiar only with Cincinnati at-large unless they visited relatives out of town once or twice. The area was populated by mostly middle class families with some better off and some worse. Some lived on farms and some in city neighborhoods. The Class of 1943 was born only a handful of years after World War I. Their parents struggled to make ends meet during the years after the stock market crash in 1929 and survived the Great Depression with help from their neighbors and friends. For many who lived in the valleys between Cincinnati's seven hills, the unprecedented rise of the Ohio River in 1937 destroyed what little progress they had made. Now those high school seniors faced an even more uncertain future with war on two fronts and Pearl Harbor still an open wound.

The best way to understand what was going on in the lives of war-time teenagers and their families would be to ask them. Since more than 70 years have passed at this writing, those options are limited. However, nowhere is the diverse nature of the students and their schools more apparent than in the content and presentations of their high school yearbooks. Frozen in time are those images and voices Cincinnati area high school students contributed to their school yearbooks. Each book clearly reflects the culture of its school and the attitude of the student staffers. Some schools, unable to produce large format glossy annuals, still managed to capture their years with dignity in the manner befitting their circumstances. Not every school was able to publish a book during the war years due to rationing and restriction of photographic materials and paper, but a cross section of those whose yearbooks were located yield vivid images of the lives of the students in their neighborhoods, in their schools, and in their world at large. Schools represented include:

- A Trade school – Central Vocational
- Suburban public schools – Deer Park, Norwood, St. Bernard, Wyoming
- City public schools – Hughes, Walnut Hills, Western Hills, Withrow, Woodward
- Parochial or Private schools – Purcell, St. Xavier
- A Semi-Rural school - Sharonville

Victory Corps

One activity common to most schools was the Victory Corps. It was founded by the National Education Association (NEA) in cooperation with the U.S. Office of Education, under the leadership of John W. Studebaker. Captain Eddie Rickenbacker, hero of World War I and II, was Chairman of the National Policies Commission. Secretary Willard E. Givens of the NEA and Secretary Paul E. Elicker of the National Association of Secondary School Principals were members of the committee, along with representatives of the War, Navy, and Commerce Departments. Excerpts from an article in the April 6, 1943 *Cincinnati Post* by Mrs. Lee Shapiro do a great job of explaining the purpose of the Victory Corps.

> "The high school students of Cincinnati are all out for Victory. In order to get a concerted effort on the part of boys and girls of the High School, Victory Corps has been established on a nationwide basis and Cincinnati high school youth are joining."

> "There are two main objectives of the High School Victory Corps, preparing youth for war service that will come after they leave school and the participation of youth in the community war effort while they are yet in school."

> "The schools meet the first objective by offering a variety of pre-induction courses such as aeronautics, navigation, mechanical drawing, fundamentals of electricity, fundamentals of machines, and the like. In addition to regular pre-induction courses, a large number of school clubs and other school groups have been established."

> "The second objective...is through various other agencies which set up the USO, the Junior Red Cross, the Health agencies...This kind of service is established to supplement the services of existing community youth agencies in carrying out war programs…"

> "The general membership in the Victory Corps is open to any high school student who is participating in a school physical fitness program appropriate to his abilities. We must make men and women who are physically strong..."

> "The students must also be studying courses appropriate to his abilities, and must be currently participating in at least one important community service. This service may be making model planes for the air service, being a blood donor, assisting in the service activities of any community agency, making cookies for the USO, or any of the worthy tasks that the community agencies need so vitally in times like this."

Meet the Class of 1943

Central Vocational

The 1942-1943 school year brought the combining of five city trade schools—Building, Electrical, Mechanical, Automotive, and Aviation—into one complete unit known as Central Vocational High School, an all male institution whose first students went about their classes with wartime tunes on their lips.

Chapter 5 – Class of 1943

The 1943 *Central Craftsman* listed five faculty members and thirty students in the armed services. Most of their students participated in the Victory Corps: Air Service–252, Production Service–12, Sea Service–98, Land Service–18, and General Membership–380.

Deer Park

Victory Corps was also part of daily life at Deer Park High School, a public co-educational school located in a suburb just northeast of Cincinnati. "Pre-Induction Courses" covering topics such as electricity, machinery, and shop work were held once a week adding to the senior boys graduation requirements. They were in line with the army training that many of the boys would have as soon as they were out of school. It was assumed that some students taking a lead role in the Victory Corps would probably wind up as officers or at least have a better chance for advancement in the different branches of service.

Deer Park yearbook staffers filled *Antlers* with student photos and activities but not many extras. As with many annuals, this one took on a military bent. With an American flag flying near a collage of the Statue of Liberty surrounded by drawings of military trucks, ships, planes, and tanks the authors wrote:

> "To Youth"
>
> "In this, the 1943 ANTLERS, we of the staff have endeavored to create a portrait of a year's life at Deer Park High School in keeping with the spirit of these warring times."
>
> "Classes, sports, and activities have all been included in this composite of school life. These material things have been recorded here in words and pictures—"
>
> "This ANTLERS is also a picture of American youth: Youth in all its glorious faith—curious youth, self-reliant and gallant—youth, fighting for the hope of its tomorrow—youth who will soon carry on our American way of life."
>
> "To youth then, we dedicate this sixth volume of the ANTLERS."

St. Bernard

The *St. Bernardian* yearbook, whose cover prominently featured an eagle, represents the co-ed public high school in the central suburb of St. Bernard (pronounced Ber-NARD). Other than the dedication, the book is very bare bones and school focused. Facing pages featured a flag with this sentiment:

> "We hereby dedicate this page of the 1943 St. Bernardian to all those teachers and former pupils of St. Bernard High School who are now serving their country. We know their training received here will help them to achieve their highest goal."

Chapter 5 – Class of 1943

"We can all remember them by buying U. S. War Stamps and Bonds. They are giving their lives for their country; let us back them by lending our money!"

Wyoming

Wyoming is an upper middle class suburb just north of the Cincinnati city limits bordering the east side of Vine Street. Almost since the incorporation of Cincinnati, Vine Street has served as the East/West dividing line as it meanders north from the Ohio River to the Hamilton/Butler County line. The cover of the Wyoming High School yearbook, *Communique*, proudly displayed a raised eagle—olive branches in one claw, arrows in the other—with E Pluribus Unum on the striped shield.

Yearbook creators changed headings such as Faculty, Administration, Students, and Activities to such titles as General Staff, Commanding Officers, Colonels, Ranks, Maneuvers, and Details in deference to the war effort. The Dedication page includes a photograph taken outside the school of a doughboy statue and Wyoming Honor Roll of students who participated in World War I. The sentiment reads:

"In this year, nineteen hundred and forty-three, the world is at war. It is not a war fought by foreign people on strange soil; it is our war, yours and mine. We must fight it then."

"Already we have suffered the loss of several members of the graduating class to the armed services, and we have lost many valuable members from the faculty. Along with these have gone many students who have graduated from Wyoming in other years. Once they walked through the corridors of Wyoming school, played on the athletic field and on the basketball floor; now they fight in the foxholes of New Guinea, the deserts of North Africa, all over the world. They are fighting so that the coming generations may continue playing on the athletic fields of the future; may continue to live the way we Americans want to live: in freedom. To these men and to all others fighting this great battle for freedom we humbly dedicate the *Communique* of 1943"

Students participated in air-raid drills, a scrap-collection drive, key-collection campaign, Victory book drive, coat hanger collection, and received instruction in First Aid. A page called "Wyoming at War" shows students buying and selling War Savings stamps and bonds, something they were particularly proud of. Sales were handled by the Junior Red Cross Council with a quota for the school year of $4000, but by March 19, 1943, sales had already reached a total of $9751.10.

Activities of the Junior Red Cross included knitting eight sweaters and ten afghans, making garments for small children, making bandages, printing New Year's napkins for the soldiers at Camp Pickett, making Christmas nut cups for Camp Pickett, sewing soldiers' utility kits, conducting two Junior Red Cross membership drives, and raising funds for the Victory Book Campaign and the Red Cross War Fund.

Chapter 5 – Class of 1943

Western Hills

The first glance at the 1943 Western Hills High School yearbook inspires gasps. The large two page spread has a nearly full page photo of Gregor Ziemer's book *Education for DEATH, The Making of the Nazi*. The cover of Ziemer's book has a picture of a hatless soldier leaning back blowing on a trumpet festooned by a large Nazi tri-color flag with a swastika in the middle. The other page shows a large German camp-like building with tables full of young men and several girls in traditional dress, writing or singing along with an accordion. Two of the young men wore Nazi arm bands. Spanning the two pages is hand drawn white eagle with the 'Song of the Hitler Youth' printed in it—a chilling start to a high school annual.

The title of the Western Hills High (often referred to as West High) yearbook is *Education for Life*. Reading on, the views of the author and the stance taken by the West High yearbook publishers started to become clear.

> "If I had the voice of an angel, and the eloquence of Socrates I could not make it any more clear than this: 'Education for Death' brings death, 'Education for Life' must bring life."

> "The education for death that Hitler is preparing for his youth is the most calculating, the most coldblooded, the most systematic debauchery of youth that the world has ever seen. Our schools are veritable manifestations of paradise in comparison. Our schools are haves, our teachers are exponents of free wisdom, our equipment is the most elaborate evidence the democracy can and does work. 'Education for Death' subordinates the individual, without elevating the state to any greater height than base selfishness. Education for life must elevate the individual, without making of him a selfish individualist."

> "We have 'Education for Life' now. Every attempt that we make to improve our methods, to produce a closer cooperation between teacher and student, every effort that we put forth to understand America, improve America, and salvage America, is a step forward in our 'Education for Life'. –Gregor Ziemer"

> "The Western Hills annual staff felt the challenge. They talked with Mr. Ziemer and learned from him personally the contrast between German and American education. They conferred with their principal, Mr. B. H. Siehl, concerning their desire that in this, the most crucial year in all recorded history, their 1942-43 annual might be not only a record of happy school days but also a visualization of an ideal. They hoped that in picture and printed word they might carry to the world a message and make a small contribution toward that better age for which so many brave boys are dying. They have tried to show how the American school educates for life rather than for death. They believe that their own Western Hills fulfills this ideal as nearly as any school in the land. Perhaps the concepts presented here are nowhere perfectly achieved; in some instances we may be merely outlining an objective. This in itself is worthwhile. As we define our aims we resolve anew that they shall be accomplished. In each of the sections, Social Contacts, Mental Stimulus, Creative Activity, and Physical Activity we have set forth the contrast between our ideals and those of the Nazis. We dedicate our annual to the preservation of the American way."

A creative ad for Indianapolis Engraving Company shows a man in a black coat and bowler hat pushing a wheelbarrow whose metal wheel is devoid of rubber and stacked full of items affected by rationing such as suitcases, a large format camera with tripod, and various metal items. The ad reads:

> "Blame Tojo [Japanese Premier]! No gas…No tires…no meat…no coffee and even no cuffs on our trousers. But who cares! Our blood goes into banks—our money into bonds…and our fathers and brothers go to war. We go to school. We work and in spite of Tojo and Hitler, we laugh and play. Tomorrow we go to war. Today the flowers are out…So is our annual. Here is the record of our year at Western Hills…That year of the Solomons, of Midway, the Aleutians, and of North Africa. Such a year of work, play and sacrifices had to be recorded. Our engraver helped us immeasurably…"

St. Xavier

St. Xavier (pronounced ZAYvyer) is an all-male independent Catholic high school run by the Jesuit order that draws students from all over the Cincinnati area. Their 1943 yearbook, *The X-Ray*, took two pages to pay tribute to all St. X graduates in service to the country, including about a half dozen who died while in service. Two photographs of alumni in uniform flank the top right and left corners of these two pages. Their only other subtle references to the war appear in the photos of Cincinnati that divide sections of the book. An aerial or hillside photo of the Ohio River contains the quote "The Ohio river, the route of vital materials". Other photos and text highlight skills and benefits the area lends to the war effort without mentioning the word 'war'.

Hughes

Hughes High School sits on top of Clifton hill a stone's throw from the University of Cincinnati (U.C.). Their large format yearbook, *Classics of '43*, is indicative of a venerable old school with a focus on classics. Dignified and eloquent, two introductory statements, from a symphony conductor and an alumnus, set the tone. Mr. Eugene Goossens, Conductor of the Cincinnati Symphony Orchestra wrote:

> "Music is the most vital factor for morale building in war time. It is the most powerful antidote to the horror and sadness of war, and the greatest inspiration to those, soldiers and civilians alike, who are called upon to make the greatest sacrifices at this time."

> "The highest medium for the performance of great music is the symphony orchestra; the great masterpieces of music have been written for it, and it alone can convey to the full their grandeur."

> "We in Cincinnati are the proud possessors of a symphony orchestra. It represents one of the things for which America is fighting. It brings us what we most need today: energy to carry on our work, and the courage and resolution to maintain the morale which is essential to victory."

Assistant Principal, Arthur J. Havlovic, summarized the school activities in the framework of culture and war with an emphasis on Victory Corps efforts.

Chapter 5 – Class of 1943

> "'A thing of beauty is a joy forever' is a quotation which has been repeated for many years. That modern society is not unmindful of this fact is evidenced by a statement observed recently in an advertisement of one of our large insurance companies. This company states, 'In a world that is torn by strife and hatred there is still need for beauty.'"

> "That the class of '43 dedicates its annual to things 'classical' indicates that it has not overlooked cultural values at the same time that its members have been participating, and preparing for more intensive participation, in the war effort. I congratulate the class upon both its achievements and appreciations."

> "In our present conflict, attention has turned to the air. This trend has brought two new subjects into the Hughes curriculum, aeronautics and navigation. Students learn the principles of maneuvering a plane from one point to another, piloting, dead reckoning, radio navigation, and celestial navigation. Piloting refers to flying chiefly by landmarks; this fundamental is usually the first to be mastered by the novice pilot. Dead reckoning is concise figuring of a destination; it involves some higher mathematics. Radio navigation is concerned with flying on a radio beam and by radio contacts. Celestial navigation depends on the sun, and to some extent on the stars; a course is plotted with methods similar to those used for sea travel. Aeronautics involves weather, meteorology, air strata, clouds, and other subjects for study."

> "To aid in the war effort, Hughes students this year formed their Victory Corps…Students collected scrap metal, paper, and silk hose. Later they brought coat hangers for the Army Air Cadets across the avenue at U.C. Some spent Saturday mornings at the Red Cross station rolling bandages and planted and tended Victory gardens."

> "All of the schools in Cincinnati gathered together 4371 games to be sent to USO camps including 1654 jigsaw puzzles, 1428 decks of cards, 247 bingo and lotto, 184 checkers, 135 anagrams, 215 board games, 93 dominoes, 150 quiz games, 28 Monopoly, 90 marbles and Chinese checkers, and 147 miscellaneous. The Hughes Victory Corps sorted, packed, and dispatched them."

Woodward

In existence for 112 years by 1943, Woodward High School held classes in a large building at the northern edge of downtown Cincinnati before moving to its current site near the center of town. Principal Dr. Leon D. Peaslee provided this introduction to the *Woodward Annual*.

> "Woodward has never failed its country. For one hundred and twelve years, this grand old institution has squarely faced the challenge of education, of citizenship, of patriotism, and has never been found wanting. The history of its alumni written in the halls of fame bears witness to its glorious achievements."

> "…The Seniors of 1943, like their predecessors…they are intelligent, serious-minded young people, ready and eager to assume their places in life. They have met the demands of changing conditions and have geared their education, not only to the ideals of fine citizenship, but also to the requirements of a world at war."

> "As they leave these halls of learning and step forward into the service of their country, whether it be on battlefields or production lines, may they go with the knowledge that Woodward is proud of them! May God bless and keep them—everyone!"

School administrator, William G. Cramer, shared these impassioned words:

Chapter 5 – Class of 1943

> "You are graduating from Woodward High School during one of the greatest crises that has ever confronted us as a nation. Our very life and liberty are at stake in the titanic struggle that is raging in all parts of the world. Greater responsibility than ever before rests upon the shoulders of every man, woman, and child throughout the land."

> "You, graduates of the class of 1943 of Woodward High School, have grave duties ahead of you. You must help in every possible way to save and preserve our greatly cherished liberty, which was obtained at the price of much bloodshed and hard toil by our forebears. And after the fighting is over and peace once more reigns over the land, you will have to aid in bringing about a wise and lasting reconstruction, which will be for the best interests of the…nation."

> "In the past Woodward graduates have played a very prominent part in national affairs in times of peace and in times of war. Never have they shirked their duty and responsibility."

> "You, the members of this year's graduating class, will also go forth and take your stations wherever duty may call. Of this I am sure. With this assurance, I bid you Godspeed."

The student publishers of the *Annual* provided this commentary on their principal.

> "Nineteen hundred and forty-three marks the third year of the principalship of Dr. Leon. D. Peaslee at Woodward High School. We, the graduating class, have come to know and respect him. He has painstakingly sought to instill in us the ideals of good citizenship of which he is a living example. We are proud and grateful to have had the opportunity of preparing ourselves for life under the leadership of one who so thoroughly understands the problems which we shall have to face in a war torn world."

> "This year our principal was faced with many grave responsibilities. In accordance with the wishes of our government, he has done everything within his power to make Woodward High School a part of the great national effort aiming at war-time education. He has given unstintingly of his time and energy. His ceaseless efforts in this and his deep concern for our welfare have impressed us greatly."

The Victory Corps was of great importance to Woodward students. The school was so serious about their scrap metal drive that their 123,390 lb fence was removed and donated.

Students mentioned how deserted that school seemed with so many older boys and girls working. Those partaking of lunch could take only one serving of meat due to meat shortages and about 250 volunteered their services in connection with rationing activities. This seemed a small price to pay knowing the sacrifices made by Russian children for their country and of American boys "who have lost their lives on foreign fronts fighting for this great land of liberty. We at home must do everything within our power to make the peace, when it comes, a lasting one."

Students worked hand in hand with the Red Cross and the USO. First Aid classes were organized as were blood drives, for those over eighteen who obtained parental consent. The Spanish Club gathered suitable books and magazines for the men in the Armed Forces. They saved paper for paper drives. Some older boys became Air Raid Wardens, in charge of

Chapter 5 – Class of 1943

the school in case of air attacks and assisting in securing shelter for the students if this became necessary. They were also in charge of air raid drills and the various air raid shelters. The Victory Corps even had a Camouflage Committee, training students for work with the armed forces, particularly the Air Force.

Sharonville

Sharonville, located on the northern edge of Hamilton County, is a small town suburb with many rural outlying areas whose student body included many kids raised on farms. The 1942 Sharonville High School *Sigma Rho*, when members of the class of 1943 were juniors, contains no glossy paper but provides insight into families not raised in the city.

"To "Our Boys in Service" fighting throughout the world to protect and preserve the American ideals of liberty and democracy we dedicate this book. The stirring accounts of their courage at Corregidor and Bataan inspired us to do our part to strengthen our defense and their morale so that we may be victorious over those nations with which we are at war."

The 26 seniors of 1942 (not a typo) "realize that we are graduating in a year of great distress and anxiety since our country found it necessary to declare war." Classmates left school to work in defense plants or enlisted in the armed services. They remembered each other for "…giggles, red skirt, golf clubs, chatter, feather-bob, tardy arrivals, bandanas, eyebrows, silver skates, bicycle, suitcase, truck, 4-H Club work, tortoise-shell glasses, smile, satire, height, blonde hair—and one young man, by his Marine uniform."

It wasn't only the seniors talking. Those juniors who would become the Class of 1943 won the award (one half-day holiday) offered to the high school class purchasing the most defense stamps by buying $167.65 worth of savings stamps and bonds. Three of the boys

Chapter 5 – Class of 1943

"...helped our country by buying defense bonds." That wasn't all. The amazing spirit of this class was reflected in what they did for their school prom.

> "It is a tradition in our school for the junior class to give a prom for the senior class. However, after (the principal) suggested that the money might be used more profitably in the defense of our country, we decided it was best to have a small, informal party at school. With the money that would have been spent ordinarily for the prom, defense stamps were bought and distributed among the juniors and seniors. We sincerely hope that this will aid our country..."
>
> "In newspaper columns, in magazine articles and over the radio, writers and speakers repeat again and again these words "All Out for Defense," but the juniors, changed this phrase and said "All In for Defense" when they gave the annual prom on May 29 at school."
>
> "Previously the students of our school have held the prom at hotels and country clubs in and around Cincinnati. This spring the class voted to have it at home so that War Saving Stamps might be purchased with that money which is ordinarily spent on prom expenses."
>
> "The unusualness of this prom made us truly appreciate it because we found that we could have a wonderful time at home and still do our part for our country."

Students contributed toward the purchase of a service flag dedicated "to the boys who have gone from our school and our village to join the armed forces of our country." The 5 by 8 foot flag hung on the wall in the center of the main hallway. On the left side of the flag was a picture of George Washington; on the right side a picture of Abraham Lincoln. Beneath the flag was suspended a roll of honor on which was printed the names of those boys who were in the U.S. Army, Navy, or Marines.

A dairy in a burg a few miles south sponsored an ad in the yearbook. It reads "To Beat the Axis, Keep Fit---Drink Our Milk Every Day."

As seniors in the small high school, they provided additional insight in the 1943 *Sigma Rho*.

> "The Sigma Rho this year has had its troubles. There was a question as to whether we would be able to get the necessary materials because of the war crisis. Other schools did not even make an attempt to publish an annual; but since many of the students were so anxious to have one, we persevered and are proud to present this book to you."

Chapter 5 – Class of 1943

"By the time we reached our senior year the class of 45 students (who began as freshmen), had decreased to 24, six of whom had joined the Armed Forces. Our pictures were taken at Young and Carl [a prominent photography studio in downtown Cincinnati]. We went earlier on account of war, for there was less material allowed for the taking of pictures."

"This is in honor of the senior boys who will soon be serving in the armed forces. The boys will be protecting and preserving the rights of freedom—our freedom and their freedom."

"To all the boys that have left and to the boys that will be leaving, the best wishes for a bright and peaceful future. We are proud to have the following leaving from our class: [the names of nine senior boys, more than one third of the class, were listed]."

Norwood

The community of Norwood is the next door neighbor of the Evanston area called home by Larry and his family. In the Norwood High School *Silhouette*, students packed innumerable activities. Their clever introduction went as follows:

1942-1943 "Halt! Who goes there?"

"What self appointed sentinels stand guard at Norwood High's Main Gate? Upper classmen greet new recruits at main headquarters, who advance shyly to swell our numbers to 1091 for 1942-1943."

"All of us went to war on the school front. We don't mean fighting with our teachers. We mean making surgical dressings, buying war stamps, pasting USO scrapbooks, collecting scrap and rags, taking first aid and home nursing classes, and joining the Victory Corps. Our boys enrolled in classes in Aeronautics, Radio, Telegraphy, Airplane Motor Repair and other pre-induction courses."

"We said goodbye to some of our senior boys who enlisted in the Marines or Navy before graduation, and to others whose numbers were called. We welcomed our alumni in uniform, who remembered us on furlough. Two faculty members left in November for officer naval training..."

First semester achievements for the war effort were roughly tallied. Students and faculty bought $4,897.75 war stamps and $3,475.00 war bonds, collected 14,020 pounds of scrap, 1420 pounds of rags, and 130 dozen coat hangers, contributed one service flag, $50.00 to the Service Flag Maintenance fund, and $58.00 for comfort kits. The school Art Department created 1,300 Christmas menus for the U.S. Navy while the Drama and Music departments collaborated on a "Road to Freedom" benefit. The April Victory Corps USO Book Collection netted 128 games, 1000 books and Readers Digests, and 400 magazines for service members. Many students took jobs during the day due to manpower shortages and attended school at night.

> "Drafting eighteen year old youths affected the Norwood schedule for upper classmen by the introduction of new courses into the...training program. Speakers from each branch of the service...visited the school to present our local 'draft bait' with inside facts of his special branch of service. After a formal meeting (November 24) where Army, Navy, and Marine officials explained their particular branches, an open house was held where more personal questions were answered by the speakers. The crowd was appreciative and inquisitive; they wanted the best decision as to which service would be the most suitable for them."
>
> "Many boys have already left to enter the armed service. Some will return; some will not. Our service flag has three gold stars, symbols of William Dahling, Robert Oberhelman, and Roy Purvis who died in service. This flag was presented October 15 in the auditorium..."

Physical education was changed to fit war necessities, to give high school boys a chance to improve their physical condition to meet service requirements. By joining the Victory Corps, students pledged to be physically strong, engage in military drills, and take classes such as those mentioned in the yearbook introduction. Other students worked on model airplanes, used by services to aid in recognition, and wrote to friends and family in service.

Walnut Hills

To the east, the closest Cincinnati Public School to Evanston is the prestigious Walnut Hills High School, a college prep school for students in grades 7-12. Students made the war, the defeat of the enemy, and the freedoms enjoyed by the public institution, a theme in nearly every section of the 1943 *Remembrancer*.

Leading off, a cartoon-style puppet show called "All the World's a Stage, Adolf" featured Hitler, Hirohito, and Benito Mussolini. Students wrote:

> "You thought by pulling the strings your millions of little heiling puppets could conquer that world. We're grasping those strings ourselves, Adolf. We intend to dangle you and your partners before our little world here at Walnut Hills High School in this proud old German city of Cincinnati, Ohio, to show you why our way of life will be victorious. No goose-stepping, no saluting, but, as you are discovering, we are not "soft and decadent.""

A photo of students hanging out near school busses was captioned "No regimentation here, Benito," and another of the school with "This is our castle, Hirohito."

Students standing in the auditorium during an assembly stretched out their arms toward the American flag as they "pledge allegiance" and:

Chapter 5 – Class of 1943

> "Our pledge is more than a mere formality, more than a patriotic blurb before we settle back to enjoy the assembly and muse happily over the chemistry test we're missing. When we hit the punch line '…with liberty and justice for all,' the chorus is strong and eyes are proud in acknowledgement of the heritage we are heir to and grim in the realization of the task which is ours to preserve it."

The school paper *Chatterbox* contained lots of war news and students used it as a forum to explain the Victory Corps.

Because of the war, fewer students were planning to go on to college so the school changed its curriculum to fit the needs of those entering the military. As in other local high schools, there was increased emphasis on math and new classes in Aeronautics and Navigation. The boys Radio Club learned to transmit and receive Morse Code and how to operate radio sets. The Model Airplane Club devoted much of its meeting time to making planes for the government to help aviation cadets learn all angles of enemy aircraft.

There was more emphasis on calisthenics and helping students pass tests in agility, balance, power, strength, and endurance. An obstacle course, consisting of hurdles, fences, ditches, and other impediments, was built to get students closer to army and navy physical standards. Exercises were given to girls as well, citing increased duties at home as well as on "the swing shift."

Withrow

Another Cincinnati public high school close-by is Withrow. The title page of their 1943 *Annual* read "The New World is Ours" "We will win the war….we will win the peace."

The two page spread that followed featured a hand-drawn outline of the United States embellished with pencil sketches representing Washington crossing the Delaware, Lincoln standing tall, and several students. The text reads:

> "The America of our Fathers has been Threatened, The America of Washington won our independence, The America of Lincoln preserved our unity, Modern Americans are fighting for survival"

Withrow students were quite defiant in their assessment of the Axis and their attitude toward the war. The students reminded everyone that:

> "Our Mothers and Fathers have experienced War in 1917 and 1918, financial crashes, bank failures, depressions, recessions, floods, bread lines---but this is our fight. That trio of destruction must stew in its own juice."

Chapter 5 – Class of 1943

Like Walnut Hills, the Withrow students chose to include a characterization of Mussolini, Hitler, and Hirohito. Their two pages featured the three as Mr. Potato Head style vegetables gathered around a casserole representing the rest of the world.

> "In a war-torn year, the Withrow *Annual* dedicates itself to the great task of winning the war. This we must do by stimulating a greater awareness among the faculty and students, and by adhering to the principles and ideals of a free, Christian nation."
>
> "We must set before ourselves the all-important effort of creating a new world; a bulwark of the Democratic Ideal where there is complete freedom from oppression, where science creates instead of destroys; where free men of all nations, all races, live in brotherhood.
>
> "With these thoughts in mind we shall strive to keep this 'ersatz god,' this 'Son of the Son,' and this 'Duce de luxe' truly stewing in their own juice."

In the late 20th and early 21st centuries, midwestern students got used to hearing sirens go off when severe weather approached—tornado drills became as common as fire drills. However those same sirens served a very different purpose during the war years. In 1943, schools conducted a very different kind of drill.

> "Remain calm! Keep quiet! Don't run! It's an air raid drill!" "One bell...two bells...three...four...five...six...seven. This signal conveys to every student a certain feeling of alarm, for it may mean enemy planes overhead. The occasion not only brings forth the serious side of the pupils, but it shows how well they can cooperate in an emergency."

They realized the seriousness of air-raid drills and the need to give up many of their former pleasures like chocolate ice cream and Lucky Strike Green, contributed generously to scrap drives, purchased thousands of dollars' worth of war bonds and stamps—grateful for the opportunity of being students in a free country. One photo depicted at least a half dozen students donating blood to "save the lives of soldiers." Victory Corps activities included knitting afghans, wristlets, anklets, and other articles and participating in first aid classes.

Withrow's junior high students collected 12 tons of scrap metal and rubber. Another 40 tons of newspapers, magazines, boxes, and other paper was "trundled to school in home-made wagons or carried by faithful pupils."

Aeronautics classes were new to the school in 1942-43 school year to train young men and women for a future in aviation. Their goal was to turn out well-trained technicians for service in the U. S. Air Corps and the aviation industry. There were also one hour daily lectures and demonstrations in navigation.

Chapter 5 – Class of 1943

"The navigator's specific job is to keep the ship or plane on its true course by a system of angles and lines. Here, extreme accuracy and neatness are stressed, for the mistake of a fraction of a degree can misdirect a bombing raid by hundreds of miles."

The model airplane group had girls as well as boys building models of various types, from all nations, to strict scale for use in identification in the Army and Navy. Pupils who built exceptional models received certificates from the Army and Navy officials.

Students paid tribute to Withrow graduates working at Cincinnati Milling Machine Company noting "Withrow shop courses furnished foundation training for these 'production soldiers'."

"Never in all history has the call for defenders of freedom been so urgent. Brave men are needed; stout-hearted men who prefer to die free rather than to live enslaved."

"This is the way score upon score of Withrow students, teachers, and graduates have felt. They have taken their places shoulder to shoulder with other men and women of action who are determined to defeat the Axis; who are not only remembering Pearl Harbor but are doing something about it. They have decided that this is their war and the armed services need their help; for all the warships and fighting planes that America can produce count for nothing without the men to man them—skilled men who know their jobs—fighting men who want action—patriots who love their country as all true Americans should."

"They are the real heroes, who ask nothing greater than the chance to help win this war, and the opportunity to show that they have the stuff to do it."

"To these men of action who are serving their flag and country, regardless of grade or rank, and to the young women in their respective branches of service, Withrow pays tribute."

"We, the seniors of Withrow High School, do hereby assert that we will voluntarily surrender a period out of our lives for the winning of the war and the re-establishment thereafter. We do this knowing that this period will be one of absolute sacrifice as far as personal pleasures are concerned. We also know that we face a responsibility doubled by present day circumstances. We enter a world ringing with the disheartening phrase, 'Too little and too late'; our motto shall be "Enough—now!"

"During a war year Withrow's two outstanding publications, *Tower News* and the *Annual*, gave full coverage to the war life and activities of Withrow's students. *Tower News* in its weekly editions brought up-to-the-minute news…on war stamp sales, Victory Corps activities, Withrowites in the service, and scrap drives. The *Annual*, faced with the fact that it may not come out for the seniors of 1944, because of a drafted printer and a scarcity of vital materials, gave a complete and lasting September-to-June report on the efforts of Withrow's teachers and pupils in 1943 to end the war."

"The Newlin Math Club undertook to teach the principles of the slide rule to a class of senior students during the last semester. This was its contribution to the war effort, since a knowledge of the slide rule is absolutely necessary for many positions in the armed forces and in industry."

"Whether through participation in a major sport or by means of general workouts and calisthenics in the stepped-up wartime gym program, the attainment of good health was the aim of Withrow's student body in this war year…Seniors were given five periods of gym a week to prepare them for induction; obstacle courses were originated indoors and then moved out as the weather permitted…All in all, this graduating class and the ones following it will be the toughest in Withrow's history."

Chapter 5 – Class of 1943

Purcell

Larry attended Purcell High School on Madison Road not far from his Evanston neighborhood. At that time, Purcell was an all male, Catholic high school.

Students got started late with the Purcell High School *Cavalier* calling 1942-43 the "most history-making year in the 15 years of Purcell." It opens with a montage of photos from Pearl Harbor and December 7, 1941 followed by pages that note "September 8, 1942… Purcell Mobilized for War." References used throughout the yearbook typically were military in nature: Commanders, Aides-De-Camp, Sergeants, and Corporals.

> "Cavaliers of '42-'43 took up the challenge of Uncle Sam in an extended and intensified physical fitness program. Lieutenant Bernard McCashen worked out the first plans for this program before he left to become a physical education instructor in the Navy; Coach Ed Kluska completed it and applied it. In the second semester the gym doors were opened for upperclassmen; and Commando training was the talk of the town. There were, at first, days of stiffness and limping; but limbs soon limbered and Cavaliers were soon 'marching along' chin up and chest out as their Uncle Sam wished."

> "On December 7, 1942, the first anniversary of the attack on the huge American naval and air base at Pearl Harbor, near Honolulu, the faculty and students joined together in attending Mass at St. Francis de Sales Church (next door to the school) and in praying for the repose of the souls of all American boys killed in a year of war. These prayers were especially intended for Purcell boys who have sacrificed their lives on the fields of battle in order to defend and protect their nation. At the Mass, Father Fee read the names of these Purcell graduates and former students and the circumstances surrounding their deaths."

They remembered Army Air Forces pilot, Lieutenant Charles W. Hughes, who was the first graduate to receive the Distinguished Service Cross, awarded posthumously by General Douglas MacArthur. Hughes' airplane was shot down by enemy fire near Darwin, Australia half a world away.

About 80% of the student body enrolled in Victory Corps activities, directed by Brother Lawrence Eveslage. Various divisions included Land, Sea, Air, Production, and Community:

> "The record Victory Corps' participation in wartime activities is indicative of the full-blooded American manner in which Cavaliers took up the challenge it offered: $20,000 in defense sales; a city-shattering record in the coat hanger drive; scrapbooks (for sick and wounded soldiers-included news and sports articles, cartoons; others contained crossword puzzles) for soldiers; Victory book drive; game drive; the savings of drippings and collection of metals. The complete record of their accomplishments was more fully told in the "Schools at War Scrapbook," compiled by members of the Victory Corps and submitted to the National Treasury Department in February."

Brother Larry also initiated a "War Activities Bulletin Board."

"Located in the main corridor and illuminated by the beam of a spotlight, it was a defense inspiration center. Of special interest were the varied bulletins on Purcell graduates in the service—letters from them, newspaper accounts of their exploits." Classes from 1929 to 1942 had over 700 graduates serving "in the Defense of Freedom."

The boys sold War Savings Bonds and War Stamps. During the anniversary week, one senior class led the way with an average purchase per boy of over $75 dollars. By late March, 1943, about $20,000 in bonds and stamps had been purchased by Purcell students. The average purchase per boy was $32. With the first purchase of any stamp, the buyer received a free album for mounting that kind of stamp.

The ten cent stamp album was used to save for the purchase of United States War Savings Bonds. Buyers filled the album with 187 ten cent stamps and added five cents in coin, for a total of $18.75. The album was exchanged at the post office for a War Savings Bond, Series E, which after ten years, would be worth $25. Stamps were sold in five denominations: 10, 25, and 50 cents, one dollar, and five dollar.

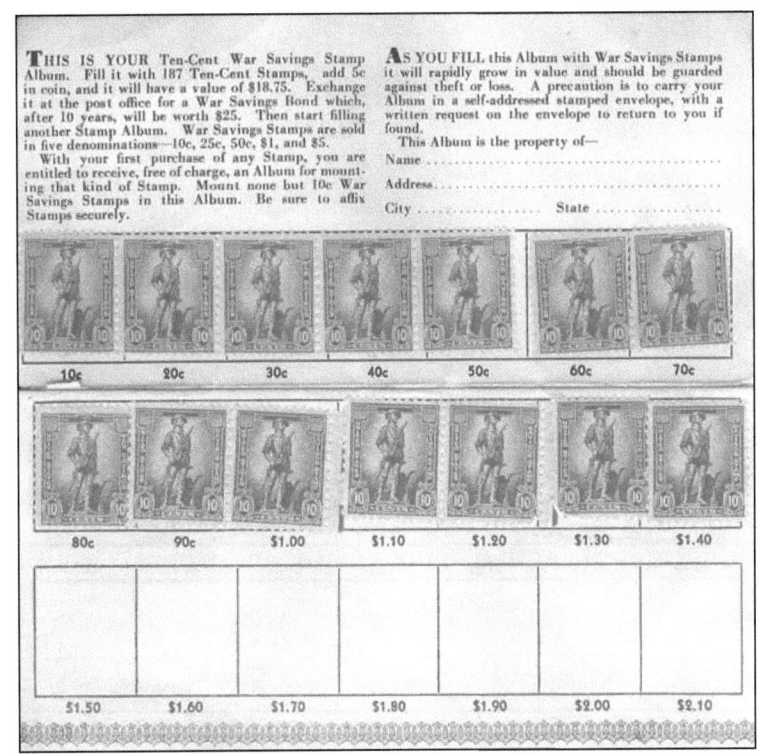

Ten-Cent War Savings Stamp Album Page

If the bond was held for ten years, the buyer received a Treasury check worth 33 1/3 percent more than the original investment—equal to an annual interest rate of 2.9% compounded semiannually. E bonds were also issued in $50, $100, $500, and $1000 denominations at purchase prices of $37.50, $75, $375, and $750.

Students held a coat hanger drive to answer a Red Cross appeal for hangers for soldiers of Keesler Field, Mississippi. Ten thousand coat hangers had been the quota set for all of the city schools. The Cavaliers won with a grand total of 15,224.

Chapter 5 – Class of 1943

Cover of 10 Cent War Savings Stamp Album

War Bond Sleeve

There were still plenty of other activities for the boys to choose from. As a senior, Larry was in the cafeteria squad, Quota Club, and Choral Group.

Purcell's Senior Choral Group – Class of 1943-Larry is in the front row, first from right

Chapter 5 – Class of 1943

Purcell's newly organized choral group "was composed of a large percentage of the senior class." Purcell was the first Parochial boys high school in the area to "undertake the initiation of this cultural operation, and intended to make the Choral Group a permanent extra-curricular activity."

Larry Eckhoff

Graduation Week

Memorial Day (known as Decoration Day) weekend, beginning Friday, May 28, was a week before high school graduation for most of the class of 1943. Two Cincinnati tennis courts, at LeBlond Park on Eastern Avenue and at Solway Park were plowed for use as Victory Gardens—to grow as much local food as possible. They were just right for conversion to the gardens due to the muddy deposits left from an often flooding Ohio river. Six other tennis courts were abandoned due to problems getting enough men to maintain them.

Most sports equipment being produced was going to the armed forces and much of the remaining 25% was allotted to war workers at home. There was "no metal for golf clubs, no bounce for tennis balls or rubber for tennis shoes, no new rods and reels, fewer fish hooks" and while new swim suits and swim caps were advertised by the department stores, only older models left in stock contained elastic or rubber.

It seemed like everything was being rationed due to the war effort, though plenty of department store ads continued to appear in the local papers. Some Cincinnati residents had their rations suspended for trying to purchase gasoline without surrendering their ration coupons. Coupons were also being bought and sold by those attempting to profit.

The Cincinnati Post reported that the Office of Defense Transportation even forbid the use of gasoline for trucks, fire engines, and other commercial vehicles in Cincinnati's 75th annual

Memorial Day parade since that event did not classify as an essential use of the resource. As a result, drivers were warned that use of their vehicles in parades "or any other non-essential pursuit" may have their gasoline allotments reduced by the number of miles of non-essential driving. As plans for the parade continued, it was announced that one of Hamilton County's two surviving Civil War veterans, Frederick Pfiester, was to be the grand marshal. The conflict at hand was still ever present as the same page of *The Post* contained the first pictures of the American tank assault on Attu Island in the south Pacific, while elsewhere, Italy was being bombed by allied forces.

Grocery ads in the local papers had weekly specials for a variety of favorite products such as Taystee Bread, Hires Root Beer, Werk's Pumice Soap, Blue Bonnet Oleomargarine, Kellogg's Corn Flakes, Heinz Genuine Stone-ground Mustard, Mrs. Grass Noodle Soup, and Butter-Nut bread "enriched with B vitamins and iron."

While ads were found for beverage favorites like Tom Collins Jr. "Lithiated Lemon" five cents for a 12 ounce bottle from The Grand Pop Bottling Company, Richardson Root Beer "Enjoy Barq's Root Beer", and "Kool Aid makes 10 big drinks - 5¢", Albers Super Market advertised "Victory Brew" "a new beverage similar to coffee in flavor and aroma" at a mere 14 cents per pound. No ration stamp was needed and customers could purchase as much of the mystery brew as they wanted. There was no mention of the ingredients in "Victory Brew".

Sips would be few and far between for those inclined to imbibe in beverages of an alcoholic sort depending on how much of the stuff they managed to stash away. The aging supply made before the attack on Pearl Harbor was carefully rationed by anyone with stock, and as often happens, was probably being sold for astronomical prices on the black market. Since late 1942, distilleries were only producing alcohol for war purposes. It was used in making smokeless powder, synthetic rubber, chemical warfare materials, and medical supplies.

Lots of War Bonds were sold to help support the war effort. During Retail Stores' War Bond Month, June 8 to July 4, heavy bombers bought by the people of Cincinnati through the purchase of War Savings Bonds actually started their flight to the battle fronts from Cincinnati. All military aircraft serving with U.S. Army forces anywhere in the world were routed to their destination through the Cincinnati offices. A goal of 12 heavy bombers was set as a goal to take off from Cincinnati. Every person buying a bond, and every person filling out a war stamp album and converting it to a bond, was given an opportunity to submit a name for one of the 12 bombers—one entry for each $25 represented by the bond.

Chapter 5 – Class of 1943

The Cincinnati Post had a regular section called "News of the Services" with small photos and blurbs about local service members. Oddly, it shared the page with ads for dancing at Ault Park, LeSourdesville Lake, and Meadowbrook Park's annual opening, plus the "At Your Neighborhood Theater" column advertising dozens of movies. Just about every neighborhood had its own movie house or a drive-in theater and many of them sold war bonds and stamps.

It was thought that continuing vehicles of entertainment, such as movies and local venues serving up dance music, helped boost the morale of the folks at home. The Palace was showing "Presenting Lily Mars" 'a high school girl's dream of success in the theater, with music' starring Judy Garland and Van Heflin. The Lyric offered a twin bill of films of opposite extremes. Radio comedians Lum and Abner starred in "Two Weeks to Live" 'a slapstick comedy with the merest thread of plot', while "Prelude to War" "'traces step by step the gangster policies of Germany, Japan, and Italy that reached a climax at Pearl Harbor. It is a grim document, originally produced for soldier consumption only, which should make everyone who sees it a little less smug over the victory in Tunisia."

Comics found in *The Post* included Abbie an' Slats, Red Ryder, Alley Oop, Wash Tubbs, Our Boarding House with Major Hoople, Li'l Abner, Nancy, Tarzan, Boots and Her Buddies, Freckles and His Friends, Joe Jinks, Race Riley and Commandos, and Out Our Way. Many of them took on light war themes. *The Times-Star* countered with Air-Spotter Anne, Bo-, Joe Palooka, Dixie Dugan, Winnie Winkle, Little Orphan Annie, Deathless Deer, Henry Moon Mullins, The Nebbs, and Dick Tracy.

Cincinnati's main AM radio stations, 550 WKRC, 700 WLW, 1360 WSAI, 1230 WCPO, and 1530 WCKY, published lists of programming for Friday night and Saturday daytime. In addition to news on the hour, WSAI carried two Cincinnati Reds baseball games vs. the Philadelphia Phillies, Cincinnati's own Ruth Lyons, radio shorts of Dick Tracy, Jack Armstrong, and Captain Midnight, The Lone Ranger, concert music, and orchestras led by Chick Mauthe, Tommy Dorsey, and Burt Farber.

Seventeen venues offered music and floor shows featuring orchestras with famous names as Louis Prima, Stan Kenton, Herman Rafalo, and Burt Farber. The venues ranged from downtown hotels like the Netherland Plaza and The Gibson, to supper clubs Beverly Hills and the Lookout House, to amusement parks Coney Island, LeSourdesville, and Castle Farm, to the band stand at venerable Ault Park.

Chapter 5 – Class of 1943

The first of June found the Reds 6 ½ games out in fourth place behind Brooklyn, St. Louis, and Boston. Former Yankee pitcher, Waite Hoyt broadcast Reds games with Lee Allen and Dick Bray.

While *The Cincinnati Times-Star* reported that new inductions were occurring at 300,000 per month, for all men of draft age (18 to 37), not all graduates would be accepted into a branch of service, often due to a physical deficiency of some kind. Often college wasn't an option and the pull of patriotism might have led them to investigate War Agency jobs offered to Civil Service employees. Persons "not engaged in war work at their highest skill" were eligible for Federal government war jobs in Cincinnati with the Army, Navy, and national war agencies. Advertised jobs and pay rates included:

- Automotive mechanics and helpers, .75 to .85 per hour
- Carpenters, for local army establishments for crating important war materials, $1620 to $2182 per year
- Demurrage clerk, $2180 per year, for duty with U.S. Engineers
- Electricians, high linemen, for duty with local army post, $2032 to $2250 per year
- Laborers, .65 per hour, needed by local war agencies
- Life guards, $4.66 per day, for duty at local government housing project, temporarily
- Packers, male, $1620 to $1860 per year, at local war agencies
- Painters and painters' helpers, $1815 to $2032 per year
- Patrolmen, $2032 per year, for duty with the U. S. Air Force
- Statistical clerk, $1970 per year, with Army Air Force
- Storekeepers, $1560 to $2180 per year
- Stenographers and typists, $1560 to $1970 per year, must qualify on U.S. Civil Service examinations
- Tabulating machine operators, $1758 to $1970 per year, for duty with U. S. Treasury Department
- Teletype operators, $1756 per year

As high school graduation drew ever nearer, *The Cincinnati Post* published a story that didn't do much to calm these soon to be soldiers and sailors. It included:

"WHEN PANIC HITS—Expert Reveals How Fear Can Rout Troops" by Marjorie Van De Water

"Panic used as a weapon or touched off accidentally 'can put to rout the most seasoned fighters'. It doesn't take much to touch off a panic among troops who are panic ripe. Then a single cry of 'Gas!' or 'Run!' or 'We're cut off' may start a mad flight."

"The enemy…plays upon it whenever possible. Sometimes agents were planted among the troops to yell 'Gas!' when a confused situation might cause them to panic. It became necessary to work out a

Chapter 5 – Class of 1943

code warning for the actual presence of gas—a code known only to trusted men. Codes…changed daily and troops were instructed not to holler 'Gas!'"

"Other means of spreading panic included the noise of dive bombers…often used to distract and frighten. Anything that makes men tense, on edge, jittery, and over-sensitive to slight noises, half hidden sights, or sudden movements will make them easy victims of panic. Prolonged anxiety, fatigue, exhaustion, lack of sleep, too much alcohol, lack of proper nutrition, hangovers; prolonged exposure to noise and stress of battle, poor morale, rumors, distrust, real or imagined threats—all increased the potential for panic."

At Purcell, graduation week started with the Senior Prom, held on Monday evening, May 31 at the Kenwood Country Club. It is unknown whether Larry attended.

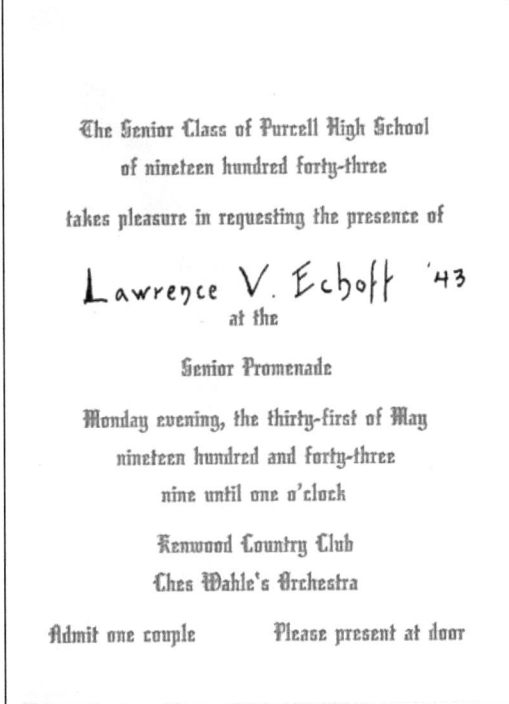
Admittance Ticket to Purcell's Senior Prom

Larry's Senior Picture, Class of 1943

Seniors were given a mimeographed sheet explaining all of the Senior Week activities from the Prom to Class Night, during which they obtained their caps and gowns and rehearsed the commencement processional. The following day, Thursday, June 3, 1943 graduation took place at ten in the morning at Xavier University Field House.

Like so many other 17 year old boys, Larry didn't wait to be drafted—though he did graduate from high school first. He went to the Cincinnati recruiting office and completed his enlistment application for the U.S. Navy. After taking down all of his information, the recruiter gave him a form for his parents to sign. For one week after graduation, Larry held a job as a laborer for Balcrank Company. The following week, he was on that train probably wondering where he would be months from now.

GRATUATES 1943

SENIOR WEEK PROGRAM

CLASS NIGHT

Tuesday, June 1, at 8:15 P.M.
Assemble in third floor corridor. Obtain cap and gown at Room 39. Vest in cap and gown, and place hat and coat in one of the empty lockers on third floor. All are expected to report at least half an hour before the scheduled time and to be in line according to height at 8:00 P.M.
Processional to the auditorium, down the northeast stairs (Vice-Principal's Office). March up the middle aisle.
The Senior Choir take places on the stage; the others on either side of the stage to the right and left of the orchestra.
Recessional after the exercises to the third floor. Remove cap and gown and dress for the street. Take cap and gown home with you. Those who wish may bring a box or bag from home, in order to carry the cap and gown home. None will be provided by the school.

COMMENCEMENT

Thursday, June 3, at 10:00 A.M. At Xavier Field House. Assemble at the place designated at the rehearsal. (Details of the rehearsal will be given later as no information is available now.) Assemble at 9:45 A.M.
Come with cap and gown. As there will be no vesting place provided, do not wear coat or hat, carry cap and gown and vest immediately before entering Xavier Field House. Remove caps during Mass and replace them after Mass.
After the cermony bring caps and gowns to the Brothers in charge and get your refund.

DRESS

On account of the warm weather which usually prevails at this time, you are not required to wear a coat below the gown. It is suggested that you wear a dark suit, a white shirt, a dark tie and polished shoes.

FEE

The Graduation Fee is $7.00; $3.00 will be refunded when the cap and gown is returned in good order. Each Senior will receive five tickets to give to his guests on class night. The two pink ones are for his parents, for whom the better seats will be reserves.

SENIOR PROM:

The Senior Prom will be held Monday May 31, 1943 at Kenwood Country Club. Obtain your bids this week at Room 26.

Chapter 5 – Class of 1943

Larry graduated 9th in his class of 195 students at Purcell High School

Larry and oldest sister Mary Jane

Larry with L-R: Unidentified, brother Donald, unidentified girl, brother Billy, sister Margie

Chapter 5 – Class of 1943

MEMBERS OF THE SENIOR CLASS
1943

Frank J. Alban	Joseph E. Harrigan	Robert T. Moorhead
Frank B. Beckman	Oscar M. Haverkamp	Ralph J. Mott
Ambrose A. Bender	Ray J. Havlin	Alfred L. Mueller
John A. Berger	Albert G. Heidkamp	Donald L. Muenich
Roger E. Berning	Ralph J. Heist	Robert J. Niehaus
Paul Boland	Robert E. Heithaus	Richard C. Nieman
Richard J. Bomkamp	Joseph P. Helmers	Frank G. Niesen
Edward F. Brandstetter	James J. Herking	Harold J. Nolting
Henry J. Brems	John J. Hirn	Edward J. O'Connell
Robert M. Brown	James C. Hoctor	Paul J. Overbeck
Joseph M. Burke	Ray P. Holley	Richard J. Pennekamp
Thomas E. Burke	Dan P. Homan	James C. Pohlman
John K. Byrne	George Hovey	Robert W. Quatkemeyer
Joseph W. Callahan	Jerome J. Hutten	Dominic D. Ranieri
Peter J. Castelli	Howard H. Istock	John S. Rengers
Vincent M. Castellucio	Clement L. Johnston	John W. Rensing
Robert J. Conlon	Frank M. Julian	Edward R. Reyering
Paul V. Connolly	Edward F. Keidel	John J. Reynolds
John L. Contadino	Eugene B. Keidel	Anthony J. Roma
William A. Crowley	William L. Kelley	Paul W. Rusche
Howard F. Deller	John A. Kemper	Edward V. Russo
William J. Dickhaus	Robert E. Kinker	Robert J. Ryan
Elmer J. Diersing	John J. Kinney	Donald J. Scheidler
Thomas J. Dillhoff	Harold J. Klawitter	George N. Schaller
Edward J. Donnellon	Charles L. Klick	Leo B. Schloemer
Arthur S. Doyle	Elmer S. Koehlke	Harry F. Schneider
Francis R. Dugan	James E. Krieger	Charles F. Schulte
Lawrence V. Eckhoff	Joseph A. Kruse	Richard E. Schultz
Charles R. Elbert	Robert P. Krusling	Roman J. Schweikert
Robert H. Ell	William R. Lambert	Charles G. Selzer
Charles B. Farfsing	Carl J. Lampe	Nicholas A. Seta
James M. Fehring	Charles C. Lang	Thomas J. Sink
Paul J. Ferrari	Paul A. Langemeier	William L. Smith
Thomas P. Flanigan	Robert R. Leen	Ben J. Stark
William S. Flynn	Ralph J. Lohbeck	Paul W. Stickley
John B. Foote	Thomas J. Mann	Howard E. Stone
Robert E. Frank	Robert G. Mannes	Francis G. Stretch
William T. Giesting	Lawrence G. Marck	John M. Sullivan
John J. Glassmeyer	William M. McAtee	Leo J. Sunderman
Thomas A. Glassmeyer	Edward J. McNeill	Charles W. Sutter
Louis G. Gruber	Kenneth J. Meibers	Carl W. Tepe
Donald G. Guilfoyle	John E. Menninger	James C. Tobin
Robert F. Hadley	Donald J. Meyer	Robert A. Waechter
Alfred J. Hagedorn	F. Vernon Miller	Kenneth E. Walter
John R. Hanlon	Gordon J. Miller	Robert J. Wellman
Aloysius A. Hare	Edward J. Montag	Harry G. Williams

Purcell High School, Cincinnati, Ohio, Senior Class of 1943

Chapter 6 – Clinton

Larry on a street in Clinton, Oklahoma
"These houses in the back of me aren't too bad
but nothing like Cincy. Larry"

Transferred 25 August 1943, to duty at NAS Clinton, Oklahoma to R.R. M. Emmet, Captain, USN, Utility Squadron Sic, Service Force, U.S. Atlantic Fleet

Date reported aboard:

August 28, 1943 Stag Three, Training Task Force, SATFOR,

U.S. Fleet

Upon returning to Great Lakes Naval Training Station following his "graduation liberty" Larry found himself assigned to a Naval Air Station in a Midwest town he'd probably never heard of, Clinton, Oklahoma. Join the Navy and see...Oklahoma?

Clinton-Sherman Air Force Base (AFB), located seventeen miles southwest of Clinton, was established in October 1943 as Clinton Naval Air Station.

The beginnings of Clinton-Sherman came in 1942 when the War Department acquired about five thousand acres of Washita County farmland by condemnation for a naval air station. Four 6000 foot runways, three hangars, twenty-four barracks, and numerous temporary facilities soon appeared next to the town of Burns Flat. More than thirty-five hundred officers and enlisted men served with the Special Task Air Groups in the operation of aircraft drones and glider bombs.

According to Headquarters, Training Task Force, the mission of Clinton Naval Air Station was "The formation, outfitting, and training of special units; tactical evaluation of equipment as directed by the Chief of Naval Operations; operation and maintenance of air stations, air activities, and outlying fields under TTF command; acquisition of target areas, and erection and maintenance of targets thereon for use in training; and maintenance of a pool of electronics equipment."

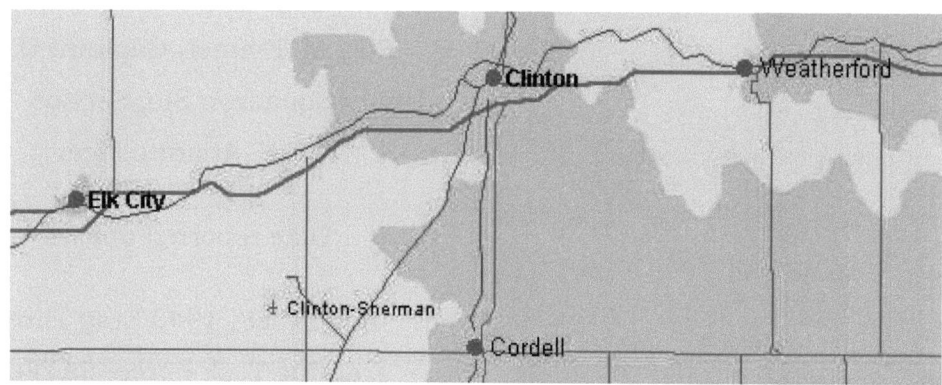
Map shows location of Clinton-Sherman Air Force Base (AFB)/Clinton Naval Air Station, Oklahoma

Up until now, Clinton's main claim to fame was probably U.S. Highway 66, better known as Route 66. The eastern Oklahoma section of Route 66 only went from dirt to a paved road in 1937. Towns along the flat, straight highway going west toward the Texas border from Oklahoma City ran in order: El Reno, Hinton and Geary, Hydro, Weatherford, Clinton (90 miles from OK City), Canute, and Elk City. How many people know there was a German POW camp just over the border from Oklahoma, between Shamrock and McLean, Texas? A guard sat on the cab of a truck while German prisoners worked in the area farm fields.

Shamrock, Texas to Clinton, Oklahoma

Lots of military vehicles and convoys of equipment, supplies, and troops plied Route 66. Unlucky motorists had to pull off the road until they passed since the roads weren't adequate to handle all of the traffic. Rubber and gasoline rationing slowed civilian traffic to almost nothing. Thousands traveled the route as uniformed service members or passed through on their way to factories on the west coast. The population of Clinton alone grew to nearly 7000 during the war but there wasn't much civilian construction since materials and workers were scarce. Persons visiting servicemen needed places to stay and while there was a building at the base run by wives of officers, most buildings by the airport were constructed of mostly tar paper.

Quite a bit of training took place in Oklahoma. The town of Norman was home to an aviation mechanic school and sailors took gunnery training at a school in Purcell, Oklahoma. Clinton NAS was known for training navigators.

As of September 9, 1943, Larry was assigned to Stag Three training task force. The following month, he penned this letter to his mom.

October 9, 1943

Saturday Nite, 19:30

Dear Mom,

Well here it is Saturday nite and I have the duty but it isn't so bad since I got myself changed today. I was supposed to have a 12 to 4 watch tonite but they took me off of compartment cleaning and now I am supposed to be working as a Yeoman. Now I stand my guard watches here in the office and do what ever I want to until about 9:30. After that I head for bed. All of the flight schedules weren't finished when the regular Yeoman left so I had to type it and then run it off on the mimeograph machine. I made it o.k. even if it was the first time that I had to do it.

I have been getting pretty much mail here of late and now I am trying to get caught up on it. I have one to write to you and one to Dot E., one to Mary Jane [his sisters], Dorothy H. [neighbor Larry sometimes dated], and since I got a letter from Mrs. Leisring [his buddy Jerry's mom] and [cousin] Bill Kemp I guess that I better answer them too, tonight while I have the time and feel like writing.

I have been doing pretty good with my vitals here since I got sick that one nite. I am getting used to being without my front tooth and now I am no longer self-conscious about being without a tooth in the front of my big mouth. [According to his sister Dorothy, Larry had an abscess and the Navy dentist pulled the tooth-abscesses were fairly common back then.]

I think you got kind of mixed up about this Bob Geiger I told you about. Bob is from Columbus, Ohio. The fellow I told you about from Blair Ave. is a guy who just came here on the base recently. He is a different guy all together. This Bob Geiger is not from College Hill. I imagine you know that by now. (I am trying to type too fast that is why I am making so many mistakes.)

You can tell everyone that I am glad to hear about them even if it does have to be forwarded through you. I know how little Mrs. Watson [next door neighbor] writes so tell her I don't mind as long as I hear from her through you anyway. Don't forget to tell her this, now.

As for the Xmas gifts, don't let them worry you because I don't know but maybe I will get to come around that time. Even if I don't get to come home just hold everything up until I find out for sure what I am going to be able to do at that time. Around here we don't always know where we will be the next day.

I am spending too much time trying to think and also try to help some other guy that is trying to type a letter to his mother or some body and he is the kind of a guy you sometimes wonder about. You know what I mean I hope, don't you? When I was stapling the flight schedules together, I was kidding him and I got him so sore that I was waiting for him to take a Punch at me but it never materialized after all. (Look at the words I can use when I type. How about that?)

I have one other thing to tell you about before I start to write to somebody else. Here we still have an inspection on Friday. We have to put on clean mattress covers and pillow covers for this inspection. Last Friday I waited until just before leaving the barracks before putting the clean ones on and I also got all of the wrinkles out of it. When I came back to the barracks at 5:30 I found a tag on my bunk and I thought I was going to get extra duty for something. Instead of extra duty I found this tag on my bunk.

Chapter 6 – Clinton

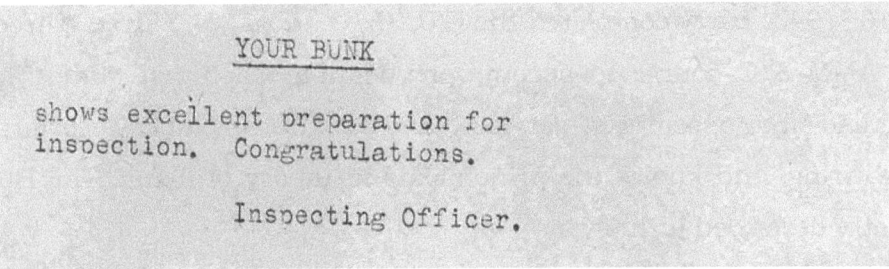

With lots of love to all,

Larry

P.S. KEEP WRITING.

The Duster was published by and for personnel attached to U.S. Naval Air Station, Clinton, Oklahoma. It received Camp Newspaper Service material: news features, and cartoons syndicated to service publications in addition to NAS submissions.

November 4, 1943 - *The Duster* – Clinton NAS newspaper

Chapter 6 – Clinton

On November 10, 1943, Larry completed the GTC (3/C and 2/C) course. Three days later he completed the AMM 3/C course to become an Aviation Machinist Mate, Third Class. An Aviation Machinist Mate assembles, services, and repairs airplanes and airplane engines, splices aircraft wiring, and knows the principles and theory of flying. The Bureau of Naval Personnel Bulletin described it this way:

> "Aviation Machinist's Mate - Maintains and repairs aircraft engines, propellers, fuel systems, brakes, hydraulic system, gears, starters. Operates machine-shop tools."

While Larry's family was sharing a Thanksgiving dinner at home in Cincinnati, he was taking part in the feast at NAS Clinton. The captain's Thanksgiving message was printed across from the menu for the day's feast.

> "Of all people in this world today, we at this station should be most grateful. Recall the privations of the first settlers of America and of the enslaved peoples of today. Then, along with gratitude for your own blessings, pray that we may soon bring this same bounty, freedom, and joy to all the sections of the earth."
>
> C.A. Bond, Commander U.S. Navy, Commanding U.S. Naval Air Station, Clinton, Oklahoma

A couple of weeks later, Larry celebrated his 18th birthday while stationed at NAS Clinton. Here was another milestone day not enjoyed with family and friends at home—and Christmas was only weeks away.

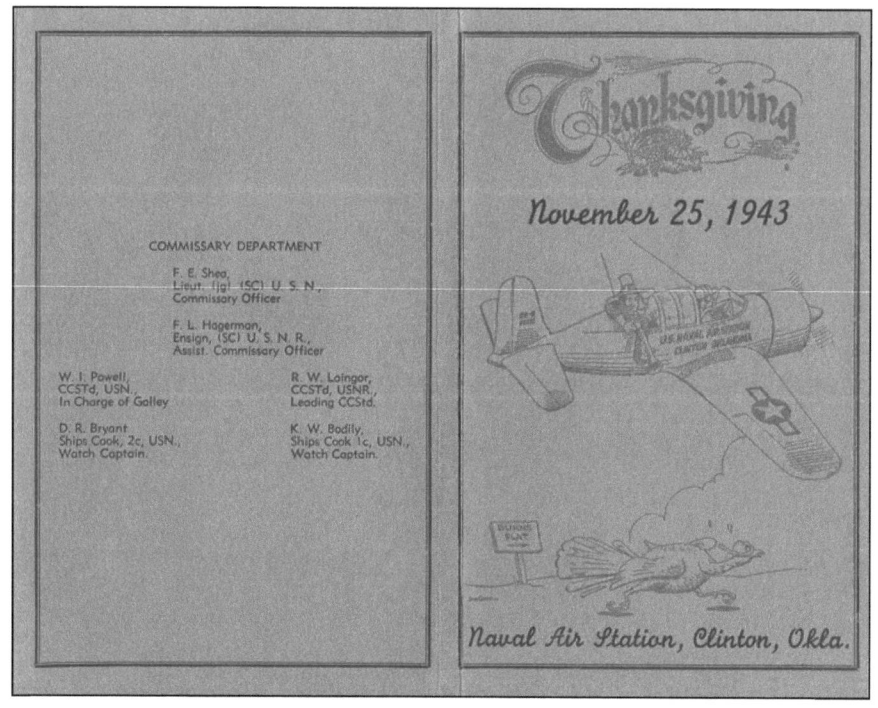

Outside of Thanksgiving Menu for NAS Clinton, November 25, 1943

Chapter 6 – Clinton

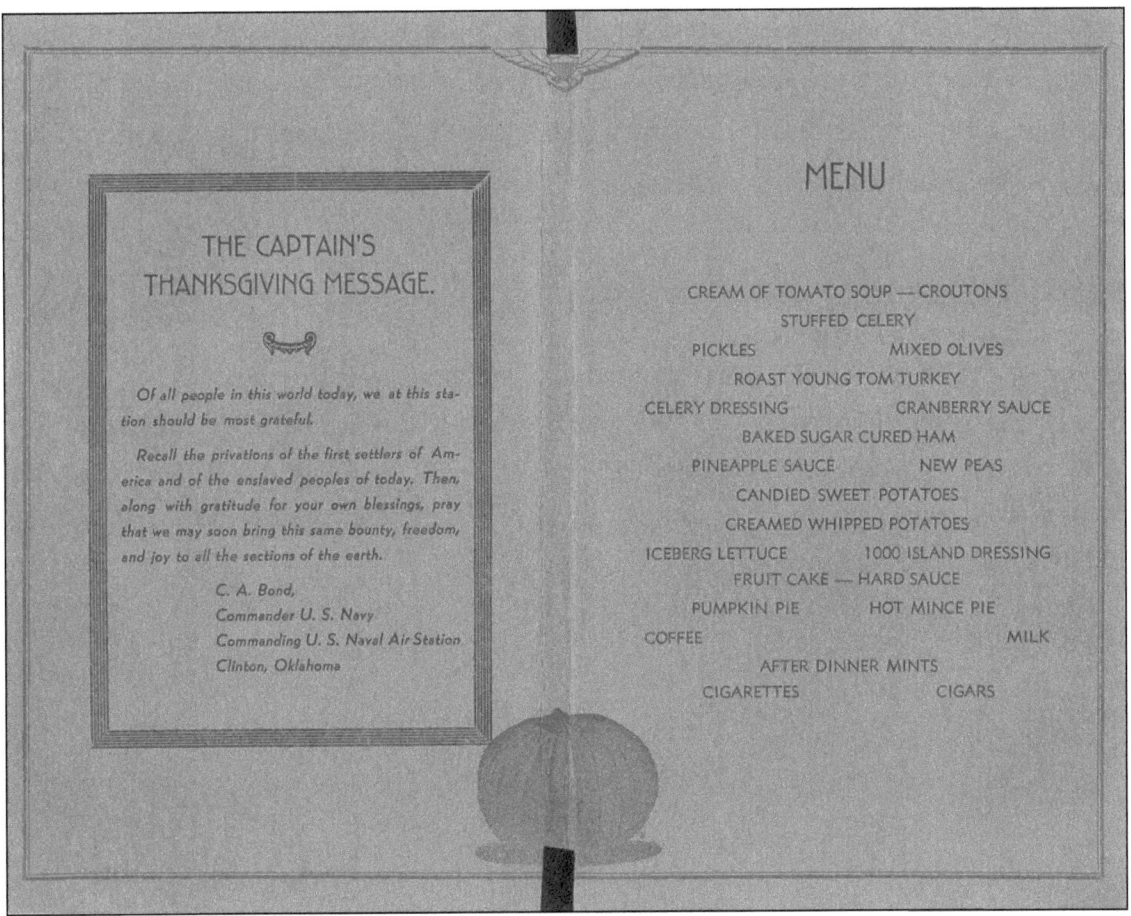

Inside of Thanksgiving Menu for NAS Clinton, November 25, 1943

Mail of all kinds, especially hand written letters, helped service members to make it through all year long but particularly during the holiday season—they were ties to home. Packages, particularly ones containing homemade food, were most popular. Mail kept morale up and often led to infatuations between service members and "pen pals" back home. It was considered patriotic to write to the troops whether they had a personal connection back home or not. In addition, letters were exchanged among service members in different places during the war since friends, neighbors, and other family members were also serving. The universal Christmas wish was "to be home, safe and sound, warm and dry."

As 1943 drew to a close, the war still raged on in the European and Pacific Theaters. By 1944, 12 million Americans were in uniform. During the war, 25,000 Japanese-Americans were in the service in addition to those in U.S. internment camps. War production made up 44% of the Gross National Product (GNP). There were 19 million more workers than five years earlier and 35% were women.

Chapter 6 – Clinton

At NAS Clinton, Larry started the new year with the apparent intention of keeping a daily activity log—often typed on small pieces of paper, occasionally hand written. Sometimes sounding like diary entries and other times like letters home, Larry tells his story as a sailor at an in-country base not quite in the middle of nowhere, in his own words.

January 6, 1944. (Day-off)

Got out of bed at 1100, went to chow. Went to laundry to pick up my dress blues. (.75) Walked out to the main gate, got ride all the way into Clinton. Went to movies and saw "NINE LIVES ARE NOT ENOUGH" Then went to H & K and ate. Went to another movie and saw "SENORITAS FROM CHICAGO". Caught 2200 bus to base and hit the sack about 2310.

No mail today. Wrote none.

Larry

January 7, 1944.

Got to work about 0745, left for dispensary at 0840. Snow and wind raising a blizzard. Plenty cold out. Walked all the way and froze. Waited in dispensary from 0905 until 0940 then had to have two teeth filled. Left there at 1100. Caught bus and went to chow then back to the office. Wrote out memo on the coffee mess. Whitt. made (jg) passed out cigars but I missed them.

Five letters today.

Mom, Dottie E. [his sister], Dottie H. (3) [girl from the neighborhood he dated]

Wrote none yet.

Secured at 1521.

Larry

Chapter 6 – Clinton

**Cartoon in *The Duster* –Servicemen crammed on a bus with Larry's handwritten note above it
"Whole truth and nothing but!"**

January 6, 1944. (Day-off)
Got out of bed at 1100, went
to chow. Went to laundry to
pick up my dress blues.(.75)
Walked out to the main gate,
got ride all the way into
Clinton. Went to movies and
saw "NINE LIVES ARE NOT ENOUGH"
Then went to H & K and ate.
Went to another movie and saw
"SENORITAS FROM CHICAGO".
Caught 2200 bus to base and
hit the sack about 2310.

No mail today. Wrote none.
          Larry
          LARRY

January 7, 1944.
Got to work about 0745, left
for dispensary at 0840. Snow
and wind raising a blizzard.
Penty cold out. Walked all the
way and froze. Waited in dispensary from 0905 until 0940
then had to have two teeth filled .Left there at 1100. Caught
bus and went to chow then back
to the office. Wrote out memo on
the coffee mess. Whitt. made (jg)
passed out cigars but I missed
them.
Five letters today.
    Mom, Dottie E. Dottie H. (3)

Wrote none yet.
Secured at 1521.   *Larry*

Samples of Larry's Log Entries, printed larger than their actual size

Chapter 6 – Clinton

Jan. 7, 1944.

After securing today a blizzard came up, and the snow piled in drifts and also it blinded anyone trying to walk in it. I went to chow and then to the movie on the base with Henry, Kasper, and another fellow. Saw the "Iron Major" thought it was pretty good. Afterwards I went to the canteen and bought some soap and stationary. Took a shower and hit the sack after reading a little of "Fast Company." Secured at 2230.

Larry

Henry Kendjorsky, a sailor at NAS Clinton hailing from the southeastern Ohio town of Yorkville, was about two years older than Larry and probably his best friend while stationed at the base. Kasper was Kasper Schiller from New York.

Larry Eckhoff on left, Henry Kendjorsky on right

Chapter 6 – Clinton

January 8. (6° above 0°)

Reveille at 0700. Ate chow at 0715, snow had stopped but drifts were so high that couldn't even walk through them. Had to walk to the tower and found that all the traffic was snowbound on the base and in towns near by. All officers calling up and giving word that they are snowbound. It is now 0930 and very few officers are on the base. No personnel in the office force here except 5 out of 17. Flying is secured, naturally.

Larry

Jan 9, 1944 Sunday 1245

We secured the office at 1500 then I wrote a letter to Dottie. After going to the barracks, taking a shower, I went ashore with Henry and to my regret KS. also. We went to Cordell and after eating a half dozen times K and I went to the show and saw "Coney Island". Met Jesse Lemons [sp-written in cursive], then sat through the show again with her. Walked her home and saw she was a very young Okie, as usual. Caught bus at 0100 and hit the sack at 0210.

No letters today. Wrote one. Liberty this evening. (Cordell)

Larry

January 10 Monday

Arose from the sack at 0715 went to chow and got to work at 0800. At 0845 went to Hanger #1 and mustered with King in Lt. Willy's office. This is the first muster for Stag III. I am going to be a log yeoman so they say. Typed out watch list then went to chow at 1110. Returned at 1230. A little bit of flying today. R4D returned with Lt. (1a) Brewer at controls.

1 letter from D.H. Wrote none yet. Larry 1305

[King is probably Roy Dodds King from Longview, Texas]

C-47 Skymaster
Photo courtesy of U.S. Museum of the Air Force

The Douglas Skytrain R4D-5 troop/cargo transport was similar to the Air Force C-47. The Marine Corps, particularly the South Pacific SCAT group used this plane in their combat transport operations.

Jan 10, 1944 Monday (later)

Then went to work on a schedule and had a terrible headache so I went down to sick bay and got some pills. Came back up and from 1600 to 1715 dozed in a chair in Ready Room. Went to Clinton with Bob Craven and ate in Harry's. At 2140 went to Del Rio to see "A Lady Takes a Chance." Not so hot. Went to Harry's again, then caught 1230 bus to the base.

Wrote no letters. Received none.

Larry   [Bob Craven was from Denver, Colorado]

Jan. 11, 1944 Tuesday.

Reveille at 0745. Mustered with Wing III at 0900 in #101. Did nothing this morning. Went to chow at 1100 returned at 1210. (It is now 1225.) Am now going to try to read "Fast Company."

(Wing III payday, (15) Saturday)

No mail this morning. Wrote none yet either. Larry

Chapter 6 – Clinton

Jan. 11, 1944 Tuesday

Went to early chow then with myself went to a movie on the base. Saw "Heaven Can Wait." Not such a good movie. Returned to my barracks and took a shower. Couldn't go to bed because there were a dozen guys playing poker so I just laid on the bunk and watched them play. At 10:00 P.M. when the lights went out I finally got to go to bed. Slept well all night.

No letters today either way.

Larry

Jan. 12, 1944. Wednesday

Got out of the sack about 0715 this morning and went to chow. The chow was pretty lousy. Beans for breakfast again. Came to work about 0800 then messed around until 0900 at which time I went over to the hangar and mustered with Stag III. Didn't do much of anything this morning. After chow I crapped out in the Ready Room until Whittington came in and said we had a lot of work to do. Came back and worked a while then until time for chow again. I drove the "jeep" up again and also delivered schedules tonight. Picked our officer up at the Officer's Mess on the dot of seven. Henry told me he made a date for me for tomorrow night with his girlfriend's sister. A blind date. That's something, ain't it. Have to do one of two things at 0900 tomorrow morning. Dentist appointment and Stag III muster.

A letter from Bob Carroll today, about time, NO? Answered Bob's letter. Duty tonight.

Larry

There weren't many who were not touched by the war. Seemingly everyone knew someone—a family member, cousin, neighbor, classmate, teacher, coworker—who was affected. Larry was no different. Bob Carroll (Army Air Corps) was one of Larry's buddies from Purcell and the neighborhood. Jerry Leisring, in the Navy somewhere in Europe, went all through grade school with Bob and high school with Larry and Bob. A few houses down on Bevis Avenue, Art Koenig had a nephew stationed in the Pacific—Sgt. Joe Ungerbuhler was Art's sister's son. Bill Ford was a neighbor of the Koenigs on Bevis Avenue. The oldest of four boys, Bill was in Japan and stationed on a ship. Jack Meyers, a neighbor who lived about four doors from the Eckhoffs, was apparently injured as the Private was listed in Larry's address book at the Second Conv. Hospital, APO NY. Larry's cousins Jack and Bill Kemp were in the Air Corps and Navy, respectively, and by June, 1944 Larry's cousin Dick (Richard Mervin Eckhoff) was part of the crew on the destroyer U.S.S. Peiffer (DE588).

Women were not just Rosie the Riveters either. When the Women's Army Auxiliary Corps (WAAC) was founded, women pilots flew planes from manufacturers to bases in the U.S. They didn't think of it as a career in the military rather as a way "to serve country, help America win the war, and get home again." Early in the war, there was a need for military clerks, drivers, telephone operators, medical technicians, cooks, and couriers. Larry's cousin Lorrayne was a secretary at Wright Aero Corp and cousin Mary was a secretary for the U.S. Office for Emergency Management.

An often overlooked branch of service was the one chosen by Larry's neighbor John Thomas "Jack" Gallenstein, Sr. He was a Merchant Marine, six years older than Larry. In 1936, Congress passed the Merchant Marine Act requiring that U.S. merchant ships be "manned with trained and efficient citizen personnel." Two years later, the Act was modified to create the U.S. Merchant Marine Cadet Corps and to authorize a shoreside training facility. The site chosen in 1942 was the former Walter P. Chrysler estate in Kings Point, Long Island, New York—completed in 18 months.

There was a great need for merchant marine officers during the early years of World War II. Cargo ships, so vital to the cause, were being sunk at an alarming rate. At the time, new vessels could be built faster than the officers and crews to sail them could be trained.

> "In response to this manpower shortage, the Academy's shoreside training program was reduced from 18 months to 12, and eventually to six. Kings Point students were sent to sea for practical training during the war. They often found themselves in combat situations, and 142 students were lost at sea in enemy action… Nonetheless, during the war, the Academy produced more than 6,600 merchant marine officers."

Larry's cousins Bill Kemp (USAC) and brother Jack Kemp (Navy)

**Sgt. Jos. F. Ungerbuhler, Jr.,
Engineering Aviation Battalion**

**John Gallenstein, Merchant Marine,
Larry's neighbor and future brother-in-law
Photo courtesy of Diane Gallenstein**

Chapter 6 – Clinton

United states Naval Air Station

Clinton, Oklahoma

Jan. 12, 1944. Wednesday

At 2130, L. L. Ashmun drove me to barracks 507. Woke up Henry and got the key to my locker. Came to 511 and took a shower, then went to bed like a good little boy.

Larry

January 13, 1944 Thursday

Got up at 0730 and ate chow. Then went to the office. What a start for the day. Went to the dispensary at 0845 and waited until 1000 before getting into the chair. From 1000 to 1030 I had one tooth filled, then made another appointment for 1300 on Wednesday, Jan. 18. Walked back to the barracks and here I am at 1110. Got a date tonight in Cordell, and have a ride all fixed up for 1830 tonight. Not bad for a start, no? Still have bad head cold.

Larry

January 13, 1944 Thursday

After chow I spent most of my time in the Ready Room sleeping. Got my laundry and forgot to take it to the barracks with me when we secured at 1700. Henry and myself went to town and had a date at 1930 with two sisters in Cordell. That blind date was O.K. We went to a show and saw "Sahara," which was pretty good. Then we sat in the Steak House for a while then went down to the girls' house and talked until 1230. It wasn't so bad.

Larry

Chapter 6 – Clinton

Jack Mueller, a pilot, was a neighbor of the Eckhoff family

Bill Ford and his family lived across the street from the Koenigs on Bevis Avenue. Bill served in Japan and on a ship.

Jack Ficker, another Eckhoff friend in the Navy, dated Larry's sister Lois

Jim Johnson was a friend of Larry's who dated his sister Dorothy

Chapter 6 – Clinton

Jan 14, 1944 Friday.

Got up ate chow, changed my mattress cover and got to the office at 0803. Went to Wing III muster at 0900 and here I is at 0930.

Larry

Division 3

Jan 14, 1944 Friday

Crapped out in Ready Room until 3:00 then went to the barracks and slept until 1658. Then went to chow and came down to tower. At 1930 Ensign Hansman/Harrison[?] joined us in the tower and at 2000 started to deliver flight schedules for the last time. Went to the canteen then came into the Ready Room until 2300 and Henry saw a movie when Henry finished pressing his clothes for the commissioning. Then returned to the barracks and took a shower then hit the sack.

Das Alles,

Larry

On January 15, 1944, Larry was transferred and received aboard Hedron, Stag Three SATFOR, U.S. Fleet, Training task force at NAS Clinton.

Jan. 15, 1944 Saturday.

Woke up at 0630 coughing my head off. Got out of the sack at 0800 and came to the tower. Went over to muster at 0900. After muster waited until all Wing men were paid which was then 1120. Practiced review until 1140. Went to chow, (grilled ham) (cherry sauce). Then to barracks, cleaned up then back to tower now waiting for 1400 for commissioning ceremony. They are going to take moving pictures when we (Henry and I) come out of the Hanger Door. Time to secure.

Chapter 6 – Clinton

Got letter from Moms "diesen Morgen." Is she sore at me. Ya?

Larry

At 1500, we lined up in Hanger 101 and the commissioning began with 5 men reading their orders to be commanding officers. At 1530 the ceremonies were over and then the muster business began. Its snafu. Henry and I are now in Cordell at 1820. (Steakhouse)

Larry

(Johnny)

Jan. 15, 1944 Saturday

At 1830, we left Cordell and stood on the highway waiting for a ride. We got one very shortly with an officer and rode in peace and comfort into Clinton. Henry and I started drinking beer in the bowling alley and then we went to the Bungalow where we met Margie and Marie as per date. We then went and had Henry's picture taken, then out to a 'Miserable' night at Sooner's. At 2400 Henry and I left and went to a preview without the girls. At 0200 we met them again in the bus station and rode the bus to the base.

Saw "Alaskan Highway" and ------ (Double feature)

Got letter from Frederich Family and 2 from Dot H. Wrote none again.

Hit the sack at 0420.

Larry

<u>Margie</u> <u>and</u> <u>I</u> <u>get</u> <u>Along</u> <u>Fine</u>. I hope.

[The Frederich family were neighbors in Larry's old neighborhood, College Hill. Their daughter went to grade school with Larry and attended Commercial School with Larry's sisters Dorothy and Mary Jane. Dot H. lived on Larry's street.]

Chapter 6 – Clinton

Clinton, Oklahoma circa 1944, probably the center of town

Left – Larry and Marie Weiss/Weese in front of theater
Right - Henry Kendjorsky and Marie

Jan. 16, 1944 Sunday

Secured the office at 1600. Henry and I went ashore and at 1945 took Margie and Marie to the movie "Destroyer." The third time I've seen the picture. Went to Saunders and eat for awhile then went to their house. Talked to them on the porch for a while then went to the Washington Hotel and waited for the bus. At 0100 the last bus came and we got to the base about 0200 and hit the sack. Had to stand on the bus all the way to the station.

No letters this afternoon.

Wrote one home but forgot to mail it.

Signed:

Larry Eckhoff

(Johnny Armstrong)

P.S.

Sat for a while and talked to Mr. and Mrs. Weiss and I liked this pretty much but I think that they thought I was crazy or something. I made, of myself, a pretty good fool, I think. My hat almost was recognized, I had a bad moment there until it was safe in my hands again.

Larry's friend Bob Carroll, Army Air Corps at home in Evanston

Larry Eckhoff, Albert J. (Jerry) Leisring, unidentified, Robert (Bob) Carroll

Chapter 6 – Clinton

Jan 16, 1944. Sunday

Henry woke me at 0730 this morning and we came to our new office. Crapped out all morning with nothing to do. Got a letter from Billy. [Billy is Larry's eight year old brother.] Went to chow at 1100 returned at 1215. Roast loin of pork for chow. Not Bad for a change. It is now 1255 and still nothing to do. What a way to spend time in the Navy.

Larry

Jan. 17 1944 Monday

Henry woke me at 0730 and we went to chow then came to the office. Did nothing all day secured at 1730. I at chow then took a shower and hit the sack at 1915. Slept thru.

Larry

January 18, 1944 Tuesday

Woke up at 0630 got up at 0700. Put my laundry out and went to chow. Came to the office and did nothing all morning. Gruber and I talked about a lot of the boys from Purcell. They got their log rack but we didn't. Went over to the Tower and had a cup of coffee and then swiped some log books. At chow at 1100 and returned at 1210. Argued with Chief Moore for about 15 minutes.

Jan 18, 1944 Tuesday

Hit the deck at 0715 and went to chow. Forgot Henry. Came to work at 0100. Went over to the tower, drank some coffee. Sat around for 1/2 hour. Returned to hangar and stood outside for 20 min. put material from tower in King's office then went to chow at 1100. Returned to Hangar. Did a little work and crapped out the rest of the time. Secured at 1730. Got dressed in the barracks then went ashore with Henry to Clinton. Met Lulu and Henry and she and myself went to the movie and saw, "Woman of the Year." Saw it before as usual. Came back on the 1230 bus. Wrote letter to D.H. received none.

Larry

Jan. 19, 1944 Wednesday

Got up at 0700 this morning. Ate chow with Henry then came to the office. Did a little work this morning, on yellow sheets then went to chow at 1100 with Henry. Went to the dispensary at 1230 and waited until 1315 for doctor to come in.

Got in the chair and he answered a telephone so I fell asleep. Slept until 1345 when he said he was too busy and would have to make a different appointment for me. Got my laundry and met Geiger there. Went to the barracks and shaved and took a shower then returned to Hangar about 1445. Got Martin to stand my watch so Henry and I went to town. Marie, Margie, Henry, me and two other couples. Movie, steakhouse, Weiss/Weese's house. stayed, (Henry and me) until 3 minutes to 1 and almost missed bus.

Larry

L-R: Larry and Henry in dungarees near Margie and Marie's house

Chapter 6 – Clinton

January 20, 1944 Thursday

Hit the deck at 0715. Went to chow and then came to the office and began a long day. Worked on the logs for a while then went to chow at 1115. Stopped in the canteen and got some weeds and candy. Typed flight schedules but naturally. NO? Got stuck at the office tonight until 1015, don't know why. Worked hard too! Almost got gypped out of tomorrow off but I think I have him foxed, I hope.

Got a letter from BC [his buddy Bob Carroll]

Wrote none.

Au Revoir.

(Warm Weather) Larry (Johnny)

21 January, 1944 Friday

Day off. Got out of the sack at 0830. Put on dress blue and headed for town. Got into Clinton at 1030. Went to the dentist and it is still $30. Went to the show then and saw "A Yank is Never Licked" also "-----". Thumbed into Cordell and ate in the "steakhouse" then called Margie on the phone and she said that she would be in the base tonight. At 1945 woke Henry in his barracks and we got ready to go to the party in the Mess Hall. (Dance, eat and drink) Met Margie there and fooled around for a while then ate and had hot turkey sandwiches. Not too bad. At 0100 everything was over and the girls all left on the buses for home.

Wrote a letter to mom in the USO in Clinton. Received one from Dottie E. and H.

<u>Das Alles</u>.

Warm Weather

Larry

Chapter 6 – Clinton

Just like the USO hostesses in Cincinnati, the volunteers in Clinton served food and coffee, usually cooked and donated by local people, sang songs around a piano, danced, and played records. Dating of servicemen was not allowed though buses filled with young women and their chaperones were welcome at dances on the base. At the USO, servicemen could wash up, rest, and write letters, just as Larry did. Each facility was as different as the town or organization that kept it running but they were all a home away from home for service members.

Some women, after working long hours in factories, still managed to join with the rest of the town to make the troops feel at home. Servicemen were invited into private homes near the bases, often for Sunday supper or to join with local families during holiday celebrations.

Postcard of "The Lounge" at the Joplin, Missouri USO Club

22 January, 1944 Saturday

Woke up at 0900 this morning and was supposed to be at work by 0800. Worked on the yellow sheets and logs all morning then went to chow. Began to work in the office with King after chow, looks as if I will be there all the time now. Worked all afternoon there, and no time for anything. Duty tonight. Saw Margie at noon chow today and Henry and I talked to her for awhile then we came to work. Henry has a date and I would too if I didn't have the duty tonight.

Got a letter from Mom and D.H. today. Guess I will write one or two now.

It is now 2000. Letter to Billy Eckhoff and Dorothy H.

2200

Warm Weather. Larry (Johnny)

22 January, 1944

Saturday

Secured at 2200, then went to the barracks and took a shower and hit the sack at about 2300. Signed:

23 January 1944

Sunday

This morning I got to sleep until 1200 noon, but I got up early, 1100. I went to chow but didn't see Henry or Margie. They did see each other. Came to the office to work at about 1300. Worked until 1730, and had none too much time to myself all day either. Henry and myself got ready and went to town because we were pretty P.O. at anything and everything in general. We stood on the road to the gate until 1945 and had almost given up hope of getting a ride into town when two Army Officers and their girls picked us up and rode us into Cordell in a big new ---(Can't remember what kind of car it was.) The date was supposed to be for 1930 but we got there at 2010 which wasn't too bad at that for not getting a ride. Henry and I went down to the Weese family's residence where we met Margie, Marie, Rosalie, and Joe, of Course. From here we went to the show, but since it was so crowded we went next door to the Cafe and got me something to eat. I am always hungry these days, for some unknown reason. At close to 2200 we went to the movie again, after waiting in the door until all the other people had gotten out of it. We sat in one whole row all the way from one wall to the center aisle. The show was, as usual, one that I had seen already, "Mr. Lucky", but I didn't mind seeing it again because it wasn't a bad show. After the show, we all walked down to the Weese family's home again, but Rose'a and Joe, who went to Rosa's house, I guess. Henry started to play with the dog again but I put a stop to that in a hurry this time. Finally he sat with Marie and I sat with Margie. It was pretty late already so there wasn't much time for anything of any kind. At 2455, I finally decided it was time for us to leave and catch the bus if we were going to catch it at all. I kissed Margie good-night and Henry couldn't break himself away from Marie but finally it was managed and we ran our tails off so that we wouldn't end up in the SP headquarters instead of in our nice beds in the barracks. We finally got the bus and talked all the way in, so the ride seemed pretty short for a change. Hit the sack about 0200.

Signed:

Larry (Johnny)

Henry Kendjorsky and the Weese family dog

24 January, 1944 Monday

This morning I got out of the sack at about 0715. I went to chow with Henry when he came to the barracks at about 0720. At 0800 this morning we all (all enlisted personnel of the Maintenance and Material Department) (in Stag III) had to take physical drill. It was some drill. I have been feeling the effects of it ever since I stopped it this morning. I worked as usual this morning, then went to chow with Henry at about 1130. We went back to my barracks and talked a little and read the letters that we received this morning. Came back to the office about 1300 and went back to work. This evening the schedules didn't come in until late so I went to chow and came back to the office afterwards and finished them up. Got finished with all my work about 1930 or later and delivered them. Now I am catching up on the diary that I am having so much trouble keeping up with. Henry has the duty and he took out a little time as per usual to make a phone call at the tower. (Guess who) I guess it is now about time to secure, I hope. 2115

Got a letter from Billy, Lois [Larry's sister], and Dottie (H).

Wrote none. Signed:

Larry

(Johnny)

Jan. 25, 1944 Tuesday (Duty nite)

Got up early as usual (0730) and ate chow and went to the office. Not much work all day. Secured at 1730. Then came back and stood my duty. Worked on engine logs with Gruber and Ens. Crites/Criter until 2300. Went to the barracks, took a shower, and hit the sack.

Larry

Got 1 letter from Margie (E) [Larry's 7 year old sister] and one from Dottie (H).

Went to dentist this morning, left at 0845, just after taking "Muscles" and had two teeth filled and he took an x-ray of the two teeth where the one is missing. Got back to the office at 0110. Good duty, no? Was in the chair for 1/2 hour.

Larry

Chapter 6 – Clinton

Jan. 26, 1944 Wednesday

Got up about 0730 went to chow and went to the office. Worked a little in the morning then went to chow. Did nothing much in the afternoon. Ran off about 2000 pages from stencils, went after the mail in the Dodge pickup. Talked King into letting me off at 1730, went to the barracks. Henry is off today. Took a shower and Henry came over and we left at 6:00 p.m. Walked out to the road and got a ride from one of the farmers going to Cordell. Got in about 0830. Ate in the "Steakhouse" with Joe and Henry. Went in and played "Snooker" until 1935, then went down the house. Margie, Marie, Rose, Henry, Joe, and myself went to the show and saw "Heroic Stalingrad." Went to their house and sat and talked (?) until 3 minutes to 1. Then Henry and I ran for the bus. Stood all the way in as usual. Got in about 0200.

Larry

Jan. 27, Thursday   Day Off

Got up about 1100 then went to chow. Returned and took a shower and prepared to go to town. Rode in the rear end of the bread truck with six other guys. Got into Clinton about 3. Got rid of my coat in the USO and then went up to see Henry's proofs on his pictures in the photograph shop. Went to the show and saw Al Pierce and His Gang. Don't know the name of the show though. From there I went to the USO and wrote a 4 page letter to Mom and then saw Eng. Crites in there. Got my coat and went out the Highway. Got a ride in a Navy car into Cordell. Ate here then called 176-W (Margie). After she woke up I told her I would be down and then I walked to her house. Talked to Mrs. Weese and Marie for a while then Margie and I walked to the show. Show was filled so we went back to her house and sat until 9:45 (2145). We went back to the show and saw "My Friend Flicka." My third time. We went to her house again after the show and sat until 2445 and talked, then I kissed her good night and left. Got to the barracks about 0200. Rode back in a blue Chevrolet convertible.

<u>Borrowed two more dollars from Geiger.</u>

Chapter 6 – Clinton

Got 2 letters from Dottie H. and one from Mom today. Wrote one to Mom.

Larry

<u>Changing my address to Section G. Division III</u>

Jan. 28, 1944 Friday Duty Day Muscles at 0810

Up at 0730 went to chow with Henry but missed it because they had closed the Chow Hall early. Only got the mail at 0945 then went to chow at 1100. Came back about one and got the mail at 1345. Ate chow at 1700 came back and typed the schedules. Left here at about 1100 [2300?].

Took a shower and went to bed. Beautiful day. (Wrote letter to D.H.)

Larry

Jan. 29, Saturday   Muscles at 0810

Up at 0715 went to chow with Henry. Did nothing much except got the mail at 1000 and made a couple of copies for King. Went to chow with Henry at 1100. (Bob Craven, also) Came back about 1300 and got mail again at 1400. No mail for me. Went to chow with Henry at 1700, came back and typed schedules. (Bad night about 2100.) Rode with an officer to the main gate in the pickup then drove it back. Delivered schedules, and returned to barracks at 2130. Took shower and got to bed at 2230. (Beautiful day from 1000 till 2100.)

Larry

Jan. 30, 1944 Sunday

Hit the deck at 0710. Stich[?] came and was going to wake me but I was already up. Johnny Meeks[?] and Henry came in later then. Ate chow and came to the office. Took muscles at 0810 and looked at the gloom outside. Got mail at 1000 with Henry, received none. (in pickup) Ate a big chow at 1100, then went to the barracks and slept until Craven came and woke me at 1245.

Day is now beautiful. No mail this afternoon so Henry and I walked around outside in the sunshine from 3 until 4:30 this afternoon. Henry and I ate chow then came back to the office. I just finished typing the schedules for tomorrow. It is now 1930 and Henry is ready to secure and go to the movie. I have one cent to my name. And $7 in the hole.   Larry

Jan 31, 1944 Monday

Hop from 1645 to 1830. Worked until 1100 Dentist at 1400 Temporary filling

February 1, 1944 Tuesday (Made the M+M) (Department Personnel Yeoman)

Letter from D. H.

Worked until 1130 P.M. Started a letter to D. H. Totaled all log books with Henry. Ate a sandwich at 1130.

Feb 2, 1944 Wednesday

Day off. (Chief M[?] off today also)

Wrote letter to Dottie last night. Mail it this afternoon. Going to town with Craven. Borrowed five from B. Geiger 1400. No letters from anyone yet.

Feb. 2, 1944 Wednesday Day off.

Went to town with Craven. Thumbed in and saw two shows and sat in the Red Shield for awhile then drank beer until 1115 and thumbed a ride to the base. Got here at 1200 midnight and went to bed.

Larry

Borrowed five more from Geiger and also his jumper.

Chapter 6 – Clinton

Feb. 3 Thursday Duty

Up early. Went to chow with Henry then to the office. Didn't do much all day as usual and got the mail at 1000 and 1400. Came back after chow last night and worked until 2115. Got paid today $19 and gave Bob G. $17 of it. Got my Laundry.

Got a letter from D. H. She must be pretty happy these days.

Wrote letter to Mom. Went to the barracks took a shower and hit the sack. Returned Geiger's jumper.

Larry

Feb. 4, 1944 Friday

Got up at 0715 went to chow and with Henry came to the office. Took King's place for the day. Made the muster report and was kept pretty busy all morning. Went to chow at 1110 and came back at 1210. Got to work again. Flight schedules all in but Hedron at 1730. Waited until 1830 for schedule and King came in and wanted to do it for me. Left office at 1900 went to barracks and changed to go ashore. Henry had gone already. Got ride to gate so did Dewey. Walked out past the school in Burns Flats and got a ride to the Hi-way. Then got ride in to Cordell in a Model-A. Called Margie on phone then went to a cafe and ate.

At 2030 got to Margie's house and Henry, Marie, Joe, and Rose had gone to the show already. Margie and I went to the show and saw "Holy Matrimony." Sat with the rest of the gang. They left and we stayed for the rest of the show. Walked to her house and just beat Marie, Rose, Joe, and Henry. Sat and talked and ------- until 0100. Ran for bus and missed it. Got ride with Rouse back to the base. Hit the sack and at 0145.

Larry

Chapter 6 – Clinton

Burns Flat, a town first developed around a school of the same name, is ten miles west and four miles north of Cordell on State Highway 44 in Washita County, Oklahoma. According to the Oklahoma Historical Society, the community took its name from a former post office, designated Burns, which had been established in 1894 and discontinued in 1904, and from the absence of hilly terrain in any direction. Burns was located two miles south of present Burns Flat. When the U.S. government acquired four square miles of farm land and established the Clinton Sherman Naval Air Station during the war, it also led to growth in nearby towns like Burns Flat.

Feb. 5th, 1944. Saturday

Up at 0715. Chow with Henry. Office to work. Henry and Harold Martin went to school all morning, Dewey, day off and Gruber, on leave.

Got mail at 1000 worked on personnel log book until 1200. Chow with Henry. Barracks until 1300. Mail at 1400.

Dentist at 1500. One tooth filled. Finished with dentist got x-ray. Back at four from Ship's Service.

File, straightened (Kardex), chow at 1730. Met Henry. Back to office. Helped him with log books all night. Now 2130. Time to secure.

Mail from Mom (2 bucks), D. E. + D.H. Wrote none.

Martin told me if I go on leave when he does I can drive home with him in his car. (Cleveland) (At Easter). Started signing out leave chits today also. Larry

Feb. 6, 1944. Sunday Duty

Up early chow with Henry then to recognition again. We started school over again today. Went on the rifle range and shot a carbine for 22 rounds. Two bulls' for a score of 120.

Chow and went ashore because there were three men down here on duty anyway. Saw show in Cordell "Claudia." Thumbed back. Got here at about 2330. Secured.

Larry

The "recognition" Larry mentioned entailed learning how to recognize aircraft, Allied and enemy, by their silhouettes, markings, and other recognizable features. Air crewmen had to identify ocean vessels below them while in flight and sailors on land or at sea had to recognize planes in the air above them. The Bluejackets' manual provided this information to all sailors and various base newspapers often printed quiz pages with plane silhouettes designed to be torn out and used for reference by men on the ground. A *Recognition Journal* was published to keep service members updated on the latest war planes and sailing ships from merchant vessels to submarines.

Feb. 7. Monday

Up at 0730 chow and to work with Henry. Worked a little went to noon chow back to work. Not much in afternoon went to late chow went to town with Henry, and Bob, Got in Clinton and started drinking. We drank all night and got feeling pretty good. Henry got sick. Went to the Yacht Club with Bob and 2 girls and one of them had her husband with her. At 2400 Bob and I went to the Red Shield Club and I typed a letter for him then we went to bed. The bed was spinning for Bob but I was O.K. Sleep at 1245 P.M. [AM?]

Larry

Feb. 8, Tuesday Day off

Slept in town last night at Red Shield with Bob Craven. Slept until 1300. Went to show with Bob and to eat. At 1730, went to Weatherford. Bob got haircut and we walked around the college. Went to show and saw "Happy Landing." Out the highway and got ride on truck to Clinton. Went to USO and got pea coats and got ride with some guy back to the base. Got in about 1130 P.M. Secured.

Larry

Chapter 6 – Clinton

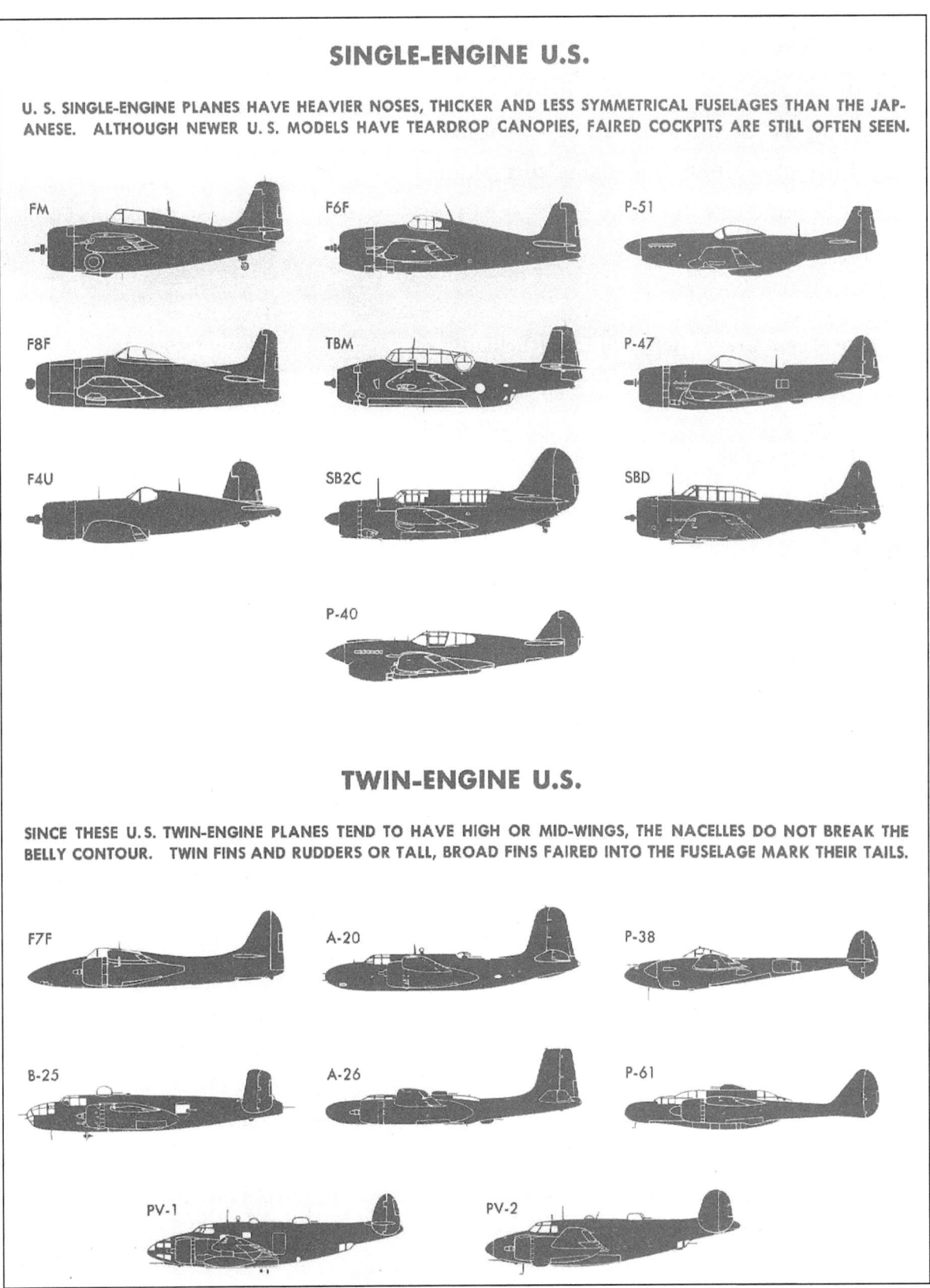

Images of Some Single and Twin Engine U.S. Planes from World War II *Recognition Journal*

Chapter 6 – Clinton

Weatherford, once a "rough and bawdy frontier town" near the turn of the 20th century, was also a "major rail hub" where "herds of cattle were regularly driven down Main Street to the railroad stockyards." "By November 1926 that same dirt Main Street became U.S. Highway 66."

Photo of Bob Craven (left) and Larry Eckhoff

Feb. 9, Wednesday   Duty night

Up at 0715. Chow with Henry. To office. Caught up on Leave and Special Liberty books then to Recognition and movies. At 1100 Craven and I went to chow and to barracks. Slept until 1245 then went to Laundry with Craven. Back to office. Worked all afternoon. Got to chow at 1700. Back to office. Worked until 2130.

Two letters from D.H. today - one didn't like so much.

Secured, Shower, and to bed.

Larry

Thursday 10 February 1944

Chow by myself this morning at 0730. Went to work. No physical drills. King and Dewey had to go to school so I was in the office myself all morning. Had to do King's work and my own. Chief and I are pretty well straightened out though. I didn't do bad. At 1145, with Craven then back to work. Wind is blowing like hell all day. 70 knots and 80 in gusts. Blow everyone and everything away, no kidding.

Secured at 1730. At chow with Bob Craven and came to the barracks. Read for a while "Lady in Morgue." Bob Geiger came over and gave me some stuff to type for him. Read some more then took shower and read until lights went out.

A letter from Mom today. John Wason is up at the Lakes. Joe Macke, fireman there. Jerry [Leisring] in Mediterranean, still.

Secure I hope.

Larry

Feb 11, 1944 Friday

Feb 12, 1944 Saturday   Duty - Wrote three page letter home.

Up at usual time. Worked, studied my book for chief all day. ("Lady in the Morgue.") Hit the sack early Friday nite, late Saturday nite.

Nothing exciting happened except records still SNAFU (Situation Now All Fouled Up)

Trouble as usual.

Larry

Die Deutschland Uber Alles! (SNAFU) "Das Alles" "We'll Fight to the Last American."

"No Letter, Today." "Die Ende" The English! "United We Stand, Divided We Fall." G.W.

"Finis"

"That's All, Folks!"

"The End"

When that's All there is, There Ain't No Mo!

"I'm Disgusted Tonight."

Larry

Delivered flight schedules and afterwards wrote a letter to Mom. Had duty with Harber and Ashmun. Linschoten came back from town about 2330 and made up a bunk in the Ready Room on the table. I played chess with Harber until 0200 then hit the sack in the Ready Room.

Finis.

Larry   [Harber is probably R. D. Harber from Fort Wayne, Indiana and Linschoten probably Chris Linshoten of Salt Lake City, Utah]

Sunday, February 13, 1944

Up with the birdies. Not in time for chow though. Came to work, did a little. Got fouled up some more. Bob Geiger went on leave today. Came me my five $$. Had to work late and Henry and Bob Craven were waiting on me at the office. Secured at 1730 and got ready for town. We got in late and had to take the bus at Burns Flat. Got into town about 2100. Started drinking beer in Yacht Club but beer was warm so we left. Had a time in H&K for the rest of the night. Won $.65 matching nickels with the waitress there. About 2300 Bob and I went to the Red Shield to sleep but they said they had no rooms for us. Bob and I left. Went out on the hi-way and he and I were both sick but couldn't throw up. We got across the street from the bus station and tried spinning around. This helped me but not Craven. An enlisted man stopped in a car and rode us back to the base then and I slept all the way in the back seat. We got here at 0100. I hit the sack.

Larry

Feb. 14, 1944 Monday Day OFF.

Got up early this morning and ate chow. Then went up and woke Bob Craven. After slinging the bull for a while I went down and hit the sack again with my clothes on. At 0930 Bob came down and lay on the bunk next to me and we both fell asleep again. He had my pea coat over him. We woke up and went to noon chow and after messing around and shooting the breeze we both finally

Chapter 6 – Clinton

got ready and headed for town. We checked our coats in Clinton when we finally got there after four different rides because it was a beautiful sunny day. Bob and I ate and then went to a movie. we saw "Government Girl." Which was pretty good. After the show it was about 1800 we walked out the highway to get a ride to Weatherford. We got one and the people said they would pick us up at 2200 on their way back to Clinton, if we waited for them on the corner, so we did.

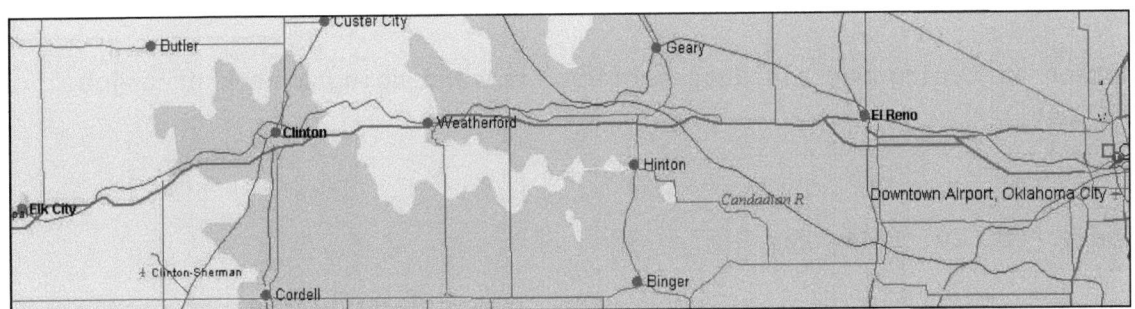

Central Oklahoma, Route 66, Towns from Elk City to Oklahoma City

We went in Ted's Cafe again and started shooting the breeze with the waitresses. One we met the last time we were there. After sitting in there for about an hour, we decided to go to the movie and see "Desert Song." It was not bad but wasn't too good either. We came out at 2200 and it was a little chilly but was pretty lively town for Monday nite. We got our ride back when we had just about given up and got to Clinton about 2300. Got our coats in USO and there was a Dance for Valentine's Day going on but we left anyway. We went out on the road but had little success. Finally a station wagon came along from the base and said we could ride back with him as soon as he saw the Shore Patrol Officer. We got in and he saw the officer, then went to the USO, picked up three other sailors and two Waves then we started back. The speedometer read 100 miles an hour most of the way back to the base. We made it in about 40 minutes, which is plenty good. We saved $4.00 along with the deal. Got back early and went to bed 2415. Larry Das Alles!

Today is Tuesday 15 February, 1944

This morning I got up at 0810 and missed a muster which almost caused me to experience my first Captain Mast. I went to school all morning and got back here to the office about 1215 where I got Hell for missing the muster. Then I had to go see the Personnel officer and get things straightened out. When

Chapter 6 – Clinton

I went in to his office, Bob Craven was just coming out and didn't look very happy. He had to go and apologize to a Chief for saying "tough" the other day when I was with him and we got the Coffee Table for the CPO's Mess. This afternoon I didn't have much to do so I wasn't very busy. I have the duty tonight and I made out the Flight Schedules and then typed out cards on the first duty section. Took muscles at 1645 this afternoon and was I weary. Got a box of candy and three Valentines in the mail. One from home, one D.H., one from Mrs. Leisring. Can't forget to write her a letter.

Whitson is typing out his duty section list and doing a heck of a job.

Sunday Feb. 20, 1944 Day Off.

Slept in Bishop's Hotel in Weatherford with Craven. Got up about 1030. Ate chow in Ted's across the street. Had bacon, eggs, and coffee and rolls. Then we thumbed out the road to Oklahoma City. Got a ride to Hydro in Buick Eight. Then, Chevy pickup to no man's land. Then in another Ford with owners of Northrup's Jewelry Store as far as El Reno. A ride with a soldier out to hi-way 66. (about 2 mi.) Then we rode into Oakie City with two old people at 35 miles per hour. From 23rd to heart of town got another ride in a coupe. We walked around for a while. Town pretty full of sailors and soldiers. Shows all crowded. Finally we went in and saw "Thousands Cheer." (not bad) Came out and had a beer then decided we might as well head back. It was beginning to get dark, too. Got ride out to highway 66 then waited. Got ride all the way to Clinton from here in an Oldsmobile. When we got to Clinton we ate in Harry's then went out the hi-way again. Got ride almost immediately with three officers back to base. Got in at 1105 P.M. Then hit the sack.

Larry

Lots of small businesses lined Route 66, the main highway. Near small towns such as Hydro, Oklahoma, during the war years, they included gas stations, sometimes with small motels containing maybe a half dozen rooms built on the property, and cafes. Old cattle trails once crisscrossed Route 66. El Reno, not far from the North Canadian River and named for the fort nearby, once marked the location of the Chisholm Trail, mostly used for

Chapter 6 – Clinton

driving cattle. Route 66 was split by another branch of the trail near the present site of Weatherford, while the Dodge City Trail crossed 66 at Elk City. Jesse Chisholm's grave is located not many miles north of the highway.

```
Tuesday Feb. 22, 1944    Went ashore.

Up with the birds. Went up and got Bob (C) out of his bunk then went to
chow. Came to work but not work to do. Sun was shining swell out and it was
plenty warm. Afternoon, I went outside for about an hour and sat in the
sun. Secured after muscles and Bob and I went to town. Rode to Elk, and
picked up his blues, then came out again. Got ride to Canute in Buick
Eight. Waited here for a while, then got ride in Army pick-up to Clinton,
Oklahoma. There were two of them and Bob got in one and me the other. They
were going to Tulsa. Bob and I went to Harry's and then to movie "??
Gunner." Out to the Hiway and got ride to Cordell and had to wait for the
0100 bus here. Got back about 0200. Secured.

Larry

Found letter from D.H. in Box

Box of candy from M.J. yesterday. Gone. [M.J. is Mary Jane, sister]
```

Canute, a small farming community settled in 1901, was named for the ancient Norse king. West of town, the terrain turns rolling and hilly as Route 66 meanders toward Elk City.

```
Wednesday Feb. 23, 1944
```

> Got up and went to chow with Bob Craven. Came to work and as usual did nothing. Chow at 1100 back at 0100. Quarters at 1645 and "Muscles". Big argument after chow about going to town. Finally Bob and I went. Got ride over the dirt road and ride in truck the rest of the way to Clinton. Ate in Harry's and went to show, saw "Underground Agent." Harry's for a cup of coffee and then out on the hi-way. Got ride with officer and had a swell time all the way to the base. Hit the sack about 1230.
>
> Larry

Chapter 6 – Clinton

Things must have gotten much busier for Larry as this was his last regular log entry. On March 10, 1944, he was transferred to Training Task Force, Clinton, OK, Utility Squadron Six. A month later, April 21, 1944, Larry transferred to PATSU (Patrol Aircraft Service Unit) 152, U.S. NAS, Clinton, OK. Records show the following air travel for Larry, most likely to participate in special training.

Clinton, OK to Dallas, TX	April 30, 1944	Columbus, OH to Houma, LA	July 5, 1944
Dallas, TX to Houma, LA	May 1, 1944	Houma, LA to Ft. Worth, TX	July 11, 1944
Houma, LA to Columbus, OH	July 5, 1944	Houma, LA to Clinton, OK	July 27, 1944

A Dallas-Fort Worth, Texas Navy Shore Patrol card was issued to Larry in April. Another record indicated a transfer to VB-152 for duty in VB-152 PATSU, NAS, Clinton, OK, June 10, 1944. In May, he apparently participated in some kind of training in Houma, Louisiana, and traveled from New Orleans to Houma per a bus ticket in his possession. He sent his family a postcard packet of New Orleans/MardiGras images postmarked June 23, 1944.

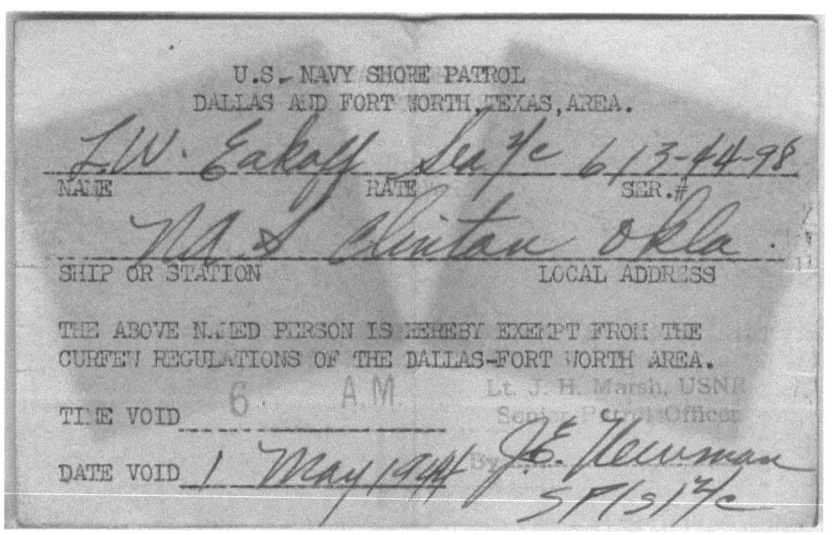
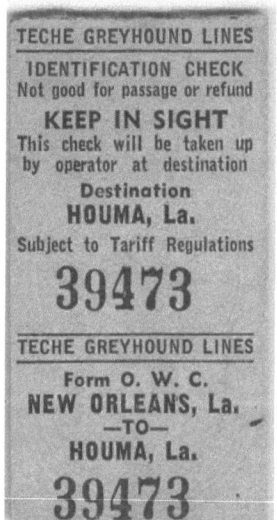

U.S. Navy Shore Patrol, Dallas and Fort Worth Texas Area curfew regulations exemption expiring 1 May 1944

Back of bus ticket stamped is June 22, 1944 New Orleans

Larry was part of the group that completed "Special air operations at Houma - August 3, 1944, PATSU 152/P18-1/MM." Then, finally, Larry was granted 10 days annual leave of absence from 1700 hours August 8, 1944 to 0800 hours August 19, 1944—he would be going home to Cincinnati. Before departing for home, he had to check in date, time, and signature with the following personnel: PATSU M.A.A., Post Office, Section Leader, Leading

Chief, Department Head, Personnel Officer, PATSU 152 O.O.D (officer of the day). Talk about red tape! The same group was notified in reverse order when Larry returned to Clinton with the signed paper delivered to the Leave Yeoman, Personnel Office, PATSU 152, Hangar 101.

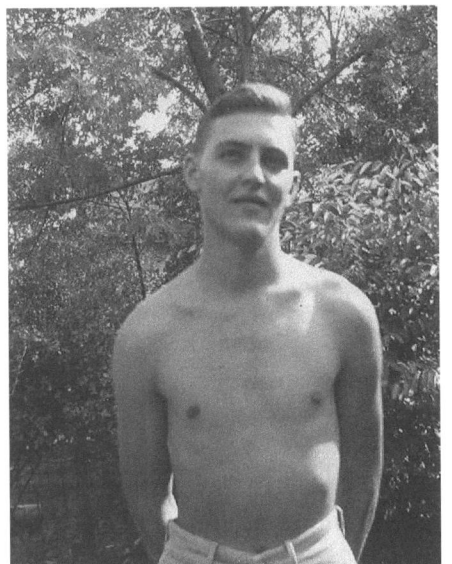 

A very lean Larry while home on leave, August, 1944

As the summer waned, September heralded the CBS Radio debut of "Ozzie and Harriet" and the Mutual Broadcasting System sounded like songs by the campfire with "The Roy Rogers Show" and the Sons of the Pioneers. Along the dusty trail at NAS Clinton, Larry wrote this letter to his mom.

```
October 16, 1944

Monday

Dear Mom,

Before I write anything I want to thank you for the box of chocolate and
also for the box I received today. Everything was in good shape and tasted
very good. The chow they are having lately make those boxes taste even
better.

I want to tell you also, first of all, about something that happened today.
Don't be surprised if this is word for word with Dottie's letter, this last
```

I mean, because I'm going to copy the letter to her from it, concerning the dog.

I think I've told you about the Squadron Mascot, a dog called Peter 1/C. Well, today, he ran after one too many cars like my dog used to do and it was his last one. He got himself run over and killed this morning by one of our officers. When it happened, some of our boys were around and they said the officer got white and nervous and looked as if he would keel over any minute. The fellows took a truck and picked him up and brought him to the Hangar. They had a casket made lined with parachute silk, inside and out. They dug a grave and set the casket on two boards right at the top of the grave, covered it with an American flag, made a white cross and inscribed it and set it at the head of the grave. Two jars of flowers were then placed in front of the cross which had the collar draped over it and three rifles were stood behind the cross. The ground that was removed was, also, covered with a green mat. We then got a bugler and a photographer. All the fellows gathered around the grass by the grave then and the photographer took a couple pictures. The bugler then blew taps and it was probably heard all over the base because at the time not one plane was turning/tuning up and it was pretty quiet, only the sound of the bugler.

One fellow remarked that that dog got more attention than one of the fellows who had been killed in a plane crash not long ago. If they publish the pictures in "The Duster" I will send you one so you can really believe exactly what some guys will do. Maybe Okla is doing it.

I'm OK and hope everyone at home is the same. You stick to that diet. Will write next chance I get.

All my love,

Larry

Chapter 6 – Clinton

Ceremony for Squadron Mascot, Peter 1/C at NAS Clinton, October, 1944

The Navy provided each service member with a form letter into which they filled in the blanks with information a family member might need to know while he was stationed out of the country. Larry completed such a letter October 11, 1944:

Chapter 6 – Clinton

Dear Mother (with her address),

"Hold on to this letter; it will tell you a lot of things you may need to know while I'm away. The Navy wants you to have this information so that you will know about, and be prepared to benefit from, the assistance and protection to which you are entitled."

"First, there's my service number: XXXXX. Always use it when writing the Navy Department or other official organizations on service matters concerning me. Give them my name, rating (or rank) and service number, like this: name, S 2/c, xxx-xx-xx."

"I've applied for family allowance and you should receive each month $37.00......"

"I have authorized an allotment of $6.25 per month for War Bonds, which are being mailed to you. I have taken out $10,000 worth of National Service Life Insurance...."

There were also such comforting standard paragraphs such as" If I am wounded...", "If I am reported missing, missing in action, or captured by the enemy...", and "If I should die while on active duty..."

The Application for Family Allowance mentioned in the letter lists three dependents for Larry in September, 1943:

Mother

Brother (age 7 ½)

Sister   (age 5 ½)

"Mother is a widow, drawing a pension of $66 monthly. There are four minor children in the family, only two of whom allowance is asked for. There are also two older girls, each of whom contributed $8 weekly, covering their board and the board of the other two minor children. Support from the subject named man is necessary."

Jack H. Spencer, Lieut. USNR

PATSU Beer Party, November 2, 1944
Right side of table—Front to back Larry Eckhoff and Bob Craven

PATSU Beer Party, November 2, 1944
Center to the right of the guy with large cup, Larry Eckhoff and Bob Craven (with cigar)

Chapter 6 – Clinton

The form letter was probably a harbinger of things to come. "In compliance with ComFair West airmailgram of 20 October, PATSU 152 departed for Naval Air Station, Whidbey Island, to report to Hedron Six for duty."

On November 13, 1944 Larry was transferred to Headquarters Squadron, Fleet Air Wing Six for duty. He was finally getting out of Clinton.

Buddies since arriving at NAS Clinton some 15 months ago, Henry Kendjorsky (left) and Larry Eckhoff getting on a train

Chapter 7 – Whidbey

postmarked

La Junta, Colo

Nov 14 1944
2:30 PM

11-14-44

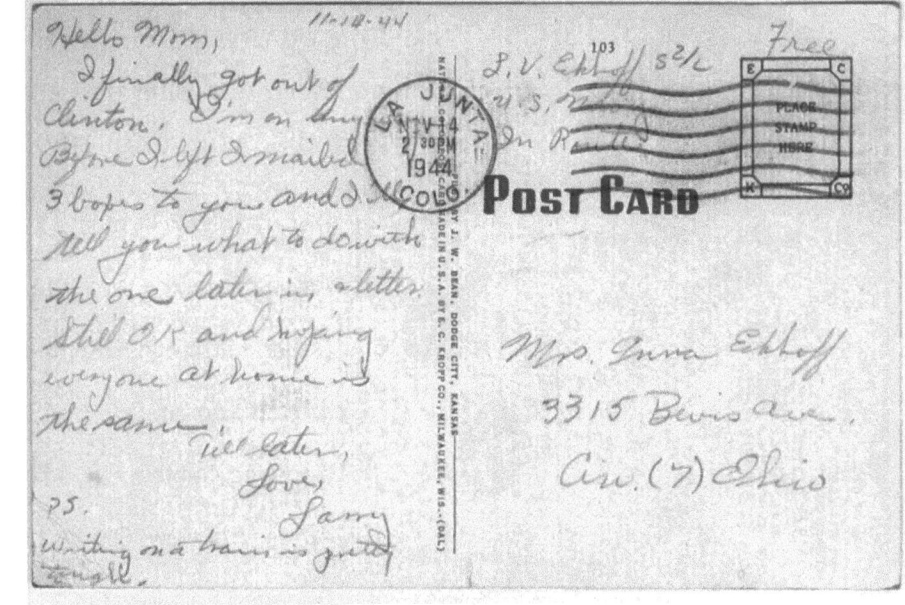

Hello Mom,

I finally got out of Clinton. I'm on anyway. Before I left, I mailed 3 boxes to you and I'll tell you what to do with the one later in a letter. Still OK and hoping everyone at home is the same.

Till later,

Love, Larry

PS. Writing on a train is pretty tough.

Chapter 7 – Whidbey

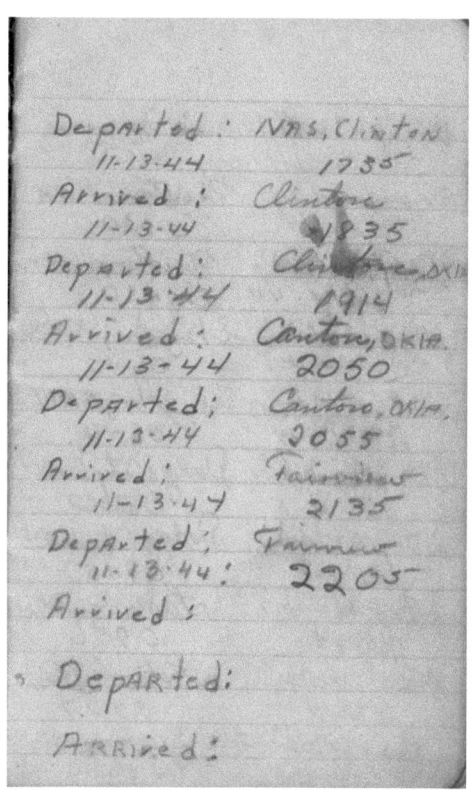

Larry kept a travel log from Clinton to Whidbey Island. Page one chronicled the trip from NAS Clinton, OK to Fairview, OK, a northern and slightly eastern route, that took from 5:35 p.m. until 10:05 p.m.

Departed NAS Clinton, 11-13-44, 1735

Arrived Clinton, OK, 11-13-44, 1835

Departed Clinton, OK, 11-13-44, 1914

Arrived Canton, OK, 11-13-44, 2050

Departed Canton, OK, 11-13-44, 2055

Arrived Fairview, OK 11-13-44, 2135

Departed Fairview, OK 11-13-44, 2205

He probably went to sleep after leaving Fairview since his next entry did not occur until 4:30 a.m. the next morning upon arrival at Newton, Kansas—merely another stop on the train route. Breakfast did not occur until 8:00 a.m. in Dodge City, Kansas.

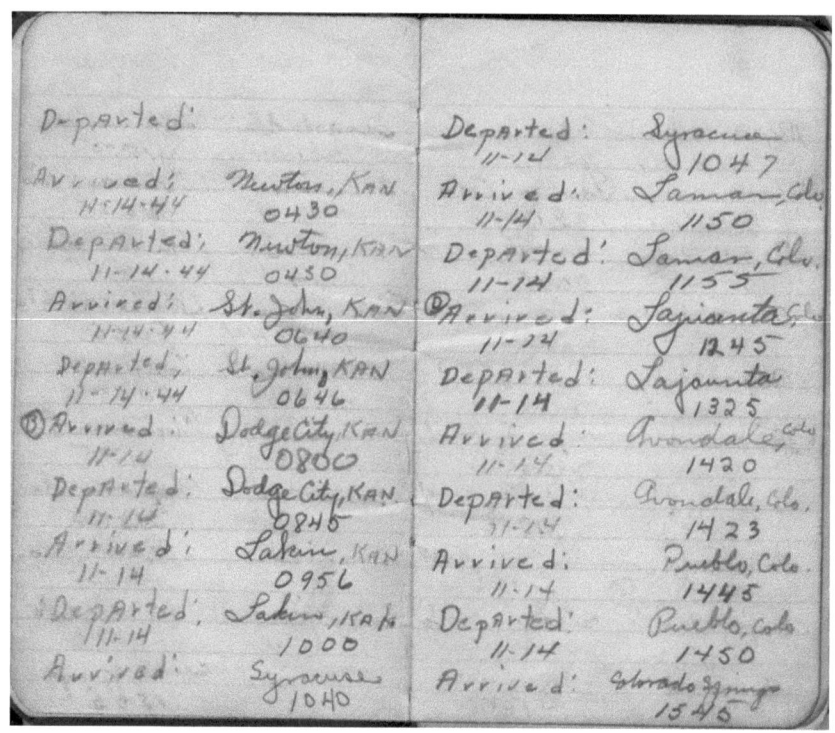

Additional pages from Larry's travel log from Newton, KS to Colorado Springs, CO

After brief stops at the small towns of Lakin and Syracuse, Kansas, Larry crossed into Colorado where he spent five minutes at the Arkansas River town of Lamar. Not quite an hour later, the train finally stopped at LaJunta, Colorado for lunch. Note the "noon chow" as Larry refers to it, is noted as "dinner" in his log, rather than "lunch." Following departure for sites west, Larry sent another postcard to his mom:

```
postmarked Denver, Colo Terminal R.P.O. Nov 14 1944 5:30 PM

Hi Mom,

Well, we are still going. Had noon chow in LaJunta, Colo. Country around
here is a little cool but still wide open plains. Train is as dirty as
usual. Probably write the next card from Denver, Colo.

Love,

Larry
```

Troop trains were not glamorous passenger cars. It took days to travel across the country on a non-air conditioned train. The trip often took even longer because every time a crucial cargo train or some other significant train came along, the troop train was shunted to a siding. As the other engines passed, they belched thick black smoke that blew in the open windows. The trains got filthy. The travelers got filthy. They had no showers so the first thing they did when they got to their eventual receiving station was take a shower—often as many as could cram in at one time. Still, 98 percent of military personnel journeying any distance traveled by train.

Due to gasoline and rubber tire rationing, Americans were forced to cut down on driving during the war but that didn't stop them from traveling. Trains were often crammed with vacationers [amazingly] as well as families visiting military bases and service members coming and going—base to base or to coastal ships. Opportunists took advantage of the dearth of Pullman sleeping car availability buying and reselling tickets to anyone willing to pay their price. Rail traffic got so heavy during the war that the railroad industry began to discourage people from traveling. At one point, Florida ran radio and print ads to prod Northerners to flee the cold of winter for warmer climes. Railroads countered with an

Chapter 7 – Whidbey

unusual anti-promotional strategy. "It's only fair to tell you trains are crowded these days," read an Atlantic Coast Line ad. "You'll be more comfortable at home."

Huge, heavy steam locomotives were required to haul the trains through mountainous terrain. The Union Pacific Railroad took delivery of an engine named "Big Boy" in 1944. It was so named since it was the largest ever manufactured—weighing in at 1.2 million pounds and stretching 132 feet. Between 1941 and 1944, 25 of the behemoths were built.

A young woman from Kansas City, Missouri noted that "Hundreds of trains would go by every day, and many were troop trains." Sometimes girls near the trains would throw notes containing their names and addresses to the servicemen hanging out of the train windows hoping they would write to them. Some actually did.

Big Boy 4004 on display at Cheyenne, Wyoming

Servicemen's canteens and other refreshment and entertainment facilities cropped up at high-traffic railroad stations across the country. They ranged from the previously mentioned USO centers to Service Men's Clubs, all providing amenities to traveling soldiers, sailors, and others. As many as 10,000 servicemen passed through Nebraska's storied North Platte Canteen during the war.

Chapter 7 – Whidbey

Larry's train tended to parallel Colorado's State Route 50 from LaJunta, through Avondale, and finally Pueblo, where it veered north toward Denver.

postmarked Nov 15 1944

Dear Mom,

Just ate here in Denver, Colorado. Bob C. [Craven] only got to call home and he lives just two miles from the station. They are plenty strict with us. Let us do nothing. Everyone is enjoying this trip though. Saw Pike's Peak this afternoon at Colo. Springs.

So long,

Larry

Following supper in Denver, Colorado and a nearly three hour layover, Larry once again spent the night on the train as it continued rolling northward. It is unknown which route they followed through the Rocky Mountains but the air was cold and crisp when they arrived at Green River, Wyoming at twenty minutes past ten in the morning.

Larry sent at least two more postcards during a brief stop at Montpelier, Idaho.

postmarked Nov 15 1944 Montpelier, Idaho 5-PM

Hello Mom,

Today we woke up going through snow country. It is pretty cold after a year in Clinton. Had breakfast in the diner a short while ago and now we are in Green River, Wyo. getting a little of the fresh cold air for a change.

Still feeling swell. Hope everyone at home is O.K. Till later,

Love, Larry

Chapter 7 – Whidbey

postmarked Nov 15 1944 Montpelier, Idaho 5-PM

Hi Don,

We are now traveling through Wyoming and it is really pretty country. Lots of mountains, and valleys, and a few rivers. Not much population though. Towns are few and far between. How's school? and where's that letter?

Your Brother,

Larry

Traveling service members had access to free postcards. This unused postcard from Larry's collection advertised russet potatoes grown in Idaho while including a humorous cartoon—strong sailors eat Idaho potatoes!

Chapter 7 – Whidbey

The train stopped at Granger and Kemmerer, Wyoming before the short stay in Montpelier, Idaho. Larry was slightly confused as to which state he was in as he jotted locations in his log possibly due to the nearness of the Wyoming, Utah, and Idaho state lines and the northwest route taken by the train. His third day on the train continued through Bancroft, Pocatello, Minidoka, Shoshone, Glenns Ferry, and Nampa, Idaho crossing into Owyhee, Oregon, just northwest of Boise, Idaho shortly after midnight on November 16, 1944.

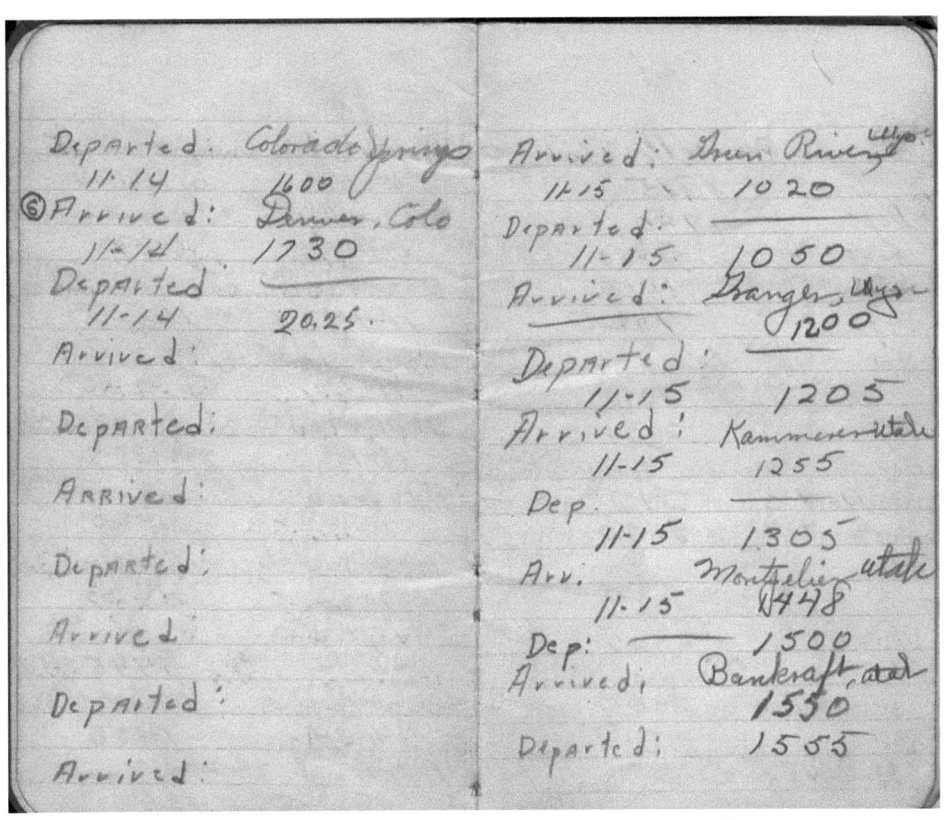

Larry's travel log from Colorado Springs, CO to Bancroft

Day four of Larry's journey began at Baker, Oregon at 4:15 a.m. and continued with only three stops listed for the rest of the day—Pendleton, Dallas, and Portland.

Overnight the train traveled north through Washington state, arriving at Mount Vernon at 4:30 a.m. Finally debarking from the train on November 17, 1944, Larry was now fewer than ten miles from his destination—Whidbey Island.

Larry was received aboard Naval Air Station Whidbey Island on November 17, 1944 as part of Hedron, Fleet Air Wing (FAW) Six.

Chapter 7 – Whidbey

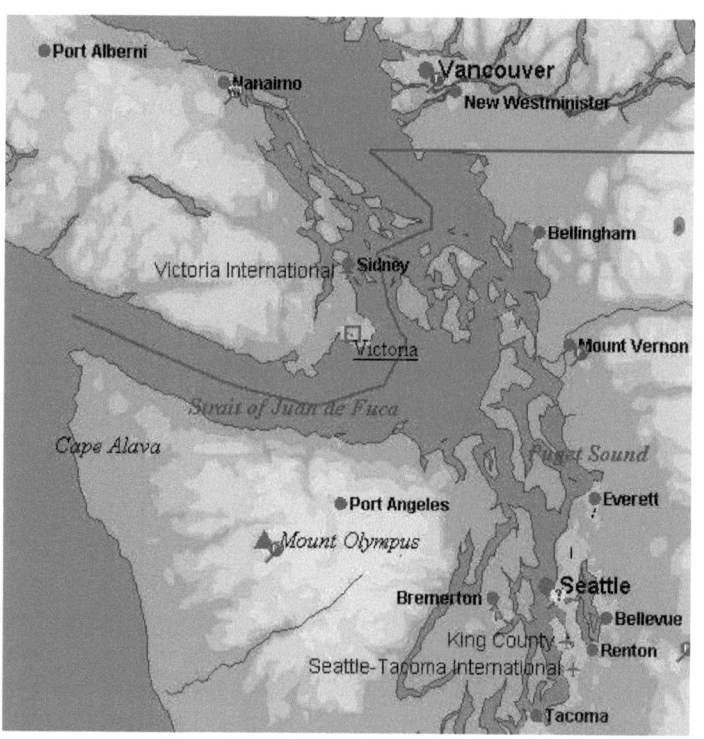

Map of extreme northwestern United States, solid line marks the border of Washington State with Canada

Whidbey Island is about 25 miles north of Seattle, Washington and about two hours south of Vancouver, Canada. In late January, 1941, the Commandant of the 13th Naval District was asked to find a location for re-arming and refueling of Navy patrol planes, particularly in the event defense of Puget Sound might be necessary. The commanding officer of NAS Seattle recommended "the site of Saratoga Passage on the shores of Crescent Harbor and Forbes Point as a base suitable for sea plane takeoffs (such as PBYs) and landings under instrument conditions."

The Pearl Harbor attack increased the urgency compelling nearly 200 men to work through all weather conditions to finish the base. Some farmers "turned over titles to ancestral farmlands so that runways and hangars could be built."

The air field, just north of Oak Harbor, Washington, which would be part of Naval Air Station Whidbey Island was far enough from populated areas to enable operational training flights with live munitions. The air field was renamed Ault Field in memory of Cdr. William B. Ault, who went missing in action in the Battle of the Coral Sea.

The Naval Air Station was commissioned September 25, 1943 as a base for recruit and petty officer training, rocket firing training, torpedo overhaul, and for sea plane patrol operations. F4F Wildcats were among the first planes to arrive at the base, followed by F6F Hellcats, PV-1 Venturas, and SBD Dauntless dive bombers.

With Hedron Stag III, Larry was a mail orderly for the Maintenance to Materials Department and was authorized to draw all mail for this department.

Chapter 7 – Whidbey

Ault Field, NAS Whidbey Island circa 1940s, Photo courtesy of U.S. Naval Aviation News, December 1947

Larry celebrated his 19th birthday that December at Whidbey Island—one of many young service members experiencing another Christmas season far away from home.

In 1944, Christmas presents were wrapped creatively to save paper needed for the war effort. At home, a gift for a baby could be wrapped and pinned in a diaper, while food items canned from the garden, as well as jars of homemade jams and jellies were often wrapped in a new kitchen towel.

It was considered patriotic to write to service members to help keep their morale up. With so many overseas, and the mail system vying with ammunition, food, fuel, and other supplies for precious cargo space, V-mail was born in June, 1942.

Chapter 7 – Whidbey

This is an actual V-Mail Christmas Greeting sent in December, 1944 from Pfc. Arthur L. Maines to his wife in the Cincinnati suburb of Reading. His short note says "Makes the third one we've been apart, Honey. I'll be thinking of you…God Bless You – Art" Note the censor's stamp in the upper left corner indicating it was safe to send.

V-Mail (short for Victory Mail) "used a one-sided form on which the writer composed the message. The message was photographed onto 16 mm black and white camera film, sent to a processing center on a reel containing many other letters, printed onto a piece of five-by-four-inch black and white photographic paper, folded, and slipped into an envelope for delivery." V-mail allowed a massive exchange of personal messages, which otherwise could not have occurred. During the course of the war, over 1.5 billion V-Mail letters were processed and the use of the small one page forms meant shipment of mail weighing about 2500 pounds was reduced to 45 pounds. V-Mail simplified the censorship operation as well. Officers in every service division were required to censor outgoing letters. Regular letters had to be opened, removed from the envelope, read, and any sensitive items cut out before they were returned to the envelope and resealed.

Writers couldn't say much. Some developed a code with their family before being deployed or while home on leave—such as the first letter of every other sentence might provide an idea of where they were when the letter was written. For example, one serviceman might mention his Uncle Mike which, in the prearranged code, would mean he was in a certain area in the South Pacific. A mention of Uncle Ralph would mean another area.

Chapter 7 – Whidbey

NAS Whidbey tried to make the Christmas meal a nice one for those who were away from home. The printed menu was designed so sailors could mail it home to family members if they wished. The feast included cream of tomato soup with toasted croutons, stuffed celery, sweet pickles, and green olives with a main course of roast young tom turkey with giblet gravy, cornbread dressing, cranberry sauce, snowflake potatoes, and buttered green beans. Also on the menu were fruit and vegetable aspic salad, hot graham rolls with butter, holiday fruit cake, ice cream, assorted hard candy, mixed nuts, coffee, and cigarettes.

Cover of NAS Whidbey Island 1944 Christmas Menu

Chapter 7 – Whidbey

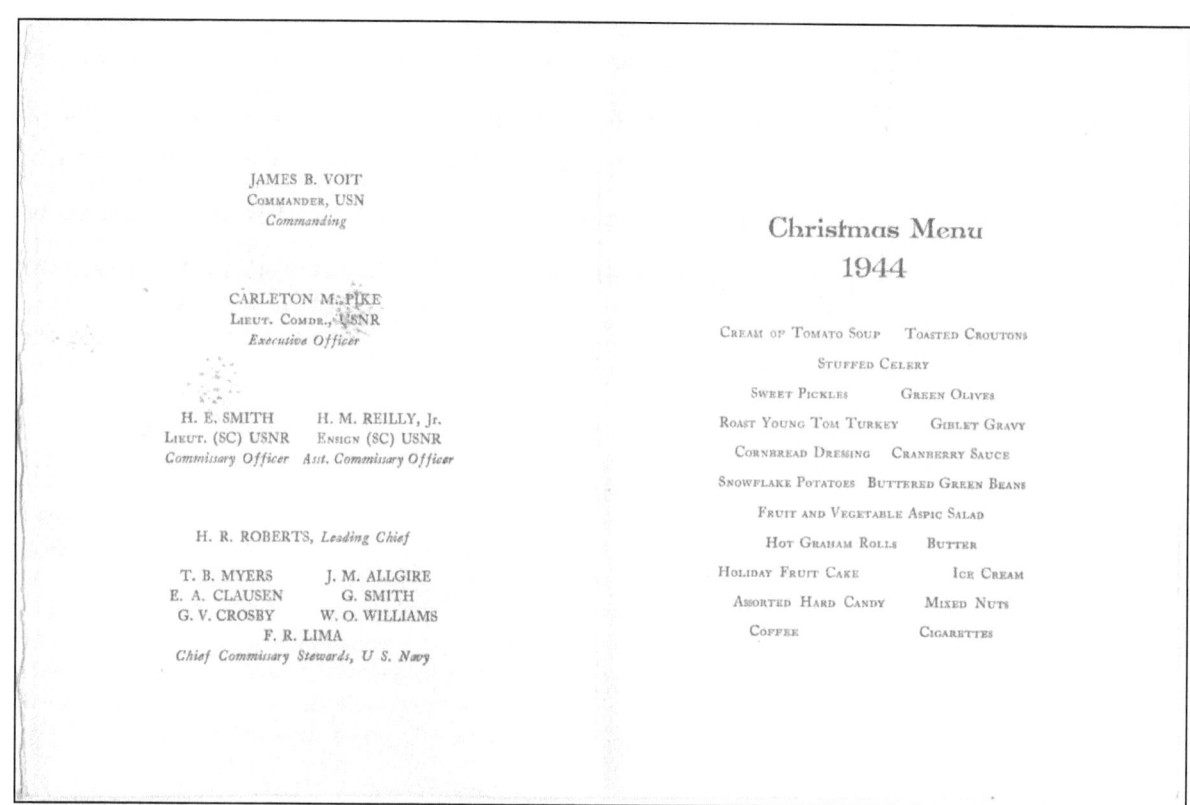

Inside of NAS Whidbey Island 1944 Christmas Menu

As another new year brought hope for an end to the war, a milestone was reached by Larry on January 8, 1945 as he completed the new AMMI 3/C training course and passed. According to the *Bureau of Naval Personnel Bulletin*, May, 1944 an AMMI—Aviation Machinist's Mate I (Aviation Instrument Mechanic) installs, overhauls, cleans, and repairs aircraft instruments; and adjusts and calibrates them for accuracy.

After midnight at the Hotel Leopold in Bellingham, Washington, Larry wasn't tired enough to sleep so he sat down and wrote a letter on hotel stationery.

Chapter 7 – Whidbey

January 13, 1945   0135

Dear Mom,

Since it has been a little while since I last wrote you I decided now is as good a time as any.

Earlier this evening I was going to write you but I didn't know I had my pen here with me. I just now noticed it in my bag which I have with me to carry my shaving gear, extra socks and handkerchiefs in.

Its one thirty in the A.M. and I'm alone here in the room and not very sleepy. I am on my usual every two weeks 48 hours liberty. I have to be back at the base this afternoon at five.

You know I only get liberty every two weeks because I work nights. I come here to Bellingham and get a room usually with another fellow and get a bottle and drink in the room so we don't have far to go to hit the sack.

New Year's Eve, Bud and I met two pretty nice women and I've been going out with the one I met whenever I got to town and she wasn't busy already. I never make a date ahead of time. That's no fun. Don't say anything to Dottie H. about this because she isn't writing to me the way it is. Not that it would make any difference to D. H.

Harold just came in and told me what he did tonight. A girl called for me before he got here and now he's gone again to try to get some soda pop(?) so we will be able to go to sleep tonight.

(By the way, the girl's name is June, 22 and very pretty. Nice girl, too.)

Well, I guess I will say so long for now, hoping everyone is O.K. and having good luck. I'm fine and am expecting lots of good luck and good changes.

Loads of love to you all,

Larry

P.S.

I'm being good.   Larry

Chapter 7 – Whidbey

Bellingham is the largest city near NAS Whidbey—roughly 30 miles from the base. June Ann Ginger , the girl mentioned in the letter, lived in Bellingham.

Old Hotel Leopold, Bellingham, WA
Photo courtesy of City of Bellingham

It was a chilly Tuesday the 16th of January when Larry's change in rate from S2/C (Seaman Second Class) to AMMI 3/C (Aviation Machinist Mate Instruments, Third Class) took effect.

Exactly one week after Franklin D. Roosevelt started his fourth term as President, a relieved Larry was on liberty in Bellingham, Washington writing another letter home.

```
January 27, 1945

Saturday

Dear Mom,
```

Chapter 7 – Whidbey

This is a fine time to be writing a letter but it is as good a time as any, the way I figure. I have a long story to tell you which I don't think I will forget for a long time. Here goes:

Thursday nite at work about eight o'clock in the evening some of the boys decided they were thirsty and that a bottle or two of beer would go well together with something to eat, toward making the evening a pleasant one. About nine of us chipped in and one of the fellows who had a car went to the town of Oak Harbor, about nine miles away, and got a case of beer along with peanuts, potato chips, cheese, cheese crackers and other stuff. (We are not allowed to have alcoholic beverages on the base.) We ate and drank. All gripes had been taken care of. That case went swell. Naturally no one was satisfied. They guys went back again and got two more cases. We were in the middle of the first case and there was a knock on the door. When the door opened, after all the bottles were hidden, there stood gold braid. 2 half inches and a quarter of it. Meaning a lieut-comdr. He strode in with pad + pencil. Tossed them on the corner of the table, which was the only place not occupied with food or remnants of food. He said, "Every man in this room sign his name on this pad." No one moved. Finally one guy put his name on it and we all followed. He was the skipper of one of the squadrons whose planes we take care of. He walked out with a guy carrying the empties which he also told us to bring out.

The next morning nine men from the radio shack were minus I.D. cards. This evening was the first time since it happened that we heard anything about it. Then we heard plenty. The div. officer and the warrant officer who just made warrant were called before the skipper and threatened with demotion. Then the guy that caught us, being a skipper, stepped up and told the skipper the whole story and asked him to forget the whole thing. The man did so, much to our amazement. We got our I.D. cards back with a lecture and warning not to make one little crooked move. Normally the men involved would have been broken without questions being asked. There were 4 first class, 5 third class and one seaman who would have been one or two rates lower today if we weren't lucky.

I came into town tonight because last night when my liberty started I was still sweating and I do mean sweating. I thought I wouldn't even be bothering to sew my third class rate on my jumper for another year maybe.

Received the candy and cards and thanks a million. The cards cost me about sixty five cents in penny ante before that night was over.

Hope everyone at home is O.K. I'm fine now that I don't have to sweat anymore.

Will write you again soon from the base.

Love to all at home,

Larry

In war news, February, 1945 saw Britain's Winston Churchill, Russia's Josef Stalin, and FDR meeting at Yalta, Crimea. With the exception of conflict in the Aleutian Islands, the war still seemed a million miles away from Whidbey Island.

As at NAS Clinton, Whidbey had its own newspaper called *Prop Wash*. The March 09, 1945 issue contained a variety of articles of interest to the folks around the base. Civilian and Navy boys could take a boxing class on Friday night at the Rec Hall and later attend a Junior League Juke Box dance. Twice a week, civilian women held Red Cross meetings at the Rec Hall work room.

Cover of *Prop Wash*, the newspaper of NAS Whidbey Island

Chapter 7 – Whidbey

There were classified ads. One Naval Officer wanted a cook or mother's helper in his home while another F1/C simply needed a parking space with electricity, water, and a rest room near Oak Harbor for his trailer home.

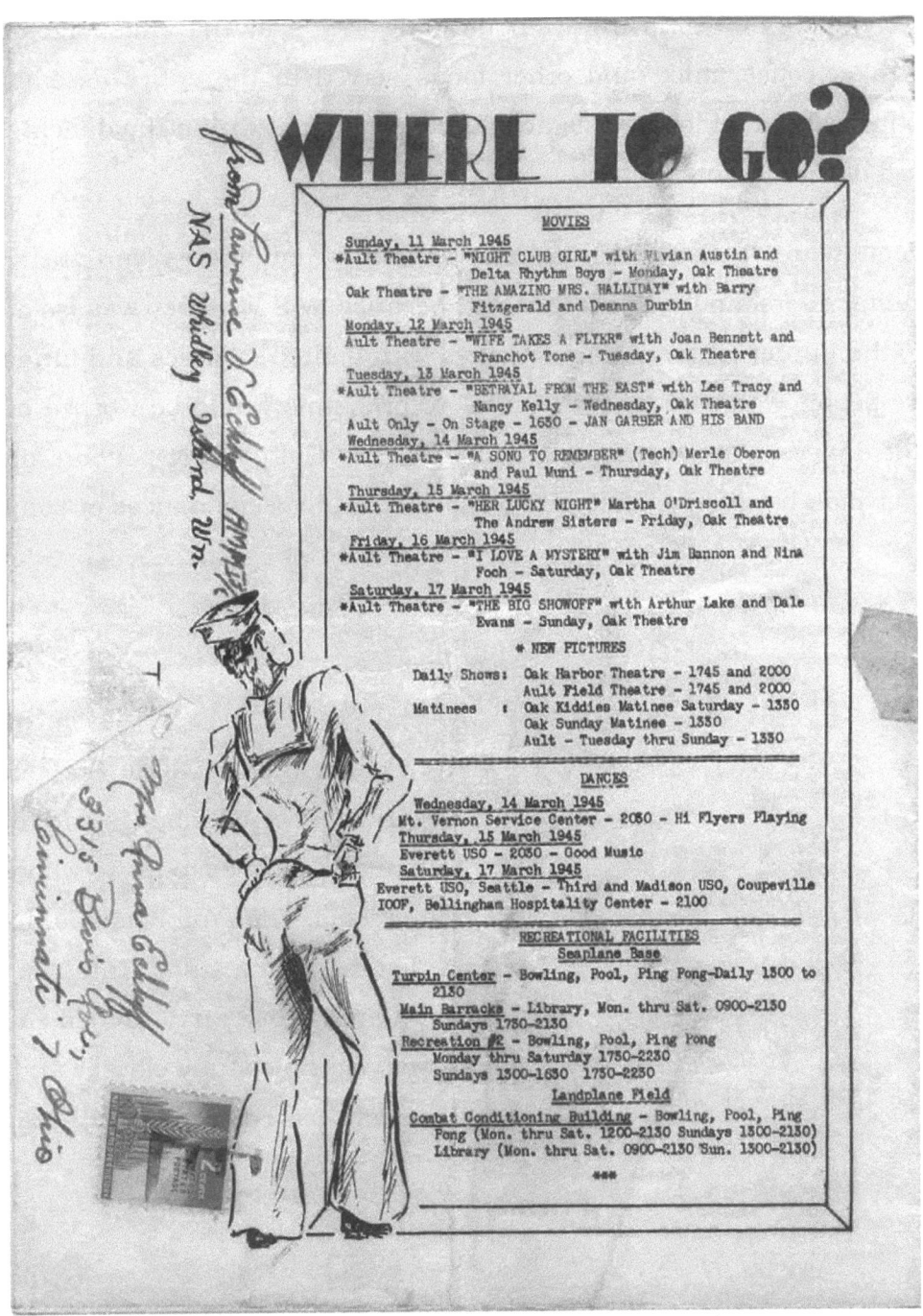

Prop Wash provided lists of weekly movies, dances, and recreational facilities along with NAS news

Whidbey's Recreation Department did its best to keep the men entertained and morale up. They announced a banner program of dance bands such as Jan Garber and his orchestra and Eddie Oliver and his swing band. Popularity of the dances was demonstrated by a Valentine dance featuring Ted Fio Rito with attendance of 2800 at the enlisted dance, 600 at the officers dance, 800 girls from surrounding towns at the enlisted ball, and 4000 sandwiches, cake, coffee, milk, and other foods served to the entire assemblage. It was strongly emphasized that smoking was absolutely prohibited within the dancing area on the gym deck at all of their events.

Providing adequate recreation for hundreds of civilian employees and their families, in addition to military personnel was complicated because NAS Whidbey was isolated from city centers. Also, the burden of arranging activities with limited facilities and funds fell upon a few. The more people who participated, the more programs would be worked out. Activities included adult dances, Saturday fortnights in the Rec Hall, young people's dancing every Friday night, civilian bowling, occasional box socials, and special dances or songfests.

Divine Services

PROTESTANT

Sunday Services
Oak Harbor Theatre	1000
Ault Field Theatre	0830
Adm. Bldg., Oak Harbor	2000

Sunday School
Ages 3-12 - Nursery Bldg.	1100

Wednesday - Bible Class
Adm. Bldg., Oak Harbor	1930

CATHOLIC

Sunday Masses
Oak Harbor Theatre	0830
Ault Field Theatre	1030

Daily Mass
Barracks Chapel, barracks 14 next to Post Office. 1700

Confessions
Before Sunday and daily Masses. Saturday afternoon and evening in Chaplain's Office.

CHRISTIAN SCIENCE
Ad. Bldg., O.H.
Sunday Service	0900
Monday evening	1700-1900

Not unlike other Naval Air Stations, there was an effort at Whidbey Island to provide church services to those who were interested. The *Prop Wash* published a listing of Protestant, Catholic, and Christian Science services held each week, as well as Bible study classes and Sunday School classes for kids 3-12 years old.

Chapter 7 – Whidbey

Purchasing war bonds was not just a civilian effort. While Larry was at NAS Whidbey Island, the *Prop Wash* reported on their efforts in the War Bond Allotment Drive for all NAS personnel. The goal was 70% participation of all civilians, enlisted men, and officers attached to the station. By March 09, 1945, they had reached 65% and extended their bond drive for another month. The Supply Department became the first Navy group at Whidbey to achieve 100% participation. Commander Voit stated "that the personnel in Supply have clearly demonstrated a strong cooperative spirit—a spirit that is necessary for the successful operation of any department and is a challenge for other activities on the station to strive to equal."

Larry's stay at NAS Whidbey Island would not be a long one. Nearly four months to the day after leaving Oklahoma for Washington, he was on his way to southern California. After nearly 21 months at stateside bases, the young sailor would board a ship bound for a base somewhere in the Pacific ocean.

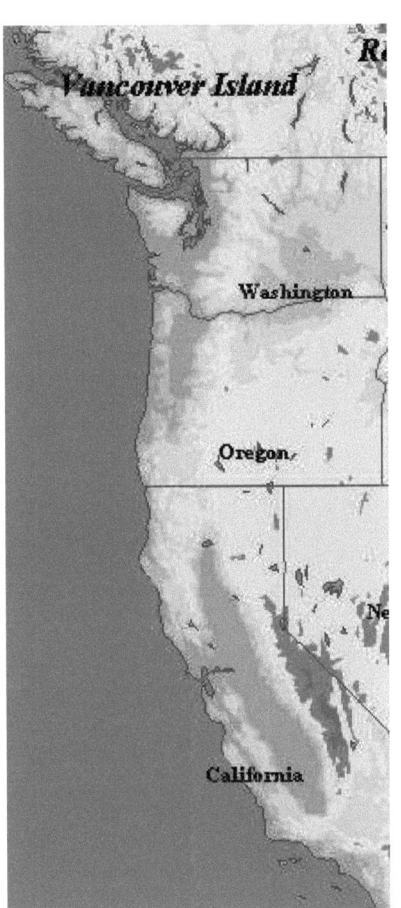

Map of the western United States coast from Whidbey Island, Washington in the far north to southern California, home of Port Hueneme

Chapter 8 – Port Hueneme: ACORNs and CASUs

March 15, 1945 – Transferred this date to the Officer-in-Charge, CASU Commissioning Detachment, Port Hueneme, California for further transfer to Combat Aircraft Service Unit (F) Fifteen, for duty.

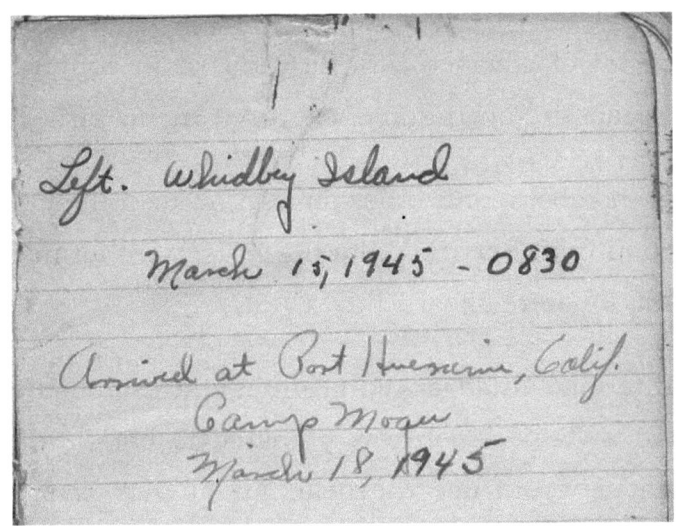

From Larry's small log book: Left Whidbey Island, March 15, 1945 0830, Arrived at Port Hueneme, Calif., Camp Mugu, March 18, 1945

Port Hueneme, California (pronounced "Wy-nee'mee") is a seaside community in Ventura County, California, about 40 miles south of Santa Barbara and 60 miles northwest of Los Angeles. The port sits directly across the Channel Islands of San Miguel, Santa Rosa, and Santa Cruz where the Santa Barbara Channel connects with the Pacific Ocean. Built in 1939, the once little-known coastal port used by produce shippers was home to a small, but busy, Naval Base during World War II. The base consisted of three units—an advanced base depot, Camp Rousseau, home of unattached Seabee units, and Camp Bedilion, the headquarters of the ACORN Assembly and Training Detachment.

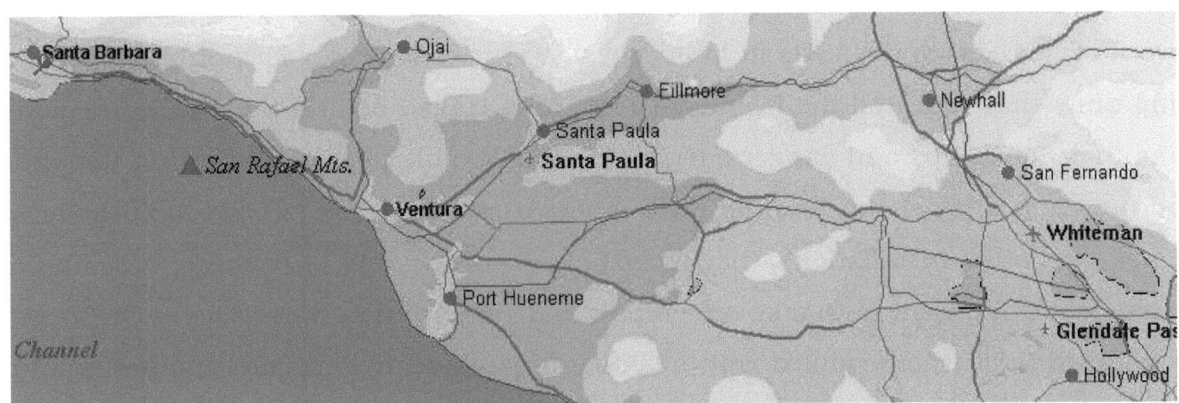

Map of Southern California coast and Port Hueneme

Chapter 8 – Port Hueneme: ACORNs and CASUs

The ACORN, an Advanced Base Unit consisting of a Combat Aircraft Service Unit (CASU), previously known as *Carrier* Aircraft Service Unit, was a wartime development providing an extremely mobile organization to keep land-based Navy planes repaired. An attachment of Seabees handled construction. Their responsibility was to provide rapid construction, operation, and maintenance of advance U.S. airfields, or in conjunction with amphibious operations, the speedy repair and operation of captured enemy airfields.

CASUs repaired fighters, bombers, and other aircraft to keep them in action. A CASU was mainly personnel. Patrol Aircraft Service Units (PATSUs) were formed specifically to service patrol-type aircraft, but many were absorbed by CASUs.

When the Navy planned to take an advanced position and establish an airfield, it put in an order for an ACORN and a CASU. Each was prepared to handle the number and type of aircraft the Navy estimated would use the field. An ACORN was created somewhat like ordering parts from a catalog. Various components, each self-contained units of equipment and personnel, were assembled according to the various jobs the air station had to perform. If it was to handle fighter-type aircraft, it was given certain components. To provide for multi-engined plane landings, other components were "ordered."

A war requiring heavy aerial activity over long stretches of the Pacific logically bestowed on the Navy the task of crafting well-equipped island air bases that could be set up quickly and operate efficiently. Air strips often were cut through dense jungle and finished with available materials from crushed coral to pierced steel planks. Operations towers, repair shops, plus fueling and rearming facilities were provided in addition to barracks and facilities supplying the daily needs of the hundreds of men who ran the air base.

The work of ACORNs and CASUs in building island air bases is far less publicized than the fighting units that captured the islands. These units trailed behind the shock troops, often sharing their hardships and dangers, trying to make livable places out of what usually was war-torn coral islands or jungle. After the Seabees attached to the ACORN built the airstrip, buildings, and other installations, they moved on. A smaller unit of Seabees, called a CBMU (Maintenance Unit), went in to take over repair and construction work. Each ACORN was so well equipped that, when coupled with a CASU, it could service, rearm, and perform minor repairs and routine upkeep for planes of a carrier group or a patrol plane squadron.

Chapter 8 – Port Hueneme: ACORNs and CASUs

Squadrons flew in and left carrying little or no equipment. CASU personnel serviced and repaired the planes with tools furnished by the ACORNs. Because it was a highly mobile unit, the CASU was not burdened with equipment. Crew complements varied widely depending on the size of the job and number of planes they had room for at the assigned island base. The usual ACORN complement, including Seabees, was 67 officers and 1590 men, with a CASU complement of 17 officers and 516 men.

The ACORN was a commissioned unit that stayed to maintain and operate the air strip. Combat missions were directed by Fleet commands, but routine operations on the base were handled by the ACORN. Air operations at the new base were under supervisory control of the ACORN, just as continental-based air stations were under a commanding officer and his staff. The CASU remained in commission as a separate entity while the ACORN could be decommissioned and absorbed into an air base after it was completed. The CASU was under the ACORN, as was the defense battalion of Marines or Army personnel that came in with the ACORN to furnish antiaircraft and ground defenses. ACORNs and CASUs received gunnery training and occasionally had to fight enemy soldiers not driven from an area.

CASU personnel were specialists in some branch of aviation maintenance. Many CASUs were formed at the Port Hueneme base where they were trained in military and technical courses, servicing of battle-experienced aircraft at Mugu Field, squadron-servicing at a nearby naval auxiliary air station, and assembly and loading of equipment at Port Hueneme in cooperation with the companion ACORN. Much emphasis was placed on loading and stowing equipment in LSTs and other ships, in preparation for the time when the CASU and ACORN would land on some distant island and start operating.

There were two types of CASUs, those based in forward areas west of Hawaii being given the designation CASU(F). They were units furnished to service the squadrons and support their shore-based operations from advanced or dispersed bases. CASU(F) 15 was initially formed at Port Hueneme December 18, 1944.

The CASU mechanics serviced, rearmed, and made minor repairs on land planes or seaplanes, large or small, fixed their radios, and helped pilots taxi around parking strips. It maintained facilities and equipment in its charge, including personnel facilities. They also furnished berthing, messing, and service to personnel of air units, both flight and ground personnel, if such facilities were not already available through some naval air station. They provided transportation, line shacks, ready rooms, slit trenches, and bombproofs.

Chapter 8 – Port Hueneme: ACORNs and CASUs

Because it was a self-contained unit, a CASU had a complete inner organization of its own, consisting of an engineering division, operations division, ordnance, radio and radar, camp, supply, personnel, and medical.

The engineering division handled aircraft repairs—the main function of a CASU. Operations handled matters concerning operation of planes attached to or visiting the CASU. Ordnance managed rearming and guns. The radio and radar division repaired electronics gear, while the camp division usually merged with the ACORN in maintaining and policing grounds and buildings of the air base. Supply division supervised supplies and disbursing. Personnel was assigned the job of taking care of officers and men of the CASU, including physical education and recreation.

Formerly, the PATSUs were trained to handle only big multi-engined aircraft, however, they stopped being formed under that name and their duties fell to a CASU(F) with special components—personnel trained to maintain large planes as well as fighters. Initially, CASUs worked mainly on carrier-type planes including F6F, TBF, SBD, and SB2C. However, when the PATSU responsibilities were folded into the CASUs, they also serviced patrol aircraft such as PBY, PB4Y, PBM, PBJ, PV, and other large planes.

While the units had all types of enlisted ratings assigned to them, most were Aviation Machinist Mates (like Larry), Ordnancemen, and Radiomen.

> "The scene is an island airstrip in the Central Pacific. Several planes are away on strikes, some are assigned to emergency standby; others are loaded with depth charges awaiting search assignments and final grooming before release to the pilots."
>
> "Suddenly a dispatch is received. 'All available planes strike-immediately!' Mechs, radiomen swarm over the planes removing depth bombs and testing each shackle. Other bombs quickly are fused, finned, and loaded. Within a short time the planes are in the air. The strike is a success. Returning pilots state that a 15-minute delay could have affected seriously the outcome."

Flight crews came to regard CASUs as their partners in operations. They shared with the fliers the rough life, bombings, and casualties.

CASUs on advanced Pacific islands endured the same rugged living conditions as frontline troops. Long hours of night work repairing planes, sleepless nights filled with bombings, cold food, disease, casualties, and foxholes. Many units landed right behind the Marines and had to build bases from scratch before they could start maintaining planes. Squadrons had a habit of dropping in before the official reception committee was all set, supplies were delayed, and replacement parts lost, but CASUs kept the planes flying.

Chapter 8 – Port Hueneme: ACORNs and CASUs

On March 22, 1945, Larry received new orders by restricted dispatch. He was transferred to ACORN 50 FFT for duty as part of the CASU Commissioning Detachment, Port Hueneme, California. A second restricted dispatch March 24, 1945, transferred Larry to CASU(F) 15 for duty as an Aviation Machinist Mate Third Class (AMMI 3/C).

Often, the journey from a coastal base to the transport ships was by paddle wheeler—steamboats like Cincinnati's Delta Queen and her twin, the Delta King. There were reports of soldiers and sailors crowded into the lower level of a ship already crammed with gear and equipment like cattle.

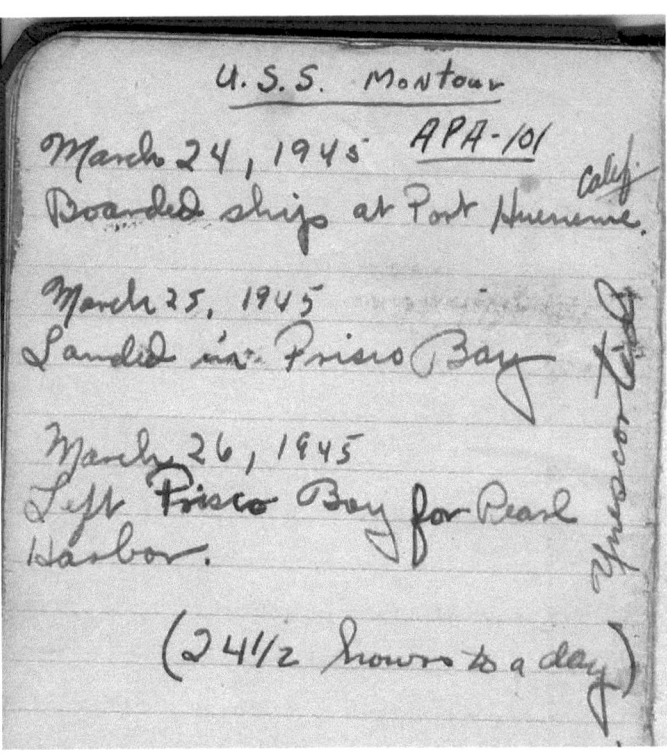

Larry's log entries: March 24, 1945 Boarded ship at Port Hueneme, March 25 Landed in Frisco Bay, March 26 Left Frisco Bay for Pearl Harbor Unescorted

Larry departed the continental limits of the United States on March 26, 1945 and crossed the 180th Meridian as a passenger aboard the *U.S.S. Montour* (APA-101).

These photos were taken by Larry but it is unknown whether they are at Port Hueneme, San Francisco, or Pearl Harbor area

Chapter 9 – Finally Left Port

Walking up to the Bayfield Class Attack Transport christened the *U.S.S. Montour*, designation APA-101, a sailor probably had mixed emotions. Some were going aboard as crew members plying the Asiatic-Pacific Theater for an unknown length of time. Others, like Larry, were essentially passengers being transported from the U.S. mainland to some yet to be announced island to establish and service a forward air field. Most had never set foot on a boat of any kind let alone a 455 foot long ocean-going military vessel.

APA-101 U.S.S. Montour on right apparently taken by Larry at Port Hueneme

APA-101 U.S.S. Montour Photo courtesy of NavSource

The ship that became the *Montour* began life in October, 1943 at Ingalls Shipbuilding Corporation in Pascagoula, Mississippi and was launched the following March. It was acquired by the Navy on a loan charter basis and placed in partial commission June 9, 1944, heading to Brooklyn, New York for conversion and fitting as an Attack Transport by the Bethlehem Steel Corporation. Finally placed in full commission in December 1944 as the *U.S.S. Montour*, designation, APA-101, with Captain James H. Thach, Jr. USN in command, the ship sailed for Hawaii after a shakedown "cruise" in Chesapeake Bay, arriving at Pearl Harbor on the first of February, 1945. Three days later, she proceeded to San Pedro, California, for yard work.

After being fitted as a Transport Squadron Flagship in San Pedro, California and undergoing a full shakedown the next week, the *Montour* headed to Port Hueneme where it was moored at Pier Two and commenced loading operations on March 19, 1945.

Chapter 9 – Finally Left Port

On March 24, a total of 30 officers and 643 enlisted passengers embarked, including CASU 15 with 7 officers and 128 men and ACORN 50 with 8 officers and 105 men. The usual crew complement of the *Montour* was 39 officers and 501 enlisted men, with capacity to transport 92 officers and 1423 enlisted. As an Attack Transport, the ship was equipped with two single 5"/38 caliber dual purpose gun mounts, four twin 40 mm AA gun mounts, ten single 20 mm AA gun mounts, and 17 boats including two LCMs, twelve LCVPs, and three LCPUs.

At 1335 (1:35 p.m.) they got underway, en route to San Francisco. The following day, while anchored in San Francisco harbor, they received five LCP(R)s and four LCM(6)s from the Naval Landing Force Equipment Depot, Albany, California, along with five LCVPs—all of the boats were received as cargo to be transferred in the forward area.

At 1202 on March 26, 1945, the *Montour* was underway for Pearl Harbor, Territory of Hawaii, with Larry on board. General and emergency drills were held enroute. Gunnery exercises expended nearly 2000 rounds of ammunition.

According to the Naval History and Heritage Command, a large number of passenger ships and freighters were acquired by the Navy in the early 1940s in anticipation of involvement in the war. They were converted into transports, outfitted so they could carry amphibious landing craft, and given AP series hull numbers. By 1942, there were already over 100 AP ships. Deciding that these amphibious warfare ships constituted a separate category of warship from conventional transports, the classification of Attack Transport (APA) was created and new numbers were assigned to the 58 APs then in commission or under construction. The need was so great that many newly constructed merchant ships were also converted to attack transports.

Service members heading out to sea usually got two meals per day while standing at a table. The food on their trays wasn't fancy but sailors who spoke about it later didn't think it was bad. Some sailors stationed on ships thought the food was great. If they had an admiral aboard, they always had a Sunday dinner. "It was just like Thanksgiving. We had a menu…a very long menu. It had everything on it that you could imagine. The food aboard our ship was great. We not only had a kitchen where they prepared the food, we had a bakery. We had an ice-cream stand. It couldn't have been much better…"

Many beds were 7 ft. long, 2 ½ feet wide, with a pipe frame and canvas matt to sleep on. Some ships had limited washing facilities and the lower deck, including the mess area, could be hot and cramped. Sleeping quarters were also hot and the stench could be pretty bad. Many tried to stay on the open deck where there was fresh air and a bit more room but the ships could roll, especially with strong ocean swells.

The water in the Pacific could be really rough. Sometimes the bow of the ship would dive into a wave and when it came back up it threw the water—completely covering the ship. Scuppers, specialized drains, took the water and funneled it back into the ocean. Some sailors thought it exciting, others got seasick and may have wondered why they didn't join another branch of service. There were times when it got so rough that they wouldn't allow people out on the deck. It was too dangerous. If they had to rescue men from other boats, they had to pull along side in those high seas and time their movements carefully as the water could fall 15 feet and then rise again.

The large liberty ships had "big holes where you put the men, and I [one sailor] was in this one roll right near the bulk, and along that one bulkhead was a rack of torpedoes. My, God, have you ever seen a torpedo close up? They're as big as a bus. They had three of them stacked up there, and three more stacked up there, three more stacked..."

Sailors stayed busy and had little time for entertainment except for the movies that some ships projected below deck in the evening after supper. If other ships were nearby, such as convoys of destroyers, they were welcome to board the ship as well. No lights were permitted top-side after dark. They made ships into targets.

The kitchen was never closed. Men on watch at night had to eat, and during the daytime, all of the shops (machine shop, etc.) were open. Basically, there was work and sleep, and occasionally they got to go ashore to play. That was life in the Navy. Most never had time to think about what was happening. They were too busy.

What little down time they might have was usually filled by playing cards, reading, writing, and watching over the side of the boat. While at sea, sailors stayed in touch with family and friends by writing letters. Mail service was usually good and arrived frequently. Men were encouraged to write home often and many wrote almost daily. Today the hundreds of letters that survived are like gold to families and historians alike, providing a glimpse of the activities going on a world away. No matter where they were, mail call was an event everyone looked forward to.

Chapter 9 – Finally Left Port

It took about 14 days to get from the San Diego/San Pedro area to Hawaii. Many crews left Pearl Harbor headed for the South Pacific not knowing where they were going. They were just kids and many didn't know anything about the South Pacific other than Hawaii. They were told they would find out after they were so many hours at sea. One man reported that "they lined us up [at the embarkation port] and they called out names. 'You go over here, you go over here.' The group I went with was altogether different fellas than ones I had gone into the service with. We didn't know where we were going until we got aboard the ship, and when we got aboard this ship they told us...we were headed for Pearl Harbor."

This letter is the only one found from Larry after leaving port.

```
Hawaiians Area

March 30, 1945  Friday

Dear Mom,

After a struggle, the usual one with myself, I am about to write you once
more. They told us that when we write we shouldn't say anything, so that is
what I'm about to do.

Am aboard ship finally and have been for a few days. When we left port it
was a little rough and kinda tough going for a lot of the fellows for the
first time out. I was among those who weathered seasickness, I was not the
only one though. It is a little rougher than riding on the Island Queen, I
can tell you that.

Before boarding the ship, we all received two shots and since being aboard
have gotten three more and still we haven't gotten all of them.

Going into the Mess Hall for chow is kind of a funny story. At first we
used to sit on benches and eat at tables sitting down but the benches would
fold up every now and then (Pretty often) from the ship's rolling back +
forth. Well they fixed that. We stand to eat chow now and every once in a
while when the ship rolls, you may be digging into someone else's tray,
since yours and all the rest of them slid to one end of the table. The
fellows, for the greater part, take it in their stride and think nothing of
it or else get a couple of laughs at someone else's expense. (A meal?)
```

Chapter 9 – Finally Left Port

Island Queen Riverboat on the Ohio River at Cincinnati, Ohio

Before leaving the States, I got to Confession, Mass and Communion and since coming aboard have gone to Mass almost every day.

They told us just about all we could say in letters and I've taken most of it in so far except the beautiful Pacific. The water is a dark blue and is actually pretty but land would look a lot better right now. Enough is enough or too much for the first time. Maybe the sea is not the life for me. We always wear life belts whenever we go on deck. Even the ship's crew has to wear them all the time. I'd hate to spend my life wearing a lifebelt.

Have you received the C.O.D. box yet? If you haven't, you should have by this time. Did you find the pictures, and what do you think of them? I guess they'll have to do for a while anyway. Received the pictures you sent, they are swell. Gee, by the time I get home those little kids will be bigger than I am. Everyone is looking good on them. Hope they are all O.K. I'm fine, never felt better.

Will write again soon. Don't forget to write whenever possible.

Love to all,

Larry

Chapter 9 – Finally Left Port

Pearl Harbor was usually a stopping point between mainland United States and everywhere else in the Pacific. Often, ships stayed in Pearl about one day—enough to get loaded or unloaded with service members and equipment. They usually loaded the ship with pineapple because Dole could not ship pineapple very often. Units being transported from the U.S. to the Pacific often were allowed up to a full day on the Island to visit or get haircuts. By most accounts, they were treated well. Damage to the harbor was still in evidence to those passing through. While the major destruction was pretty well cleaned up by this time, there were still ships sunk in the harbor.

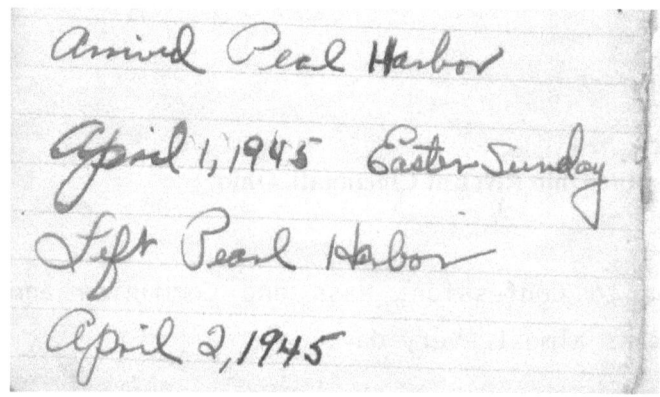

Larry's Pearl Harbor log entries noted they arrived on Easter Sunday

At 1400 on April 1, 1945, the *Montour* was moored to berth A-12, Bishops Point, Naval Reservation, Pearl Harbor. They exchanged four LCM(6) and three LCP(R) for four LCM(3) and five LCVP (landing crafts) at Waipio Boat Pool, Waipio Point, Pearl Harbor.

A Pocket Guide to Hawaii was prepared by the Special Projects Branch, Morals Services Section, Central Pacific Base Command and produced by the Army Information Branch in Washington, D.C. for the use of Military Personnel only. The little 46 page booklet with the royal blue cover starts "This is about Hawaii, to introduce you to a new country."

It goes on to briefly describe the islands and the civilian population on the islands, including Japanese-Americans, native Hawaiians, Puerto Ricans, Chinese, Koreans, and Filipinos. It provides a history of the islands, their culture, including the Hula, and describes the government, business, and industry on the islands.

Each branch of service—the Army, Navy, Marine Corps, and Coast Guard had a section devoted specifically to them. In the discussion about recreation and things to do it states "girls are scarce in Hawaii" and tells what they can say when they write home, wire, or phone, plus how to stay in good health and save some money.

Chapter 9 – Finally Left Port

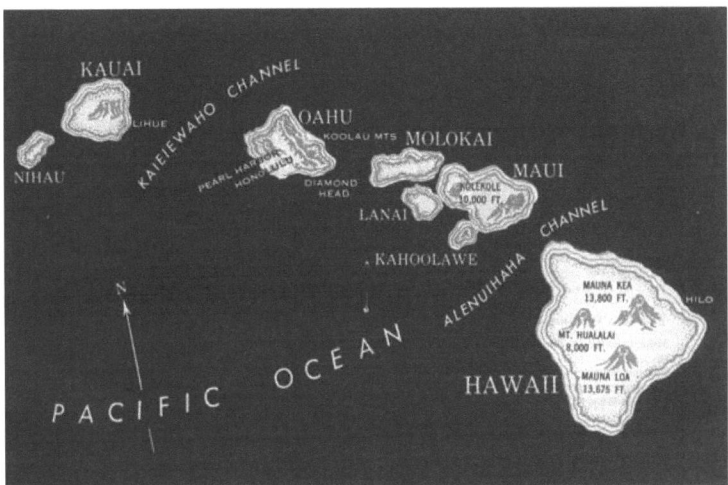

The guide, with the background of the cover and map printed in blue, contains two maps- this one identifies Hawaiian islands and towns for service men

How to get homesick in one easy lesson? Gaze at the second map clearly showing that Larry and his fellow Ohio sailors were now 2100 miles from San Francisco and another 2000 miles plus from home.

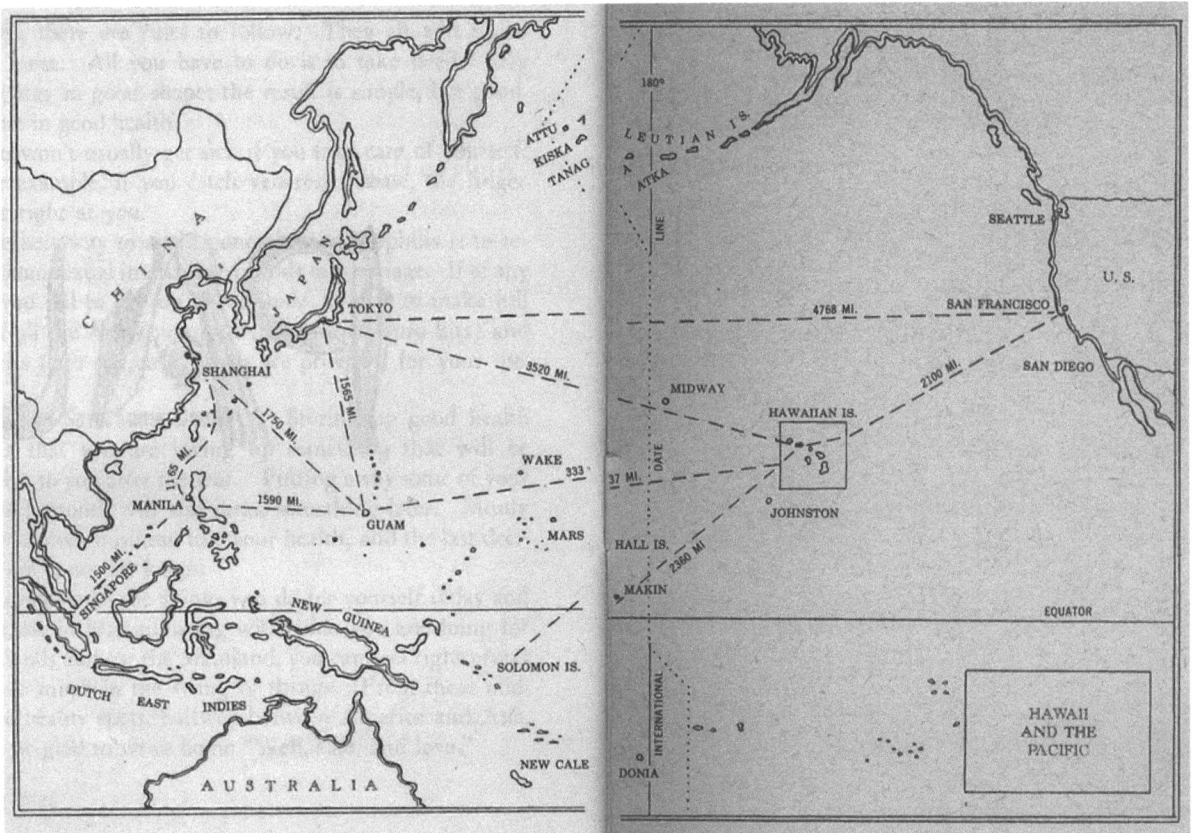

Second map in the Hawaii guide with distances from the U.S. to key locations in the Pacific

147

Chapter 9 – Finally Left Port

While in Honolulu, servicemen could have their picture taken with a "hula" girl, complete with palm trees in the background. Larry took advantage of the opportunity, possibly on the return trip since he is wearing two stripes on his uniform.

Larry posed with a "Hula girl" while in Honolulu

After disembarking one officer and 15 enlisted passengers, they were underway at 1452 on April 2, 1945 for Eniwetok, Marshall Islands—all pursuant to orders contained in Cincpac secret letters.

Chapter 10 – Destination Unknown: South Pacific

With Hawaii behind them, the passengers and crew of the *U.S.S. Montour* could see nothing but water all the way to the horizon.

Crews of ships dispatched around the beautiful islands might have "liberty parties" during the day. Before they could leave the ship, a team would first check for land mines and booby traps. When the all clear was given, they could go ashore. Sometimes they would dive off the fantail. A destroyer sat low in the water so they could go swimming. Someone would take them to the island beach in boats, generally with a beer or two. "If you had a buddy, or knew somebody that didn't drink beer, you could probably buy his beer for a dollar a piece if he wasn't a good friend and would give it to you. Sometimes you'd get two, three, four beers, and go swimming." Guys would play ball—get some exercise—there wasn't a lot to do. They tried to have fun when they could. When the Red Cross was present, they would distribute doughnuts and coffee and write letters for injured sailors that couldn't.

Reportedly, some of the men liked to have something to drink around holidays, but weren't allowed to have alcohol aboard the ship they were serving on. However, that didn't stop a few determined lads who somehow managed to break into the locker where they kept alcohol for the torpedoes. Yes, the fuel for the torpedoes was pure alcohol. The contraband alcohol was mixed with grapefruit juice and within a half hour, they were all out cold. They didn't last long drinking pure alcohol, but they got away with it until a captain made them stand watch in front of the alcohol locker to make sure that it wouldn't happen again.

At 1000 on April 6, 1945, the *Montour* crossed the 180th meridian at 16-32-OON. All clocks were advanced 24 hours. Larry's log noted they crossed the International Date Line on Friday, April 8-9, 1945.

If a Navy ship crosses the equator or international date line, an initiation ceremony generally took place. These could be quite elaborate, depending on how safe the ship was from a pending attack. A shellback was somebody who had already been across the equator, so they were the ones that did the initiating. Sailors who never before made the crossing were known as pollywogs.

The extent of the initiation could be different for passengers on a ship versus those who were part of the crew. One story told how pollywogs with painted faces stripped down to

Chapter 10 – Destination Unknown: South Pacific

their shorts and then ran through a gauntlet of Marines who slapped their behinds with sticks as they passed. Some of the stunts could be quite painful. Another mentioned sailors having their heads shaved and being told to drink vinegar.

On one ship they dressed like buccaneers and went through a "crossing the line" ceremony. Another described having a royal barber—everything to do with the ceremony was "royal." Each pollywog was brought up in front of a royal court where they were accused of something. Then they covered their body in gun grease, picked up all of the hair from the royal barbering, and threw the hair on them. As they were initiated, they formed a line from amidships to the fantail, the stem of the ship. Then they had to crawl under everybody's legs where they were paddled all the way to the end. It was maybe 4 or 5 o'clock in the afternoon when it was all over.

If sailors were bored, it could be a rougher initiation. When there were ten or fifteen at a time, they got it much worse because there were so many. It was left to the imagination of the crew how to initiate. Reportedly, it was kind of a funny thing and a fun time, at least for the ones doing the initiating.

Postcard picturing "Neptune's Barbers" at work shaving some of their 700 victims

Chapter 10 – Destination Unknown: South Pacific

The hazing applied to officers as well as enlisted men. Photos on one ship showed pollywog officers eating their lunch with boxing gloves on. They were quite humiliated during many of the ceremonies that were involved; walking the plank after drinking a horrible concoction was typical. Shellbacks created a roughly 30' by 30' swimming pool with four or five feet of water in it. They would send the pollywogs out walking on a short board before they would be pushed into the water.

After completing the initiation, participants received a certificate showing the latitude and longitude of the ship at the time they crossed the equator, along with notice that the bearer was now a shellback (no longer a lowly pollywog).

The middle of the ocean was not the place to be during bad weather. On board ship, some sailors tied themselves into their bunk at night so they didn't end up on the floor during rough seas. Those who fell on the floor might be joined by men in the upper bunks as they tumbled on top of them. Some types of ships were worse than others. In Liberty ships, it was hard to know exactly what was happening. Filled with men and equipment, the whole ship could be tossed around like a rag doll. Propellers, often the size of a house, rattled the ship terribly when it came out of the water. The bow dove under water then rose back up throwing water stories high.

As if the weather wasn't enough, there was a risk of being torpedoed at any time while on board ship. One sailor related:

> "Two days out of Pearl Harbor I had volunteered on the ship to do whatever they wanted done, and I got a job standing watch. So I would stand on the bow of the ship with binoculars looking...[for]...something like airplanes, submarines, or whatever. Well, about two days out of Pearl, towards the evening, I spotted something off the one side and this other fella was with me and we called in and they said 'Yeah, we know what it is, it's a submarine.' We found out that sub had followed us for two days and the ship that we were on was loaded with dynamite and hand grenades, and that's not a nice thing to be torpedoed with, so they found out that it was a Japanese submarine and the destroyer pulled around beside us and started chasing."

The weather, especially typhoons, could toss a destroyer like a toy boat in a bathtub. Typhoon winds were sometimes 100-115 knots. During one storm, a sailor estimated the waves were 108 feet high. A freighter about 300 and some feet long was picked up by the waves so he could see daylight from stem to stern.

> "That ship was completely in the air. It sounded like a cannon went off when it come down. We had to go climb the wave. Then we got to the top, we had to start turning the ship. One engine flank ahead, one flank back. And we sailed down and turned and got pointed the other direction by the time we hit the top. Our diesel engines were fresh water, but they were salt water cooled. And we were rolling

Chapter 10 – Destination Unknown: South Pacific

> over so far that these salt water intake to cool the diesels was sucking air. A lot of them washed up on the beach. Some of them were even sunk in the harbor. During a bad storm a ship might roll 52 degrees at one time. Some ships would roll so much, they would take in water through the ventilators and wind up with water in the crews quarters. Sometimes they lost lifeboats and life rafts in a bad storm."

The crew on the ships were some combination of full-time Navy and reservists and the weather could always be a concern in the open ocean. When the typhoons came in, everybody looked around for their bunks. "...They heard the anchor chain coming up because they knew there was a big storm coming, and probably 90 percent of them were seasick from the terrible storms out there, but our ship was so big and powerful that we just plowed right through them. All the small ships...would be going full speed ahead, but were moving backwards because the storms were so violent."

Another sailor reported sailing in a 90 mph gale where the sea was terribly rough.

> "Our flying bridge was 35 ft. off the water and I was standing on the flying bridge looking at waves coming in at eye level. It was kind of spooky, and we had an instrument on there I call the rollometer but that's not the right name for it. But it is gravity operated and it has a dial with an indicator on it that hangs straight down from gravity. Well as the ship rolls, this thing would show the degree of roll. And I was on the flying bridge during this storm, and there was another lookout on the opposite side of the bridge. And when the ship would roll, I'd look over his shoulder directly into the water and I watched this rollometer one time and it went over to 35 degrees, then it went to 40 then to 45. Now 45 degrees is halfway over, 90 degrees and the ship capsizes. I thought, 'Man! This not going to come back up!' it kept on going, and it went to 54 degrees. We were 9 degrees over halfway over and it righted itself but we had guys on there that had been in the Navy, like I say career sailors, that got sea sick, They were throwing up every place..." Sometimes storms raged on for a day or more. A 180-foot vessel in heavy seas would "shinny up" a wave and then fall over the wave with a resounding crash. Bigger ships had maybe two or three waves underneath the vessel."

Many ships had a degaussing cable that ran along the hull. When the ship fell over a wave, the water rushed between the hull and that degaussing cable making a groaning sound. The purpose of the cable was to set off a mine [yet another sailing hazard] at a distance before it could blow the ship out of the water. Sailors "prayed a lot...especially when the seas were 35 or 40 feet...you do a lot of praying."

Chapter 10 – Destination Unknown: South Pacific

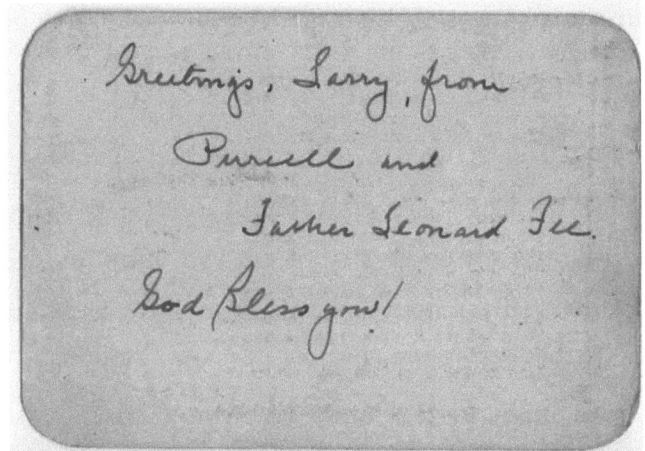 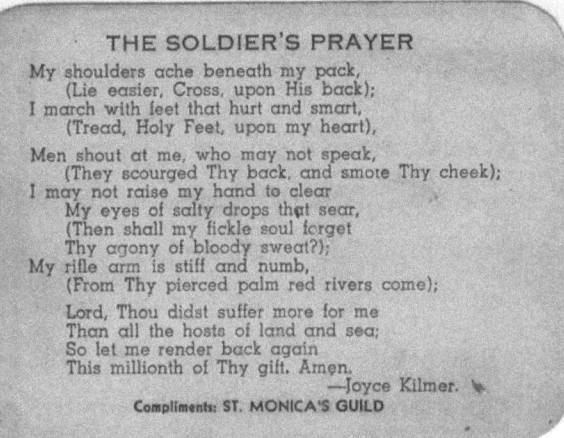

At some point during Larry's service, he received this wallet card "The Soldier's Prayer" from his principal at Purcell with a note on the back "Greetings, Larry, from Purcell and Father Leonard Fee. God Bless you!

Navy ships transporting troops in the Pacific were always in danger from attacks by air or by sea as well as from the weather. Sailors were constantly on the lookout for Japanese aircraft, particularly kamikazes (suicide pilots). Even when Navy anti-aircraft (ack acks) met their marks, not all planes blazed into the ocean. A single-seat kamikaze hitting a ship often caused many casualties even though the bulk of the ship was undamaged. Men were hit by falling booms and shrapnel, as small as rivets like buckshot, or as large as a wing from the disintegrating plane. Stories are told of men frozen with fear and helpless as they watched fellow crewmen strapped to their guns or caught on deck endure the unthinkable—body parts blown away. Wreckage often rained down fuel and oil and set fires on deck. Some men who seemingly survived the [event] later died of shock. Medics, including MDs, and supplies were stretched to the limit. Some injured were transferred to hospital ships, while the dead were buried in island cemeteries.

At sea, there was always the risk of submarines, coastal landmines, and torpedoes. Minesweeper ships had the task of finding and safely detonating sea-based mines. A direct hit from a mine could be devastating. After V-J Day when censorship of mail was no longer in force, sailors wrote of hearing the screams and other noises and seeing men blown up on a ship only yards away. Sweeper companies often sustained a higher percentage of losses than others in the Navy. They had "Ping duty" around the islands waiting for Japanese subs trying to sneak through. Sonar equipment was used to send out a signal and if it hit metal, it would echo back. If they pinged a submarine, they would report it to the squadron

Chapter 10 – Destination Unknown: South Pacific

commander, who would take action to determine who the sub belonged to. It could just as well be American as Japanese.

Of the service experience one man said "It helped me grow up...when you are seventeen years old and then to serve something like this, you know it's completely foreign to what people normally do, you mature a lot and I think that helped me, of course you have to learn when you are living in those close quarters with that many people, you have to learn to get along with people pretty well and I think it's just life experiences like that. You learn to make friends. To serve between the ones you like and the ones you don't care to be around, just like any other thing."

At 0855 on April 10, 1945, the *Montour* finally anchored in Berth Baker 93, Eniwetok, Marshall Islands. The following day at 1425, they were underway again—this time for the island of Saipan in the Marianas.

Chapter 11 – Saipan, Mariana Islands

The Northern Mariana Islands consist mainly of Saipan, Tinian, and the southernmost island, Guam. Saipan, the peak of a submerged mountain, is the largest of these at about 13 or 14 miles long and 5 miles wide with Garapan its largest town. It was a well developed tropical island for the time and location with towns, sugar plantations, refineries, a railway, terraced hillsides, and a large Japanese civilian population. A hospital, built before the war, served both Japanese and islanders. It was the most industrialized island of the Marianas.

A volcanic island, Saipan rises more than 36,000 feet above the floor of the Mariana Trench, the deepest in any ocean, with 1554 foot Mt. Tapotchau at the center. To the north and east, were a "series of high plateaus and rolling hills which ended abruptly in pinched, steep coastal flats or sheer cliffs that dropped hundreds of feet to the sea," while to the south and west ranged a "long coastal plain fringed with beaches."

Saipan is 1700 miles north of Papua New Guinea, 1650 miles east of Manila, 1344 miles from the Marshall Islands, 3700 plus miles west of Hawaii, and 1250 miles from Japan.

Guam was described as a "rugged 30 mile long chunk of limestone riddled with ridges and ravines and cloaked with dense, nearly impenetrable jungle verdure broken only by occasional rice paddies and patches of smooth table land." Saipan is about 100 miles closer to Japan and a more practical base to use for an attack on Japan. It was less costly for the U.S. and cut off Japanese air support to Guam.

"Discovered in 1521 by Ferdinand Magellan on his last trans-Pacific voyage to the famed Spice Islands, Saipan and its neighboring islands were variously, over the centuries, colonized by the Spanish, influenced by the Germans, and occupied by the Japanese," though there were very few Japanese military personnel on any of the Mariana Islands until just before the Americans landed June 15, 1944. Much of the island consisted of sugar cane cultivation and processing by civilians.

Before the war, Japanese leaders viewed an oil embargo against them as an offensive action due to a government dominated by Army officers who got involved in an aggressive war in China. They could not afford to abandon the China war as it was their justification for being in power but since the embargo would cripple the Japanese armed services within a year, they decided to take "defensive" action. The Japanese Navy went along with it as they

Chapter 11 – Saipan, Mariana Islands

depended on control of the seas as a maritime nation. The basic Japanese plan was to destroy Allied forces in the region, seize all Allied colonies and possessions, then sue for peace. They figured the Allies would go for a settlement versus a long war in the Pacific.

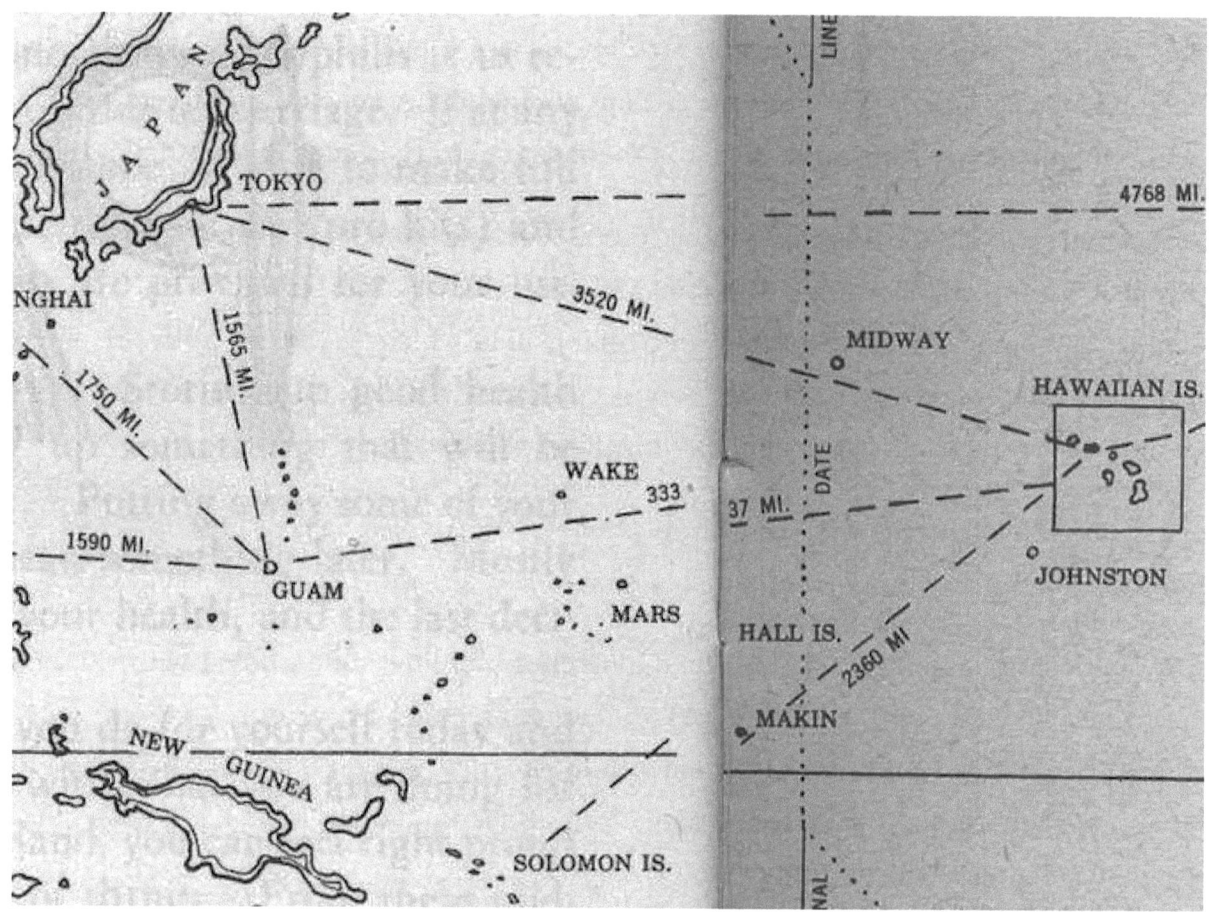

The line of dots north of Guam are the northern Mariana Islands including Saipan

At the time, Japan had about 250,000 ground troops available; the rest were in the China war. There were about 500,000 Allied troops on the Pacific islands but many were poorly trained, inexperienced, local recruits. When the war started, the Japanese Navy vs. the Allies was pretty even except for carrier superiority. Most of the areas targeted by Japan were not heavily garrisoned—many had just "token" forces while the Japanese in the area were better trained and had better air support.

The initial Japanese attacks in December, 1941 and January, 1942 overwhelmed the resistance. Japan used Naval superiority to isolate the Allied forces cutting them off from supplies and reinforcements. In six months, they had seized all central Pacific islands, all of

Chapter 11 – Saipan, Mariana Islands

southeast Asia except western Burma, most of New Guinea, and the adjacent islands, including Saipan.

By May, 1942, Japan began to lose carriers due to more U.S. carriers in the Pacific and the U.S. began sending land-based aircraft. Japan lost five carriers in the first seven months. The joint chiefs had the Marianas as their next objective after taking the Gilbert and Marshall Islands. Japan had an exclusion of all outsiders policy, so retaking the islands required complex planning and a larger force.

In November 1943, the central Pacific Campaign included Tarawa, Saipan, Iwo Jima, Tinian, and Okinawa. The Marianas, 1500 miles east of Manila Bay and 1300 miles southeast of Tokyo, were key Japanese defensive strongholds that would provide land bases to support the Pacific fleet. The Japanese bound for Saipan were slowed down by a lack of merchant shipping to move their troops and supplies due to American submarines that wreaked havoc with them. The stretched Japanese resources enabled General Douglas MacArthur to concentrate on the Philippines and Japan.

The liberation of Saipan was a sad chapter that included fanatical military defense and civilian deaths. The Battle for Saipan took three weeks during June, 1944. Admiral Ernest J. King was the Chief of Naval Operations and Commander-in-Chief of the U.S. Fleet. The policy had been "Europe First" with about 85% of naval manpower deployed in the European Theater and 15% in the Pacific Theater. The theory was the defeat of Germany would eventually lead to the defeat of Japan, however a Japanese surrender would not necessarily end the war with Germany.

Admiral Nimitz' goal was to take Saipan first, then Guam on D+3. By June/July 1944 when the Marianas were invaded (Guam, Saipan, Tinian) the Japanese had about a 50,000 man garrison. The allies sent the 2d, 3d, and 4th Marine Divisions, Marine brigade, and Army 27th and 77th Infantry divisions. It was the largest transoceanic invasion ever launched: 105,000 assault troops, 29 carriers, 891 aircraft, 14 battleships, 25 cruisers, 152 destroyers, and hundreds of freighters, tankers, and amphibious ships.

On June 15, 1944, the Navy illuminated the sky with "star" shells—very bright when they exploded. The island was the first objective of the 2nd and 4th Marine Divisions of the 5th Amphibious Corps with the Army's 27th Infantry Division in reserve. The Japanese had observation posts atop Mt. Tapotchau (1554 ft). Snipers were everywhere. On the eve of the

Chapter 11 – Saipan, Mariana Islands

U.S. invasion, Lt. General Yoshitsugu Saito, island army commander had *only* 25,469 soldiers on hand—two times those estimated by U.S. forces. In addition, Admiral Chuichi Nagumo had 6100 naval troops.

A relatively large island at 72 square miles as opposed to the atolls taken previously, Saipan has varied terrain: flat sugar cane fields, swamps, coconut groves, mountains, and cliffs with caves—multiple cave openings with one protecting another—some had reinforced metal doors. One, designated Hill 767, had tunnels built into the hillside by the Japanese. Many of the island's caves and coral were tunneled—Japanese soldiers and civilians using them to hide and fight against the American forces. For many, it was their final resting place.

Twenty thousand U.S. troops went ashore on the south of the island under heavy Japanese fire. There were approximately 20,000 men in each division—a total of about 70,000 including outfits such as shipboard marines thrown into the fight and the 29th Marines, also known as the "Bastard Battalion." They went ashore on D-Day with roughly 1,200 men and were pulled off the line a little over two weeks later with only 200 men left, not counting replacements. There were lots of casualties in the first wave of Marines that landed on the island. Many of the Marines were fresh from boot camp and knew only the bare essentials. By the end of the battle, there were 3,500 U.S. casualties. Japanese counter attacks and Banzai charges bloodied the U.S. forces as they fought their way to the north.

Before reaching the enemy on shore, men had to contend with coral in the shallow water along the shorelines. Men wore their leggings, "cause the coral was live and if you would get cut get they had to have certain, special stuff to put over the cuts to heal em' up. Snakes were bad too, a lot of those...[especially at] night time."

A man who survived the invasion recalled the Marines hitting the beach in LSTs and LCIs being picked off by Japanese fire as they landed. He was troubled by the number of men lost and the bodies floating by their ship—unable to be recovered.

> "On that first day of Saipan, we got ready to send a message back to MPM which was Honolulu, where we communicated, and the captain had me sending this message, and he said 'few casualties.' Well, I said, "Few? Captain?' He said, 'You do what I tell you.' I learned again, get back in your place buddy, but I thought it was very strange that we had all those Marines, bodies floating around and they're talkin' about 'few' casualties. From then on, every landing we had, there were always large casualties of Marines. I've got a picture where...after we got on our way, a person died aboard ship. We had a ceremony, it was...push him overboard, and that was the thing that always kind of made me conscious of you might go in there too buddy."

Chapter 11 – Saipan, Mariana Islands

"Well I'll put it this way. If a man was never on his knees, you were on your knees a lot at that point, a lot of prayers were said for everybody...I was so young that you couldn't even visualize in your own mind going to war at eighteen years old, you're just a kid."

The civilian population of Saipan committed mass suicide by jumping off cliffs at Marpi Point or committing suicide with hand grenades in caves. An estimated 22,000 civilians died in the battle. The Japanese committed suicide in at least two different locations on the north end of the island Banadero "Last Japanese Command Post." Lt. General Saito and Navy Admiral Nagumo committed heri-kari in a cave on July 9, 1944, the day the island was declared secured by the U.S. forces.

According to the official War Diary, U. S. Naval Base, Saipan:

"Landings on Saipan were effected and beachheads established by elements of the United States Marine Corps on 15 June 1944."

"The island of Saipan was declared "secure" 9 July 1944. On 28 July 1944, three (3) Base Companies, #4, #27, and #31, with six (6) officers and seven hundred and fifty-one (751) men (negro) arrived on the island. These companies were used for stevedoring work, supplementing the Army Port Battalions already on the island."

On Saipan, 2/3 of Japanese civilians died and most of the nearly 30,000 Japanese troops fought to the death with 16,525 Americans killed or wounded.

Unfinished states of the Japanese defenses and the success of U. S. Navy submarines blockading the delivery of construction supplies and replacement Japanese troops was critical to the U.S. victory. According to one POW, "If the U.S. assault had come three months later, the island would have been impregnable."

After the island was declared "secure" Navy Seabees built air strips all over the place. Saipan provided a U.S. staging area and artillery support for the attack on Tinian, a smaller, less rugged island with gentle terrain containing mostly sugar cane fields only 3 ½ miles to the south and easily visible from observation posts. Japan had three air fields on Tinian and one under construction. They had gun placements on the beaches. U.S. air forces used napalm from Saipan-based P-47s on Tinian Town.

Possession of the Marianas air fields, particularly those on Tinian, would allow the U.S. to deploy B-29s against Japan. Guam with excellent air fields and the best deep water harbor in Marianas, was also a prime objective. It had been a U.S. possession for 40 years but was seized by Japan two days after Pearl Harbor after overwhelming a small Marine garrison.

Chapter 11 – Saipan, Mariana Islands

Initially, Saipan's "inner harbor, Tanapag, afforded anchorage for only a few ships. The usefulness of the harbor further was diminished by Japanese ships which had been sunk therein. A tremendous amount of dredging resulted in making Tanapag Harbor one of the best deep water ports in the Marianas." The Port of Saipan grew in importance far beyond original expectations. At times, as many as 400 ships were anchored in the harbor.

Port Battalions had the job of unloading ships. Reportedly supplies were sometimes stolen either for personal use or to trade for other items. One sailor noted lots of stealing, one soldier from another, and inconsiderate behavior on some ships: "...half of them act like animals...they stole books from the base library, appropriated food they were supposed to be unloading..."

> "At the time the island of Saipan was captured, a Naval Supply Depot was not included as part of the island development plan. The Naval Base was to have a supply department large enough to take care of island naval needs."

> "The Naval Supply Depot, Saipan, was created and commissioned on 1 December 1944 when it was found that this Base unit was not equipped to service Fleet needs. It occupied 7,200,000 square feet of space just east of the main island highway at Garapan."

Build up activities on Saipan continued for months. On April 12, 1945, while Larry was on the *U.S.S. Montour* somewhere between Hawaii and Saipan, President Franklin Delano Roosevelt collapsed while in Warm Springs, Georgia. He died that afternoon leaving the country and the war in uncertain condition. The man who had served as Assistant Secretary of the Navy under President Woodrow Wilson in the first World War, presided over the state of New York as governor during the dark days of the stock market crash in 1929, and was elected President of the country in 1932—eleven years after being stricken with polio—who used every tool in his power to pull America out of the Depression and, having been reelected to unprecedented third and fourth terms, as commander in chief guided the country through the war being fought in across the Atlantic Ocean in Europe and in a multitude of islands in the vast Pacific, succumbed to a massive cerebral hemorrhage. That day, Harry Truman was sworn in as the 33rd President of the United States. The Kansas City native, World War I combat artillery captain, county administrator, and U.S. Senator had been Vice President for a mere 82 days. One serviceman remembered his thoughts upon receiving the news:

> "FDR we heard about right away. That was devastating. Right then and there we thought, Uh-oh, this is it, the war is over, we've lost."

Chapter 11 – Saipan, Mariana Islands

> Arrived Saipan April 14
>
> Unloaded Cargo for three days. (15-16-17)
>
> Left due ship (nite 17)

The page from Larry's log book notes his arrival on Saipan, April 14, 1945. He spent the next three days, from April 15 through April 17, unloading cargo before finally leaving the ship on the night of April 17.

```
14 April 1945 (Zone Minus 10)

Anchored at 1127, Berth I-66, Saipan Harbor, Mariannas Islands. Displayed colors
at half-mast in accordance with orders issued by SecNav as a tribute to the late
President of the United States. Disembarked 3 navy officer passengers.

Position           0800
Latitude           14-57-00N
Longitude          146-09-00E
```

U.S. Navy War Diary for 14 April 1945 for the U.S.S. *Montour*

Chapter 12 – NAB Kobler

```
CONFIDENTIAL

U.S.S. MONTOUR (APA-101)

16 April 1945 (Zone Minus 10)

    Underway at 1525 for Tanapag Harbor. Moored at 1624, port side to Pier A-3,
Tanapag Harbor. Disembarked 10 officers and 491 enlisted navy passengers. Embarked
as passengers, 2 army officers, 23 army enlisted men, 1 marine officer, 123 marine
enlisted men, 9 navy officers, and 133 navy enlisted men. Discharged all cargo. Re-
ceived 24 LCVP, 1 LCP(R) in non-operable condition from Guam Boat Pool (Saipan
Branch) in exchange for 3 LCP(R), 2 LCP(L), 4 LCM(3), 16 LCVP. These non-operable
boats to be returned to Pearl Harbor for repairs.

Position                          2000

Latitude                        15-10-52N
Longitude                       145-40-57E
```

Naval air bases had been established in a handful of locations around Saipan. A sea plane base was established at Tanapag. It included the Marianas Air Sea Rescue Unit and a Naval Repair Base. Other Naval air bases were set up at Marpi Point and Kagman Point along with a Naval Supply Depot. Located west of the town of Aslito, Naval Air Base Kobler Field, still under construction, was the home of CASU(F) 15.

Kobler Field, Saipan, April 25, 1945; Photo courtesy of U.S. Naval Aviation Museum

Chapter 12 – NAB Kobler

On February 25, 1945, while Larry was at Whidbey Island, CASU(F) 15 "A" Component arrived on Saipan. This component had the unusual distinction of being the first complete component to be moved from it's home port to it's destination by air. A group of 116 officers and men were carried by NATS in PB2Y aircraft from Alameda, California to Saipan. The "F" Component for CASU(F) 15 was transferred from CASU(F) 43 at Guam and arrived on Saipan, March 12. *The "D" Component (Larry's group) was transported by ship from U.S. Naval Air Station, Whidbey Island, Washington, finally arriving on Saipan, April 20, 1945.*

> "On 21 April the second Naval Air Base on Saipan came into existence with the decommissioning of ACORN 50. Personnel of ACORN 50 immediately became that of Naval Air Base, Kobler, which was commissioned with ceremony on this date."

Larry was officially transferred to CASU(F) 15 on April 16, 1945, and received aboard from ACORN 50 on April 20, 1945 as an AMMI 3/C (T) Class V-6, stationed at Kobler Field on the island of Saipan. He was one of 448 enlisted men who arrived with four officers.

CASU(F) 15 Kobler Air Base, Saipan
Photos from Larry's collection

Timing is everything. Just days after the *Montour* disembarked Larry and the rest of the passengers and left Saipan enroute back to Pearl Harbor, the weather map of April 20, Radio Guam, gave indications that a typhoon was developing just south of the routed track of the ship. At 08:00 a.m. GCT, a typhoon warning was received from Cincpac. The vessel's course was changed to northeast to avoid the storm, which then passed well to the west.

The War Diary Report for April, 1945 described CASU(F) 15 this way:

Chapter 12 – NAB Kobler

"Combat Aircraft Service Unit (F) Fifteen is a mobile class "C" aircraft maintenance and repair facility, designed to support carrier air groups and land squadrons in shore-based operations. The tactical mission of [CASU(F) 15] is to establish an organization ashore in the forward area in the shortest possible time to maintain fleet aircraft."

In April, CASU(F) 15 set up a complete system of aircraft service area and shops at Kobler Field, improving the entire service area for aircraft maintenance.

The Navy was gradually assuming the duties of the Army commands on Saipan. The process was slowed by a lack of personnel and equipment, which was either en route, uploading, or awaiting commissioning. Staff quarters were shaping up, personnel were arriving to coordinate various tasks, and construction at Marpi and Kobler Fields had progressed enough to enable complete operation.

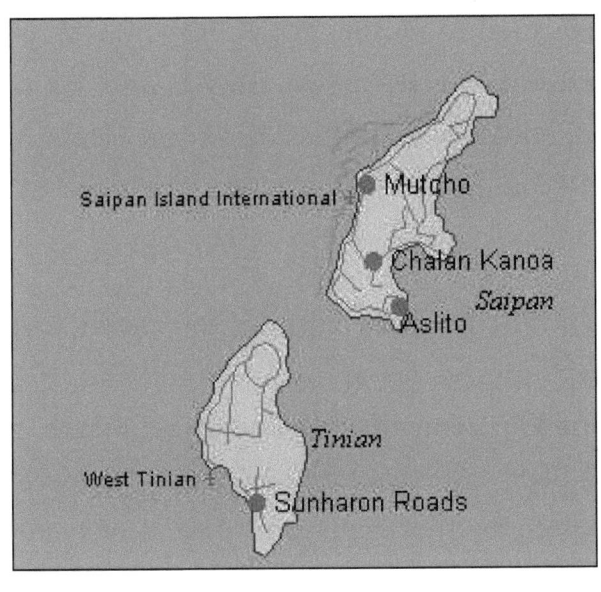

The islands of Saipan and Tinian are shown in the adjacent map. The U.S. operated a half dozen airfields on Saipan.

- Aslito Field (also known as Isley Field)
- Marpi Point (North Field) with CASU(F) 47 on the northern end of the island
- Kagman Point (East Field)
- Kobler Airfield (home of CASU(F) 15, west of Aslito
- Susup (Chalan Kanoa) an emergency airfield
- Tanapag Seaplane base located at the city of Garapan

On April 23, Vice Admiral John H. Towers, Deputy Commander in Chief of the U.S. Pacific Fleet and Pacific Ocean Areas, visited Saipan on an inspection tour.

For the month of April, 1945, the war diary report noted the following services furnished by CASU(F) 15 to the U.S. Army Air Force:

- Loading, rearming, and servicing 318th and 413th Army Fighter Groups for numerous strikes on Truk and Marcus Islands
- Rendered 3rd echelon service to the 318th and 413th Army Fighter Groups and other AAF Squadrons
- Installed rocket launchers, 163 sets, for the 318th and 413th Army Fighter Groups which resulted as reported by the United Press in the sinking, by rocket attack, of two small transports and one large cargo vessel

- Third echelon repair to the 4th Emergency Squadron, TAG, ATC, and all other squadrons and itinerate aircraft not having 3rd echelon facilities on this Air Base

In addition, they furnished the following service to Naval Air Groups, Squadrons, and itinerate aircraft:

- Serviced and maintained VC-98 and VC-99 during the period of 11 April through 30 April 1945
- Serviced and maintained Air Group Sixteen during the period of 26 May through 10 June 1945
- Maintained and serviced the Combat Air Patrol while it was based at Kobler Field
- Maintained and serviced an average of approximately 170 naval aircraft
- Accepted and combat-conditioned the new aircraft received by VC-98 and VC-99 prior to launching them for carrier rendezvous, enroute to the combat zone
- Increased the War Bond Allotment of the crew from 51% to 72%

Sixteen days after the death of FDR, big changes were occurring within the Axis powers in Europe. On April 28, 1945, Italian partisans executed Mussolini. Days later, on May 1, Hamburg radio announced Hitler's death. The end was in sight across the Atlantic. Finally, Germany signed surrender at Reins, Germany, on May 6, 1945. The Allies celebrated Victory in Europe (V-E) Day on May 8, 1945. They could only hope that the situation in the Pacific might be influenced by these events.

Americans in the Pacific had to keep half an eye on the calendar because the enemy had a fondness for launching attacks to commemorate anniversaries and other traditions. High-priority dates on the list were January 1-3, a period for remembering ancestors; March 10-Army Day, March 11-Empire Day, March 21 and Sept. 23, days for honoring the emperor's ancestors; April 3 and November 3, days of respect for the births and deaths of famous emperors; April 29-Hirohito's birthday, April 30-Japanese Memorial Day, May 27-Navy Day, and November 23-Thanksgiving.

Meanwhile, construction of the base started at Kobler in May, 1945. Base Operations at Kobler Field were finally assumed by the Navy, relieving the Army of this function. During the month of May, many Army Air Corps units arrived and departed at Kobler Field. In addition, "mopping up" operations were still continuing on Saipan. The first week of May, a dozen prisoners of war (POWs) were taken captive and 21 Japanese were killed. During the same period, four enemy were captured on Guam with 18 captured, and 44 were taken prisoner on Tinian.

Chapter 12 – NAB Kobler

The use of Avgas (airplane fuel) increased significantly due to accelerated air operations from the Marianas. Avgas consumption for the second week in May was 9 1/2 million gallons and for the third week, 11 million gallons. Four additional harbor fueling craft were added to service the fleet in the area. In addition, BEAGLE (IX-112) was transferred to this command and sailed between Saipan and Iwo Jima carrying 1,700,000 gallons of Avgas and 24,000 bbls of fuel oil on each trip.

The services tried to make use of local food as much as possible:

> "There are 893 acres of growing crops in the Marianas, and an additional 831 acres cleared and ready to plant. A small amount of produce continues to be shipped by air from Tinian to Iwo Jima. Livestock consisting of 70 dairy cows and 1000 hogs has arrived at Guam. The pasteurization unit is being installed for the supply of fresh milk to hospitals. Three Yps have reported to Saipan for duty as fishing craft."

While Larry was acclimating to Kobler, life went on at home. His youngest sister Margie made her first communion in Cincinnati on May 6, 1945. The family gathered for photos which they sent to Larry on Saipan. Imagine how he felt seeing his little sister holding his official Navy portrait while he was half a world away.

Larry's siblings on Margie's first communion day, May 6, 1945; from left Lois, Mary Jane, Margie, Dorothy, Donald, and Billy

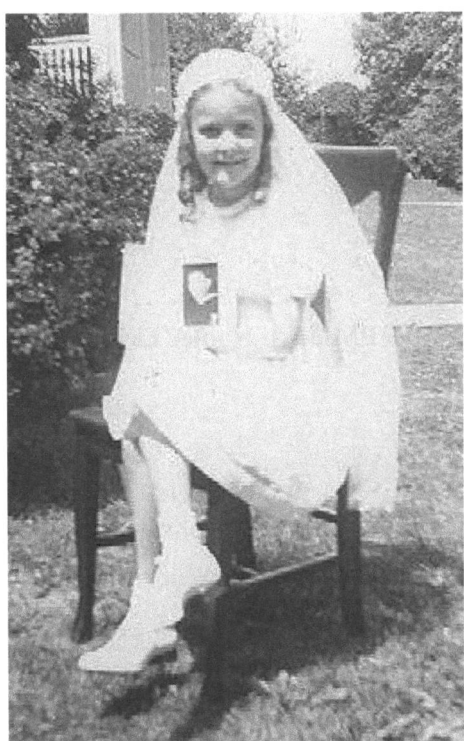

Larry's sister Margie holding his official Navy portrait

Chapter 12 – NAB Kobler

Construction work on additional necessary facilities, including laundries and mess halls, and a base hospital at NAB Kobler, continued concurrently with the training of units at the various naval air bases on Saipan. Athletic and recreation facilities were receiving some attention. Inter-field contests had a desirable effect on morale and sufficient equipment arrived to give promise of an even better situation in the future.

During the month of June 1945, the CASU(F) 15 was occupied as follows:

- Until June 10, Air Group Sixteen was still based there; 107 aircraft were made available for the training purposes of this group
- After the departure of Air Group Sixteen, CASU(F) 15 received orders to strike and salvage 22 TBM-1Cs and to "long time preserve" 11 SB2Cs. In addition, 139 aircraft were checked and placed in top operating condition for use.
- Made alterations on B-24 airplane belonging to General Jarman
- CASU(F) 15 of the U.S. Pacific Fleet, temporarily based ashore at Kobler Field, Saipan, Marianas Islands. Nothing is known as to it's approximate date of departure or destination.

TBM-3E at Kobler Field

SB2C at Kobler Field

CASU(F) 15 Strength Report
Officers, Authorized Complement 25, On Board 27
Enlisted men, Auth Comp. 733, On Board 696
Total 758 and 723

Chapter 12 – NAB Kobler

F4F-FM2 at Kobler Field

F6F with Aviation Machinist at Kobler Field

While no correspondence to or from Larry, including logs, were found after the one near Hawaii, many photos were taken on Saipan and Larry took the time to identify most of the people in them—many by nickname. He also had an address book which helped piece together some of the names and hometowns, though some are still speculative without additional research.

Instrument Shop – KOB 588 at NAB Kobler

A. C. Black "Blackie" from Oakland, California

Chapter 12 – NAB Kobler

**Inside Instrument Shop – KOB 588
at NAB Kobler**

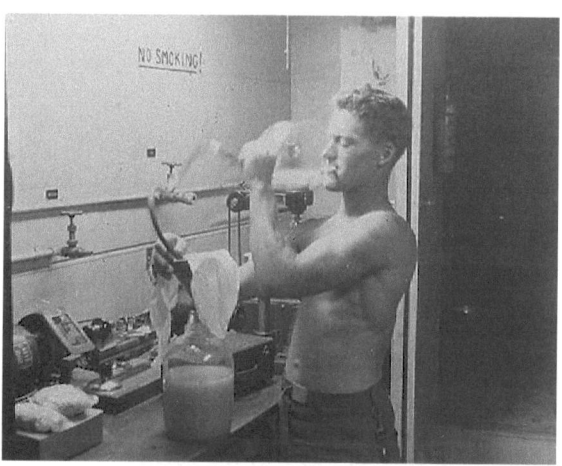

**Jake, "Raisin Jack" smoking under the No
Smoking sign (M. E. Jacobson, Weiser, Idaho?)**

**Alex, Instrument Shop boss at NAB Kobler
(H. E. Alexander, Kirkwood, Missouri?)**

**Larry Eckhoff on dirt bike by Instrument Shop
at NAB Kobler**

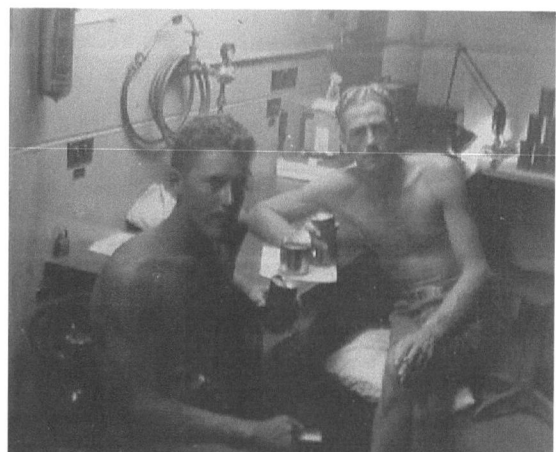

**Jake and Murray, Instrument Shop
(D. L. Murray, Slater, Missouri?)**

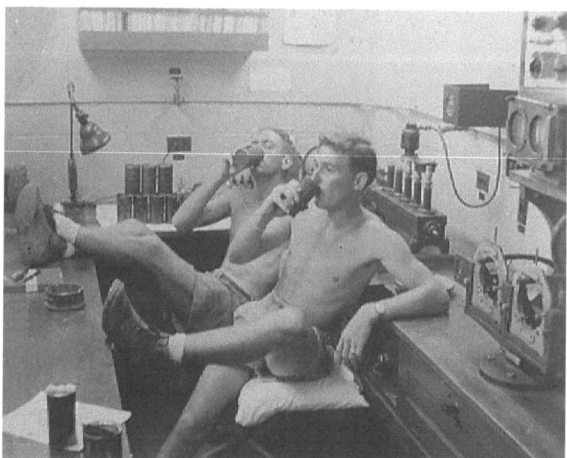

**Murray and Larry (front)
in the Instrument Shop at NAB Kobler**

Murray, Instrument Shop
(D. L. Murray, Slater, Missouri?)

Larry in front of a PV-1 with ID U540

Instrument Shop Crew at NAB Kobler
Front L-R: Larry Eckhoff and Jake "Raisin Jack"
Back L-R: Murray, Blackie, Alex

From the time Larry and the others arrived, there was still some concern about Japanese snipers. They survived in the caves for months after the U.S. retook the island. One serviceman reported that "they never wanted you to go somewhere by yourself. If you were gonna go to visit somebody, you had to go with another person." Those snipers probably had no idea the United Nations was organized at San Francisco on June 26 as an effort to achieve and maintain World Peace.

The 59th AAA Brigade provided AA protection for Isley and Kobler airfields in July, 1945. They also provided a force for mopping-up operations against enemy personnel still at large on the Island. During this period, 23 enemy were killed, 65 surrendered or were captured, and 34 civilians interned as a result of the operation. Yes, there were other people on the island. The Chamorros were the native people. Chamorros and Koreans were used by the Japanese as slave labor in the cane fields.

Children in a Saipan village

Clothes drying in a Saipan village

Conditions varied among the Pacific island groups. In general, they were tropical regions with hot humid days, chilly nights, and frequent rain. The largest base in the South Pacific was in Milne Bay, New Guinea (1700 miles south of Saipan) where they averaged 300 inches of rainfall each year. Sometimes servicemen were housed in tin-roofed Quonset-hut style facilities with concrete floors, others were in canvas tents or transitional housing of some sort. Some tents had no floors and some islands had no running water or electricity depending on fleet supply ships for their needs.

Moran and Ray "Pete" Peters (from Detroit, Michigan)

Larry Eckhoff "Me in front of our tent. (91) My sack is directly behind the tent number."

Paul Doresky (Ski), Cleveland, Ohio and Larry Eckhoff

Nelson in front of tent "Nelson. Just coming from the 'gyp joint' (candy in pockets)"

Due to the heat and dampness, everything "rotted or rusted." Skin fungus could be a problem and any break in the skin was ripe for infection. While islands like Saipan did have some towns, the vast majority were remote islands of stark contrast. On one hand there were exotic islands, beaches, and tropical fish, and on the other, dense jungles providing homes to lizards, parrots, huge spiders, scorpions, snakes, plenty of insects, and diseases such as scrub typhus and malaria—an environment totally different than the one experienced by those fighting in Europe.

The greatest danger in the tropical jungle environment was the mosquito which spread diseases from malaria to dengue fever. Dengue, while not fatal, caused so much pain for three or four days that it was also known as break-bone fever. Epidemics on Saipan and Guam in the fall of 1944, were quickly brought under control with generous sprayings of DDT. Some men in island service were required to take atabrine "nasty yellow pellets the size of a quarter and bitter as Brasso" that also turned skin temporarily yellow, to ward off malaria. Issued at breakfast, the anti-malaria pill was gulped down by many, gagged, and subsequently vomited back up, or simply palmed and never taken by others. It is unknown whether those serving on Saipan endured this requirement since it was not the scourge that it had been in the early days of the Pacific war. Thanks to atabrine, DDT, and other precautions, the rate of infection was down to around 50 a year per 1000 men in the Pacific areas and only one case out of every 2000 treated resulted in death. Shots generally protected service members from diseases like cholera and plague.

War diary reports by the 115th Malaria Control Detachment describe detailed efforts to control insects on Saipan. A three-day insect control course for Army and Navy units continued until mid-July, though units arriving on the island afterward were also instructed in a condensed version. The entire island was sprayed with a 5% DDT kerosene solution during the month. Field work on the spraying of breeding areas was continued and a drainage project was started, using native Japanese laborers. The following list summarizes mosquito control activities during the month:

Cisterns destroyed	5
Dumps sprayed	11
Dumps destroyed	1
Buildings sprayed	19
Tires sprayed	6500
Acres brush and woods sprayed	5
Gallons DDT sprayed	740
Acres sprayed by airplane	48000
Gallons DDT for Airplane spray	24252

The 743rd Medical Sanitary Company was even more specific.

"Mosquito Control - During the month of July a total of 956 buildings or tents were sprayed with 5% DDT in kerosene. Total area covered was 1, 406, 500 square feet; 4,294 quarts of spray were expended with an average coverage of 400.25 square feet per quart. The square feet coverage per quart was increased because of the fact that most troops are now billeted in wooden buildings, and a normal coverage of 250 square feet per quart caused excessive run-off. 815 gallons of DDT were issued to other organizations for their use in insect control."

"Fly control - Routine fly control was practiced through-out the area during the month."

"Disposal of Enemy Dead - A detail of men was used at various times during the month disposing of the bodies of enemy killed by the patrol activities of different units."

"Rodent Control - Prebaiting was practiced as the principal method of Rodent Control on the Island." In the six areas mentioned, an approximate total of 3862 rats were killed.

"During the month the entire Island was sprayed from a C-47A type airplane, 25,000 gallons of DDT in kerosene being used. The plane and pilot were furnished by the 9th Troop Carrier Squadron, this Island."

Servicemen were not the only ones dealing with the disease carrying insects and the island medical facilities had a mission beyond caring for service members. Some civilians on the island had leprosy, dengue fever, yaws, and elephantiasis. The military provided medical care for the civilian Japanese, Chamorros, Koreans, and Kanakas living on Saipan. In addition to making sure contagions were not a threat to military personnel, good physical condition of the civilians enabled them to help the military effort as laborers, clerical workers, domestic and hospital aides.

Sign in front of the Military Government Leprosarium on Saipan

Gate 2 entrance to Camp Susupe, the POW camp on Saipan

While an article in *Yank* indicated the Army didn't view the chances of getting leprosy as a problem "you have to live with lepers a long time to contract it" there actually was a leprosarium on Saipan.

Chapter 12 – NAB Kobler

The Fifth Military Police Battalion handled guard detail at Camp Susupe, a POW camp for Japanese prisoners built by U.S. forces after landing on Saipan.

CASU(F) 15 stayed busy during July. Their work included:

- Establishing a CASU Dispensary at Kobler Field airstrip which, when completed would provide 24 hour daily service to personnel in the area
- Rendering service on R5D and DC3 aircrafts which had been damaged by machine gun fire
- Providing service to Patrol Squadron VPB-128 from Tinian Island making relocation and new installation of radio equipment on PV aircraft
- Rendering services to 4th Emergency Squadron, T.A.G., and all other Squadrons and itinerate aircraft not having facilities at NAB Kobler
- Repainting a B-24 aircraft belonging to General Jarman
- 37 F4U-4 and F4U-1D aircraft were temporarily assigned by CASU(F) 15
- Temporary assignment of 16 SB2C-4s and 4Es completed

C-54 Skymaster (R5D)
Photo courtesy of U.S. Museum of the Air Force

The C-54 Douglas Skymaster, a large four-engine transport, was used by the Navy as the R5D. The cargo version (C-54A) could carry a maximum payload of seven tons, while the standard version normally carried 26 passengers.

On July 10, 1945 Air Group 92 arrived and started operations. An average of 120 aircraft were made available for the training purposes of this group. Two pilots from Air Group 92 were lost due to operational accidents. CASU(F) 15 painted the interior of all Quonsets assigned to them and equipped all Air Group and Squadron offices with furniture, tables, desks, chairs, and racks for gear. All equipment was built in the CASU carpenter shop.

CASU(F) 15 also had to eat. During July, 997,080 pounds of bread were produced. Plans called for the production of doughnuts for regular issue in addition to normal bread production. Construction of the doughnut shop was in progress. Construction was a constant at NAB Kobler. In July alone, the Construction Battalions completed the G-7 dispensary along with general maintenance of housing and operational facilities. At Kobler

Field, progress was made on enlargement of the terminal apron and the Rocket Assembly Shed was completed.

F4U-4 with tail number 40 and R designation on fuselage at Kobler Field, Saipan

B-17 Bomber at Lunken Field, Cincinnati, OH, September 09, 2012

Airplanes were the other constant—takeoffs and landings, and maintenance to keep them flying. The aircraft everyone seemed to be talking about was the B-29 bomber.

B-24 Liberator
Photo courtesy of U.S. Museum of the Air Force

While the B-17 and B-24 were workhorses, they didn't have the range to reach Japan. The B-29, also known as the Superfortress, was the first pressurized heavy bomber. This was a huge deal as pilots in other large bombers had to deal with the elements—without electric flying suits, gloves, and boots pilots would easily get frostbite at high altitudes. Designed as a replacement for the B-17, it contained fully automated gun turrets remotely controlled by crew members with a periscope sight and the largest radial engines of the time. They had a maximum range of 4100 miles and a wingspan of over 142 feet. The performance of the new B-29s was admirable despite some engine issues. Their firepower, speed, and general superiority had so far been too much for most Japanese fighters and ack-ack crews. B-29 losses had been as low as one in a 200-plane raid, compared with losses of nearly four in every 200-bomber sweep in the European and Mediterranean theaters in 1944.

B-29 taken at Ellsworth AFB by the author in 2006

One former serviceman recalled being assigned to the 819th Bombardment Squadron of the 30th Air Group on Saipan, flying out of Kobler Field. "Our squadron had its own mess hall and an outdoor movie theater." Prior to that assignment, he found himself not too far away on Guam:

> "They were unloading bombs and stuff for the air fields, the B-29, so we went down there and unloaded 500 pound bombs. They unload 500 pound bombs three at a time. They have hooks that hook into them and raise them out and put them in a truck and take them to the airfield.

"No pressure or stress, no, I don't think so, and I tell you why I think this. Maybe because of being young or something...you gotta remember that most of the kids were raised during the Depression. You know, we didn't have a lot and you know most of the time I didn't have a lot of food either, so there was pressure and stress like that, but I don't think it ever bothered me. I think the pressure and the stress might have been from maybe the long hours that you might have to be on duty."

B-29s carried out 3200 mile over-water flights from the Marianas to Japan. In addition to carrying out bombing missions on areas such as war factories and industrial areas of Japan, their crews proved to be highly important components of military and naval intelligence. On-board cameras continually assessed bomb damage, located new targets, spotted anti-aircraft emplacements, and reported the whereabouts of the Japanese air force. One of the main problems for B-29 crews was recognizing the ships below them. They usually cruised at 4000-8000 feet, the most economical altitude. This allowed them to burn some of their heavy fuel before climbing to their daylight bombing altitude of 16,000 to 19,000 feet. B-29s didn't attack ship targets and they could not circle for a better look.

P-51 Mustang at Lunken Airport, Cincinnati, Ohio in 2013

They usually maintained their course at about 240 mph and had to depend on a quick, sidelong glance downward. Proficiency in high-altitude ship recognition, knowledge of formations, and hull shapes was key.

During bombing runs, P-51 Mustangs, many of which were based on Iwo Jima, screened the B-29s and stayed close to the bomber formation.

While the CASU serviced aircraft day and night, there were some men who would not go to the air strip when planes landed after a mission. Even though the men at the fields were not in combat, some of them were greeted with horrible sights in returning bombers hit by enemy fire. The trauma was nearly too much for some young men to bear and they would not go back after that.

Chapter 12 – NAB Kobler

Larry, Black (Blackie), and Murray in front of a PBY-5A at Kobler Field

Larry Eckhoff in front of a B-17 bomber at Kobler

By August, 1945, the Fifth Military Police Battalion was *still* engaged in offensive operations to destroy or capture the remaining hostile military and civilian Japanese on Saipan. There were 31 Officers and 513 men at NAB Kobler and Larry received a promotion. As he was "qualified in all respects as required by current BuPers instructions" effective August 1, his rate was changed from AMMI 3/C to AMMI 2/C (T) to fill a vacant position.

The new air terminal at NAB Kobler, occupied shortly after August 1, was cleaner and provided more comfort for passengers. A new 3000 man laundry was put into operation. While CASU(F) 15 was servicing air groups and maintaining aircraft, they also installed tie down posts in Kobler revetments to secure 120 aircraft against Typhoon season storms. In July, many planes were sent to Saipan for safety when typhoons threatened Okinawa.

Bigger things were happening nearby on Tinian. On August 6, 1945 the B-29 Enola Gay took off from North Field, Tinian for Hiroshima, Japan carrying an atomic bomb. An estimated 70,000 Japanese were killed and thousands wounded. Eventually more than 100,000 died. Years later, Larry looked at Saipan on a world globe and saw how close Tinian was to where he was stationed. He said he didn't realize he was that close to the island where the bomb was. The Enola Gay normally held about eight bombs but had to be retrofitted—parts of the bay removed and the tunnel where the crew crawled through above it modified—just to fit one A-bomb. A serviceman on one of the Mariana Islands recalled:

Chapter 12 – NAB Kobler

"...when we heard about that bomb, what it did, we weren't happy, we were terrified. Because our thought was then, my, God, do they have one too? We saw that bomb in *Yank* magazine...we heard what it did, we heard the reports on the radio on what it did, and saw what it did. You can't imagine how terrified we were."

"August 9-10...Superfortresses based in the Marianas kept up their methodical pounding of prime Jap targets. B-29s of Lt. Gen. James H. Doolittle's Eighth Air Force also arrived at Okinawa to bring operations so close to Japan that they could carry full loads of 10 tons of bombs."

The Air Defense Command conducted two air raid alert drills for Saipan and Tinian and on August 13-14 conducted exercises testing plans for the defense of Saipan and Tinian against a large scale air raid. Then, President Truman announced that Japan accepted surrender terms. The news was announced to all hands on August 15. The following day, Ronald T. Lyman, Jr. (A)L USNR, reported aboard for duty as the new Commanding Officer of CASU(F) 15. Work on Base Development continued. Progress was made on a new mess hall as well as ten 20x56 quonset huts used as living quarters in the Kobler Camp Area.

Fugitive Japanese made every effort to remain in hiding in the most inaccessible areas of the island. On one occasion, they exchanged fire with a Marine ambush which had located a bivouac. However, there were no indications of an offensive spirit, opening fire only when trapped. Some fugitives possessed small quantities of rifles and hand grenades and were inclined to use them rather than be captured.

On August 16, a ten day surrender campaign was inaugurated to replace the combat patrols. Four mobile broadcast teams were organized, three operating on land and one at sea, designed to reach the overhanging cliffs along the east coast. They conducted intensive day and night broadcast activities. In addition, fifty thousand leaflets were scattered over the island in an attempt to reach every fugitive. The cooperation of the

Chapter 12 – NAB Kobler

Japanese POWs was enlisted in making these broadcasts and in contacting holdouts directly. The broadcasts were discontinued on August 25, when it was decided that sufficient notice had been given to all those continuing to resist.

There was a substantial increase in the number who surrendered—127 military and 18 civilians—mostly as a result of the ending of hostilities. Many fugitives readily believed the broadcasts and leaflets announcing the Japanese surrender and were relieved that they could honorably end their jungle life. Those remaining at large were relatively few although they remained a nuisance and were capable of minor acts of sabotage and resistance. They were divided into small disorganized groups unable to move about as freely as before. Food supplies and sources had steadily been eliminated so life was difficult for all but the most fanatical diehards. Some were in such inaccessible hiding places that they probably didn't know the war was over.

One memoir noted that about two weeks after the bombs were dropped on Japan "a typhoon hit Tinian, taking [some tents] and throwing [some to the ground]." Due to the proximity of the islands, the storm probably hit Saipan as well. Again, timing.

Bob Craven, Denver, Colorado (was also at NAS Clinton, OK) (AMM2/c) and Gene Proshold in camp

View of CASU(F) 47 at Marpi Point— CASU at the other end of the island

As a result of V-J day, many work projects on Saipan were cancelled because they were no longer necessary. During this transitional stage from war to peace, plans for the development of the base were undergoing considerable change and policies for future construction not well defined. A decrease in personnel due to men eligible for discharge was noticeable in Army and Navy construction units since then.

All requisitions for technical supplies were cancelled other than emergency requisitions and parts for grounded aircraft. The effect of the surrender of Japan had been felt in only one way, the release of personnel. Fifty-eight (58) enlisted men (not Larry), and seven officers were eligible under the demobilization program.

The Island Water System was producing 2,213,000 gallons per day. Water storage to date was 6,446,000 gallons. The rehabilitation of the eight million gallon Japanese storage tank was 97 percent complete and two wells were under construction.

The water situation in the Marianas was critical due to increased demands and the reduction in supply due to the dry season. The Island Commander, Saipan, had committed the island to supply 200,000 gallons daily for the Fleet, but due to leakage from the main storage tank he was only able to supply between 60,000 and 70,000 gallons. Facilities on Guam were taxed to the limit to supply Fleet requirements, which were first priority. They were also trying to supply Eniwetok from Guam. Temporary relief for the water situation was provided by forwarding the CALAMUS (a distilling ship) to Eniwetok and sending the SEVERN (a water tanker) to Manus from Saipan for a full load.

Fresh water for drinking, cooking, and bathing proved to be one of the most difficult supply issues for the Navy to remedy in the Pacific—comparable to providing food, fuel, and ammunition in large quantities. The only reliable natural supplies of fresh water in the vast stretches between Hawaii and the coast of China were found in the Philippines. Large fleet ships had water distillation equipment but hundreds of smaller ships had to be supplied with water for their crews as well as those they put ashore on undeveloped islands. Navy Service Squadron 10 set up fleet water ships, tankers, and water-making ships, moving them around the Pacific, often just behind the fighting lines held by the warships.

By this time there were 35 miles of paved roads and 103 miles of coral surfaced roads on Saipan. Improvement and paving of existing roads was being stressed to the point that it was mandatory for all roads to conform to good standard highway practice as to fill, grade, shoulders, and drainage. Seal coating was being increased.

Chapter 12 – NAB Kobler

All air fields were operationally complete with minor construction and maintenance on-going. Many work projects at various stages of completion were cancelled after V-J Day. At Kobler Field, paving of taxiways and aprons was 85 percent complete.

An island-wide housing survey revealed the following housing facilities on Saipan:

    Number of Mess halls – 232   Number of shower heads – 2978
    Number of latrine holes – 4998   Barracks - Number of prefabs – 750, Number of Quonsets – 785

At NAB Kobler, shower and latrine huts with sewer systems were finally in operation. A 250,000 square foot enlargement of the terminal apron at Kobler Field was completed.

Of course, the biting insects did not care about the cessation of hostilities. Saipan was almost continually sprayed with DDT. Beginning August 27, this mission was carried on through the end of the month, spraying every day that weather permitted.

Island Command was thrilled as the use of C-46 aircraft was started on regular flights. By the end of August, Naval Air Base Kobler showed a gradual decline in personnel with 25 officers and 421 men on site.

Indigenous people on the island just wanted to live their lives in peace.

A potter in a Saipan village   **Village woman carrying water and a child**

September 02, 1945 was officially designated V-J Day (Victory in Japan).

Chapter 12 – NAB Kobler

A Saipan village man

Villager with his cart and ox and Army Jeep

As always, mail was a big deal on Saipan. The Island Commander report for August showed 1037 pouches and sacks of mail dispatched and received from the Base Post Office. During down time, 16,000 took advantage of stage shows and about 75,000 attended movies at ten locations on the island. There was increased participation in basketball, table tennis, badminton, horseshoes, boxing, softball, and baseball. There were 215 recreation buildings across Saipan.

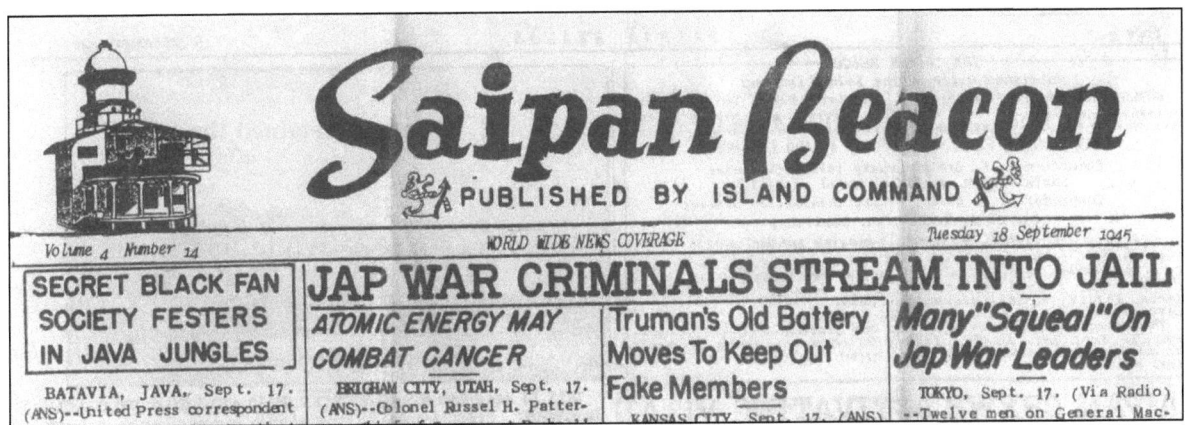
Masthead of the *Saipan Beacon*, Tuesday, 18 September, 1945

The *Saipan Beacon* was published daily by the Island Command. It provided "world wide news coverage" through the various national and international news services along with the Navy and Army news services and was distributed free to Navy, Marine, and Army personnel. The September 18, 1945 issue included reprints of the Blondie and Joe Palooka comics and big sports news. Baseball great Joe DiMaggio was medically discharged from the Army with stomach ulcers, and boxer Jack Dempsey, a Coast Guard Commander, was released from active duty.

Apparently Larry wasn't convinced that more than 51,000 sailors had been discharged from the Navy under the point system as of September 12. He crossed out the zeroes in the *Saipan Beacon* article.

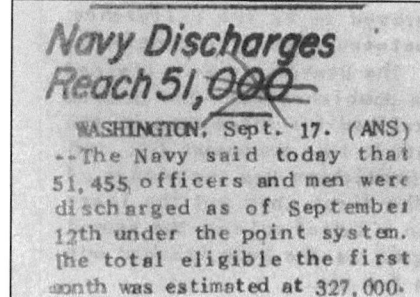

A full house at the Arvy Theater on Saipan; Joe E. Brown entertained the crowd

A photo in *Yank* showed a crowd being entertained on Saipan. While Joe E. Brown was a well known actor, often it was civilian groups entertaining servicemen. Civilians did audition for places with USO troupes, some of which could be touring islands in the South Pacific for six months. Some had official wool clothing tailored at Saks 5th Avenue in San Francisco but often the fancy uniforms were set aside due to the hot, humid conditions that would mildew stage clothing. Cosmetics were rare and often just melted. USO performers put on hundreds of thousands of shows during the war with a musical repertoire that ranged from popular show tunes, to classics and Gershwin—anything that would make kids feel like they were not so far from home.

The U.S. Army published the Western Pacific edition of their weekly newspaper called *Yank* on Saipan. The September 14, 1945 issue contained pictures and short stories from the Marianas including a feature about Japanese POWs in Manila. Most were surprised by the kind treatment they received and it was easy to tell how long they had been at the camp by "the amount of meat on their bones. The newest looked…awful." Many had been holding out in the hills north of Manila until malaria-ridden and starving, they gave up. Most were happy and relieved the war was over but were hesitant about going home as they felt disgraced.

Just because the war was "over" didn't mean everyone on the islands was safe and sound. The headline in the Saturday, October 6 *Saipan Beacon* read "Fifty-Knot Storm Lashes Saipan Thursday Night; Damage Moderate." A 50-knot tropical wind and rain storm hit Saipan uprooting tents and tearing off the tops of Quonset huts around the island.

Chapter 12 – NAB Kobler

Yank **photo of a Coca Cola plant on Saipan**

A tent containing a sleeping officer was blown over 100 feet. Hilltop and wide open installations suffered the most damage having received the full force of the gusts as did communication lines. About 15 percent of the teletype lines were out and 20 percent of the islands' telephone lines were inoperative.

As if that wasn't enough, *The Saipan Daily Target*, published by the Western Pacific Base Command, shouted out this headline "SIXTEEN KILLED, FOUR HURT AS HOME-BOUND B-29 CRASHES, EXPLODES AT KOBLER FIELD IN STORM."

Larry underlined "Kobler Field" and "All Shipping Halted" adding Mail!!

The article explained:

Chapter 12 – NAB Kobler

"Widespread Damage Caused As High Winds, Rain Sweep Island…Sixteen men were killed and four injured when a B-29 bomber crashed in front of the Air Terminal Building at Kobler Field at 0230 Friday morning. The plane had just taken off when a right engine went out, soon followed by a left motor. The plane exploded on striking the ground. Eleven crewmen and nine passengers were on their way to the States."

One can only imagine the range of emotions experienced by the personnel at Kobler, most awakened by the horrific crash of the substantial B-29 in the middle of the night.

The tropical rain storm damaged a small escort vessel on the reef and LCMs were standing by to take off the crew if necessary. Another small transport boat wrecked on the reef in Tanapag Bay and was later abandoned. All shipping in and out of the harbor was stopped. Between 0600 and 1000 that same morning, winds reached 55 miles per hour. Larry underlined the part about "blew down tents in all parts of the island." Anything that happened causing a delay in the mail was a blow to morale. Mail call occurred every day. Not everyone received letters every day, but sailors couldn't wait for mail call.

As November marked one year after leaving NAB Clinton and he was serving outside the continental limits of the United States, Larry became authorized to wear the American Campaign Ribbon and the Asia-Pacific Campaign ribbon. He was also eligible for a World War II Victory Medal. [None of these were ever found with his war memorabilia. It is not known whether he ever received them.]

Finally, Larry got that one piece of mail he had been waiting for.

Standard Transfer Orders US Pacific Fleet, Combat Aircraft Service Unit (F), 15

Transferred for discharge December 10, 1945 first available government transportation. These orders are RESTRICTED, their contents or the whereabouts of ships and personnel will not be divulged to unauthorized persons.

Chapter 13 – Going Home

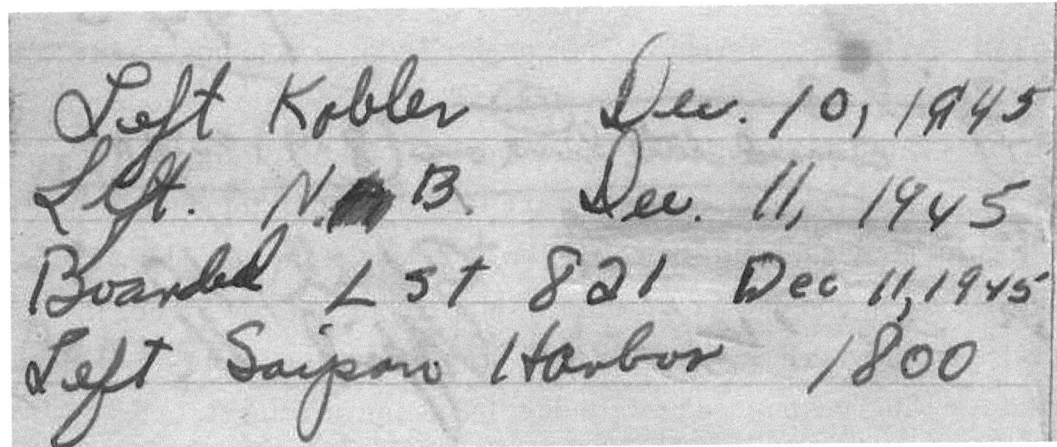

December 10, 1945 Left Kobler, Larry's Log

Although the peace treaty was signed in August, many remained in service for months. A point system helped determine who was discharged and when. Factors included a sailor's age, how long he had been overseas, and how big a family he had/familial dependencies. There may have been differences for reservists versus career men. All Larry knew was he finally received his orders—the best 20th birthday present he could ever have asked for—he was going home.

He reported to the naval base Staging Center Saipan at 0900 December 11, 1945 and his transportation order was verbally designated. The same day Larry boarded *LST 821*, finally leaving Saipan harbor at 1800 (6:00 p.m.).

The Sailing Report, List of Passengers, Report of Changes of *U.S.S. LST 821*, 11 December, 1945, date of sailing from Saipan, Mariana Islands to Pearl Harbor, Territory of Hawaii., page 4, included:

> "Eckhoff, Lawrence V. AMMI2c, USNR"

> "Received aboard as passenger, 12-11-1945; For transportation to nearest Rec. (Intake) Sta., Coast, USA, FFT to Personnel Separation Center"

> Ultimate destination: nearest receiving ship or station within the continental limits of the US FFT FSC – Great Lakes, Illinois

Landing Ship Tanks (LSTs), also known as Higgins boats in those days, saw extensive action in both the European and Pacific theatres. Built in Evansville, Indiana, *U.S.S. LST 821* was launched, October 27, 1944 and commissioned November 14, 1944 at New Orleans, Louisiana, with Lt. C. J. Rudine, USNR in command.

Chapter 13 – Going Home

Designed to carry military equipment and some personnel, the 328 foot long craft typically hauled cargo weighing between 1600 and 1900 tons, depending on the mission. They contained two Landing Craft Vehicle/Personnel (LCVP), a Landing Craft Tank (LCT), artillery, wheeled and tracked vehicles such as tanks, construction equipment, and other military supplies. Armament varied depending on retrofitting during the war. A forward ramp or elevator permitted vehicle access to the tank deck from the main deck. They were also outfitted with sectional pontoons carried on each side of the vessel amidships, used to build Rhino Barges or for use as causeways. Married to the bow ramp, the causeways enabled payloads "to be delivered ashore from deeper water or where a beachhead would not allow the vessel to be grounded forward after ballasting armament."

With a maximum speed of 12 knots, the usual crew complement of seven officers and 104 enlisted weren't going anywhere fast. Along with the designated cargo, there were troop accommodations for 16 officers and 147 enlisted men.

Island Queen II, Ohio River Steamboat	285 feet
LST 821	**328 feet**
U.S.S. Montour and U.S.S. Gosper, Attack Transports	455 feet
Edmund Fitzgerald, Great Lakes freighter which went down during a storm in Lake Superior in 1975	729 feet
Titanic	882 feet 9 inches
Queen Mary	1019 feet
QE II	1187 feet
Oasis of the Seas Royal Caribbean cruise ship (largest in 2009)	1187 feet

Comparison of the Length of LSTs and Attack Transports to Other Ships

LST 821 "was assigned to the Asiatic–Pacific theater and participated in the assault and occupation of Okinawa Gunto from April through June 1945. Following the war, she performed occupation duty in the Far East until early December 1945. *LST 821* earned one battle star for World War II service."

One sailor recalled a journey on an LST to Okinawa.

> "They're just a big hull, you know, and...just huge inside when they're empty." A team of engineers picked up from Saipan "stacked that LST full of steel drums of airplane gas...all the way to the front, and then they put a bulldozer in there...and some other piece of heavy equipment—right in the bow. We were to take it into Okinawa [where they were} supposed to have a place to unload it when we got there. But the Japs had done took it back away from them before we got there, so there we were. We went in to hit the beach before we found that out, I guess. Before you go in, about a hundred yards or so, you drop a steering anchor. It's on a winch on the steering of the ship. [It is used] to help get you back off of the beach...when you're ready to get back off. But [with] all that weight in there, we hit the

Chapter 13 – Going Home

bottom before we got a hundred feet or so from the beach, because the load was so heavy. The main deck was sticking out of the water about two and a half foot... Just thank the Lord that the Japs didn't get into that. That much airplane gas would have had everything in that harbor blown up and on fire."

The day Larry stepped off of the tropical island of Saipan and onto *LST 821*, it was a cold and windy 21 degrees in Cincinnati, Ohio—the coldest morning of the winter so far with snow flurries expected the next day.

The masthead of *The Cincinnati Times Star* shouted "Patton is Paralyzed Below Neck" and "Vertebra Broken and Another Dislocated in Crash Near Heidelberg". By page four, everyone knew there were only 12 shopping days until Christmas. What better way to celebrate Christmas and the end of the second World War but with a vacation trip to Florida? The Delta Air Lines ad read "Fly to Miami via Augusta-Jacksonville–8 ¾ hours-$47.15 plus tax." I'll bet many returning servicemen had no desire to travel for a long time.

Those wanting to spend time at home with their returning family members might spend $2.99 for a pair of comfy men's leather Romeo Slippers at Rollman's Department Store touted "The Happy Holiday Store of Cincinnati."

THE place to shop for returning soldiers and sailors near Larry's neighborhood was McDevitt's at Peebles Corner. "Choose his gift from a man's store" read the ad for Beau Brummell and Arrow ties $1.00 to $5.00. Don't forget the Interwoven socks (knit to size, reinforced toe and heel, no harsh irritating materials used) 45 cents to $1.00 and anything else the new civilian might need—Pajamas, Sweaters, Robes, Belts, Handkerchiefs, and Gloves. Make plans to see "State Fair" with Jeanne Crain at the Evanston Theatre if he gets home in time. Yes, life goes on.

Even in the light of the holiday season, the Op Ed pages ruminated about the possibilities of future wars. Should there be a standing army? How long should rationing continue? Frugality reigned in an ad for Nu-Way Dry Cleaners: "Attention! Service Men – Your uniform dyed blue, brown, or black and you'll have a high-quality civilian suit or overcoat."

One can only imagine why this story was all the way down on page 11.

Chapter 13 – Going Home

"500,000 Servicemen Home from Pacific"

"Tokyo (AP) – Gen. MacArthur reported today that approximately 500,000 servicemen have returned to the United States from the Pacific since Japan's surrender."

"MacArthur, in a statement, commended all echelons of his command 'for the efficient and expeditious manner in which the readjustment program has been carried on...'"

"The statement asserted that 'despite many obstacles incident to the rolling up of far-flung bases in the Pacific and to the redeployment of shipping' the Pacific theater increased numbers returning to the U. S. from a 'feeble 6,000 during June to a figure of 341,104' in November."

"MacArthur requested units under his command continue to 'exert all efforts' to insure return of eligible servicemen 'with the least possible delay and upon the most equitable basis.'"

Perhaps the most poignant story occurred right in Larry's own neighborhood.

"Patrolman Charles Frick asked fellow officers Monday to aid him in search for 'Sarge,' an eight-month old Cocker Spaniel which disappeared Sunday from his home, 1936 Clarion Avenue, Evanston. Frick obtained the dog as a present for his son, Charles Jr., who has been in the maritime service. The patrolman bought Sarge to replace his son's dog that was killed. Charles Jr. has never seen 'Sarge', Young Frick has seen service in all seas and is now returning from China. Frick left the dog out Sunday for a romp and he failed to return."

Sports were not overlooked in the December 10 issue of *The Cincinnati Post* with the biggest news happening in the world of tennis.

"Riggs Wins Pro Title"

Los Angeles, Dec. 10 (UP) " Bobby Riggs was world professional hard court tennis champion today after defeating Don Budge, 9-11, 6-3, 6-2, 6-0. The two Los Angeles professionals battled for more than two hours yesterday. Budge, took time out during the game to have a cramp in his right hand massaged." "Budge eliminated veteran William Tilden in the semifinals yesterday. Riggs got into the finals by beating Fred Perry. Tilden, at 52, won the consolation round yesterday by downing Perry 4-6, 6-3, 7-5."

On Thursday, December 20, 1945, Larry arrived at the International Date Line. There would be no initiations on this journey.

According to his log, the next day, Friday, December 21, 1945 the VE-Steamer Bay, took aboard an appendix case from his ship. It took 20 hours for aid to reach them.

The same day Larry wrote that entry in his log, news agencies around the world reported that General George S. Patton died of the injuries he incurred in the car crash and in Philadelphia, Gimbel Brothers department store "became the first department store to demonstrate a television set to the public; in three weeks, over 25,000 went to see it." Larry spent Christmas Day on board *LST 821* drawing ever closer to Hawaii.

Chapter 13 – Going Home

Though they were still in the tropics, winter weather in the Pacific could be just as unpredictable as any other time of year. One sailor on an LST mused about the weather conditions while docked at Okinawa during the U.S. invasion.

> "Them old LSTs weren't fit to ride a storm in. We were in Okinawa...after the invasion was about over—just sitting there—and one of these typhoons was coming up late one evening just before dark...we were sitting there empty [having already unloaded everything]. LSTs are flat on the bottom, so they can go in and hit the beach. [They are] just like a tub sitting in the water when they're empty. ...The winds got so strong, the ships got to dragging anchor on the bottom, and they...started bumping together. So they made us head out to sea into that storm in that old LST. Man, I'm telling you [I'm glad we] made it. Some of them didn't. They guesstimated the swells to be 75 foot high. That's a pretty good-sized wave, ain't it? And them old LSTs, they ain't made like a ship on the bow. They're round...and when they hit one of them big swells, you'll stand on your head if you don't grab something...And then they'll stop for a few seconds and then raise up, and then that swell would run out from under it, and it falls and hits the bottom. Man, I'm telling you, jars your teeth... a heck of a ride."

Sleeping racks in *LST 325*-four per row, three rows on each side-24 in the compartment

Chapter 13 – Going Home

Larry's log counted the days spent on *LST 821* from December 12 to 26, 1945. Finally, at 8:00 a.m. on December 26, they arrived at Pearl Harbor.

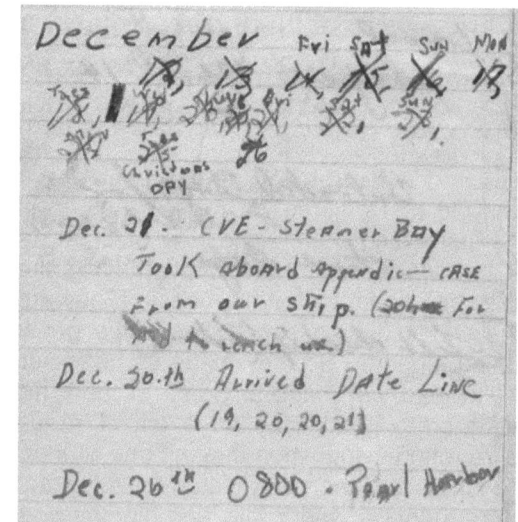

"Eckhoff, Lawrence V. AMMI2c, USNR"

"Disembarked passenger [U.S.S. LST 821], 12-27-1945; Transferred to Rec. Sta. Pearl Harbor, T.H. FFT to West Coast U.S.A."

Larry's log states:

Dec. 27th (1945) 10:30 A.M. – Left ship and came aboard "The Receiving Ship" at "Mauna Loa Ridge."

Met all the guys from the other drafts at Camp Calhoun, Saipan.

Physical Examination

Bunk Assignment

10:30-1530

Stateside Gyp Joint

Beer Every Day

Liberty Every Other Day

Muster Twice a Day

All Satisfactory

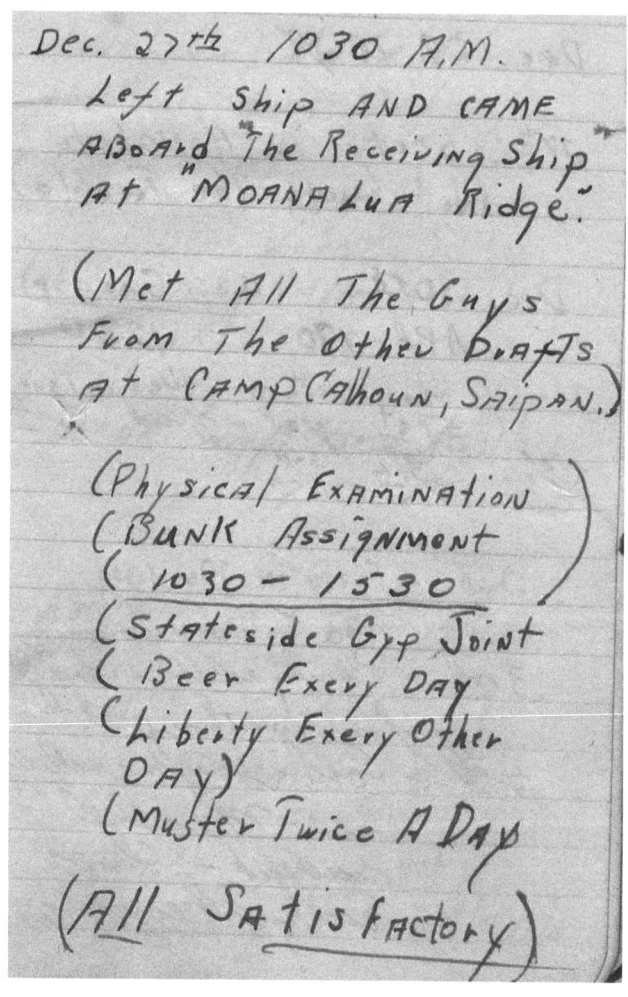

Chapter 13 – Going Home

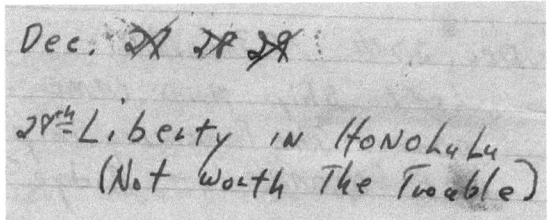

December 28, 1945 Liberty in Honolulu, Hawaii on the island of Oahu

"Not worth the trouble" – Lots of bars, few beer joints, shooting galleries and arcades all over, novelty and tattooing shops, large dept. stores too

...and no, sailor Larry did NOT go home with a tattoo.

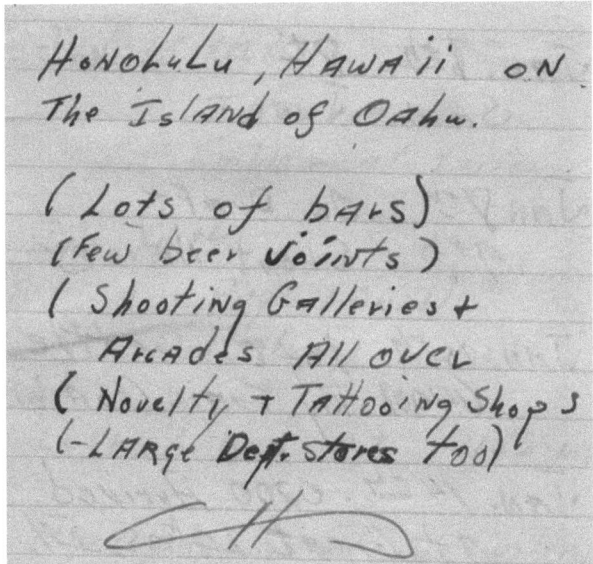

At 12:30 p.m. on December 30, 1945, Larry boarded the *U.S.S. Gosper* (APA-170) for the rest of the sailing voyage to the U.S. mainland. Though Larry did not seem particularly enamored with the layover in Hawaii, he was probably thrilled to finally board the ship that would take him to the continental United States.

The *U.S.S. Gosper*, designation APA-170, was an attack transport similar to the *U.S.S. Montour*. Commissioned in November, 1944, the *Gosper* carried out two logistics voyages to Pearl Harbor, arriving there the second time in late February, 1945. Prior to the Okinawa invasion, the ship was equipped as a casualty evacuation transport, furnished with operating rooms and other hospital facilities. Five days after the initial assault there in April, the *Gosper* began taking on casualties, caring for them for 11 days, then transporting them to the Naval Hospital at Guam. During her first day near Okinawa, the ship was almost constantly under suicide (kamikaze) attack as the Japanese tried desperately to stop the invasion. The *Gosper* shot down at least one attacker that day, while transports *Hobos Victory* and *Logan Victory* and *LST 4W* were sunk. In May, 1945 the ship returned to Okinawa with over 1000 reserve troops from Saipan, remaining nearby until mid-July, caring for casualties and fighting off the never ending Japanese air raids before returning to San Francisco for repairs.

Chapter 13 – Going Home

U.S.S. Gosper **image courtesy of Dept. of Navy, Naval Historical Center**

Following a three month assignment to pick up (from Manila in the Philippines) and treat a large group of former American, British, and Canadian servicemen who had been prisoners of war on Japanese-held islands, some since 1941, and return them to Seattle, the *Gosper* ended up in Hawaii carrying out two voyages under Operation "Magic Carpet", returning veterans, including Larry, from the Pacific theater to the West Coast. Unlike the smaller LSTs, the 455 foot *Gosper* could accommodate 80 officers and 1440 enlisted men.

While Larry relaxed on board the *Gosper*, the New Years Day *Cincinnati Post* celebrated local soldiers in their weekly column listing local men and their home addresses who had been discharged from the Army at Camp Atterbury, Indiana and Indiantown Gap, Pennsylvania. They also noted the following schedule at some local USO centers:

Tuesday, Jan. 1

DoNut Center—Buffet lunch served all day.

Fenwick Lounge—Refreshments served all day.

Y.W.C.A.—Open house all day and evening, refreshments, dancing.

Y.M.C.A.—Open house all day and evening, refreshments, dancing.

Jewish Center-Y.M.C.A.—Read your favorite magazine, listen to your favorite radio program.

Chapter 13 – Going Home

Another *Post* article hailed the 78,323 veterans enrolled in 539 colleges and universities across the country as of November 1, 1945.

> "According to Dr. Raymond Walters, University of Cincinnati president and statistician on higher education…the enrollment [is] the 'first influx of veteran students,' those discharged before last October 1 (1945). He believes an equal number or more may be seeking midyear admission in February, now that overseas troops are being transported home at the rate of 600,000 a month."

There was really big news for folks making due with worn out soles on their shoes. Most of the sole and upper leather that had been rationed for creation of service shoes and for other military uses would finally be going into the normal production of civilian footwear. *The Post* reported that "Plenty of shoes in all sizes and styles should be available early in 1946, according to the Civilian Production Administration. Production estimates call for approximately 550,000,000 pairs during the year—the largest U. S. production in history."

Shoe manufacturing wasn't the only long awaited production item. The Studebaker Corporation announced the first passenger car shipments since January 1942 when assembly was suspended to enable concentration on military goods such as vehicles and aircraft engines.

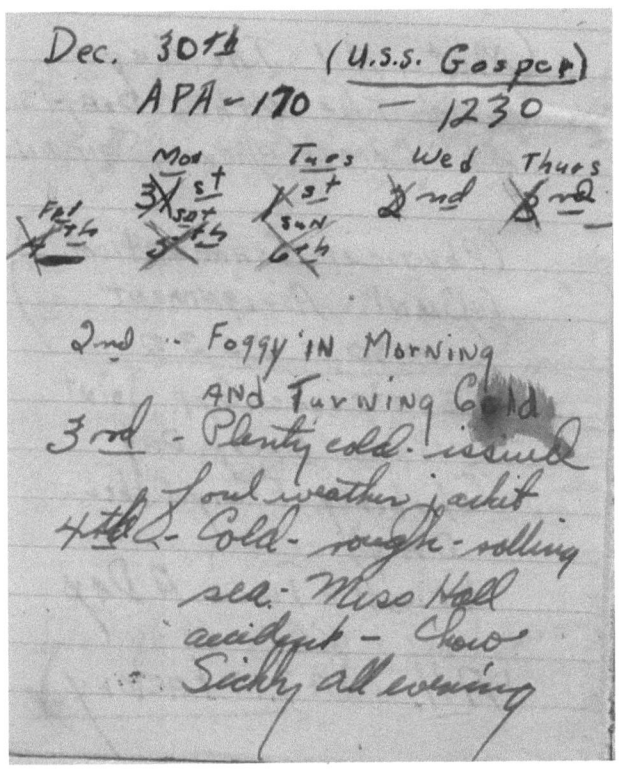

Larry was still crossing off the days. January 2, 1946 dawned foggy and it was turning cold. After months in the tropics, the change in temperature would take some getting used to.

January 3, 1946 – "Plenty cold-issued foul weather jacket"

January 4, 1946 – "Cold, rough, rolling sea-Mess Hall accident-chow"

"Sickly all evening"

Chapter 13 – Going Home

Finally, at 2:30 in the afternoon on Sunday, January 6, 1946, the *U.S.S. Gosper* pulled into port at Seattle, Washington. Larry slowly walked down the gangplank with his gear and stepped onto firm ground in the United States for the first time in almost a year.

Sailors debarking had three days liberty in Seattle until east bound transportation became available. The next day Larry visited with his friend June. The following day, January 8, he was listed as "On Draft" and spent more time with June. Living across the country in Ohio, this was probably the last time he saw June and her family. The next day he was on "Short Notice" travel status—ready to travel at any time.

At 2:00 p.m. on January 10, 1946, Larry boarded a train ("coach") in Seattle to begin the last leg of his journey as a sailor. Four and a half days later, at two o'clock in the morning, he arrived back at the Great Lakes Naval Training Station in Illinois where it all began. At the Great Lakes USN Personnel Separation Center he began the tasks of processing for discharge.

January 14, 1946

1000 – 1100 Physical Examination

1300 – 1400 Railroad Fare (lecture)

1500 – 1630 Chaplain, Insurance (lecture)

At the time of his honorable discharge, Larry was rated as an Aviation Machinist Mate Instruments, S2/C (T) V6_USNR. He received a final paycheck of $165.28 and a Travel allowance of $16.50.

Chapter 13 – Going Home

January 15, 1846

Interviews

Emblem at tailor

January 16, 1946

Pay (final)

Railroad ticket

Just before noon on January 16, Larry left Great Lakes on a train headed to Cincinnati. According to *The Cincinnati Union Terminal Company, Arrival and Departure of Trains* schedule effective Sunday, December 2, 1945, the most likely train home was the New York Central System #408 from Chicago via St. Louis, Peoria, and Indianapolis, arriving at Union Terminal at 9:25 p.m.

New York Central System Daily Arrivals at Cincinnati Union Terminal

Some nine and a half hours after leaving Chicago, Larry arrived at the train station in Cincinnati. It is unknown whether anyone knew he was coming or how he got from Union Terminal to his home in Evanston.

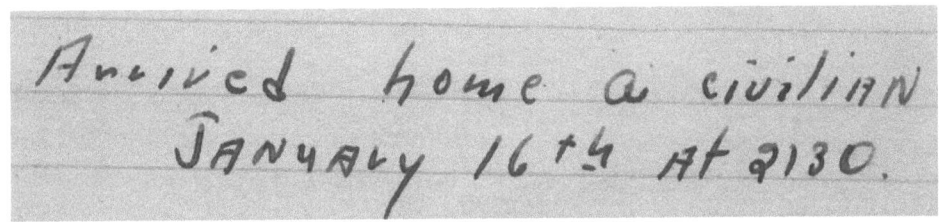

Larry's last traveling log entry January 16, 1946 at 9:30 p.m.—a civilian again

Chapter 13 – Going Home

Many families still had service flags hanging in their front windows. In the Army, blue flags meant the soldier made it home. Gold flags indicated the worst. Neighbors would go by and wave, and they would holler a greeting or update everyone on news from other neighbors or family members.

While Larry was back home, he still had a few post-enlistment items to take care of as his To Do list indicated.

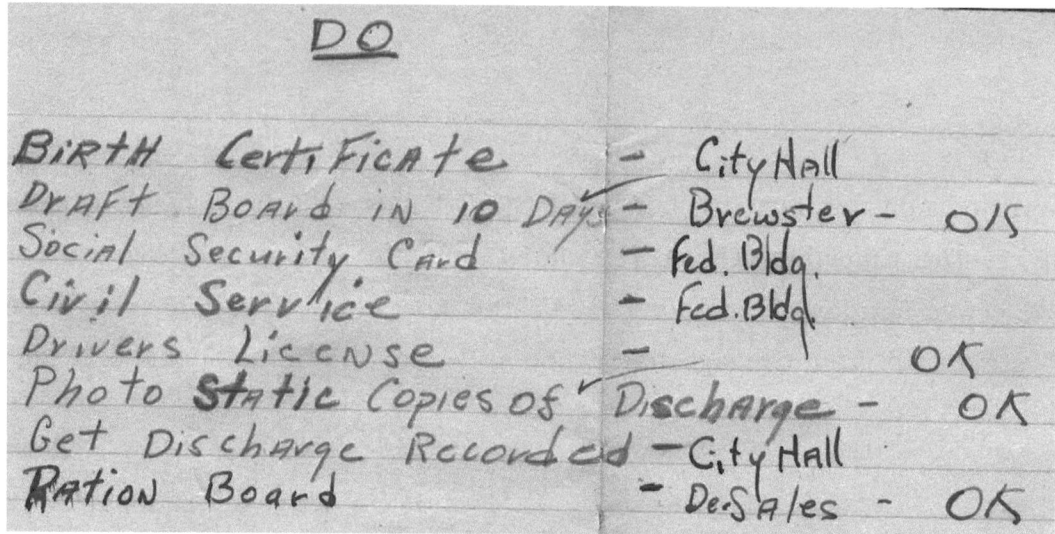

Larry's Post-Discharge To Do List from his log book

Larry served in the U.S. Naval Reserve for two years, five months, and 18 days. It is interesting to note that men serving less than 18 months were eligible to be recalled into service during the Korean Conflict.

Larry's Honorable Discharge Button

He had an Honorable Discharge 4.0 conduct rating but for some reason was not recommended for a Good Conduct Medal. He was however recommended for reenlistment. He received his Honorable Service lapel button, honorable discharge button, honorable discharge emblem, and a certificate of satisfactory service.

Chapter 13 – Going Home

Like so many others, Larry was initially undecided as to what to do when he was discharged. Taking advantage of his educational benefits as a veteran, he registered at Xavier University in February, taking a class during the Spring and Summer semesters. Apparently not finding what he was looking for at Xavier, he enrolled at New York Technical Institute in Cincinnati for a year of training from August 1948 until August 1949.

At some point, he and another man co-owned Highland Radio Center service shop until they sold the business in October 1950 to another veteran—a former Prisoner of War. Larry then started Larry's TV Service, taking advantage of the growing interest in television, working out of the family home in Evanston. Eventually he went to work for General Electric where he remained until retiring some 35 years later.

Personally, though Larry was engaged for a time, he remained a bachelor until 1957. Eleven years after returning home from the war, he married Marilyn Koenig, a girl from down the street who grew up playing with his younger siblings. Together they raised three children—the author being the eldest.

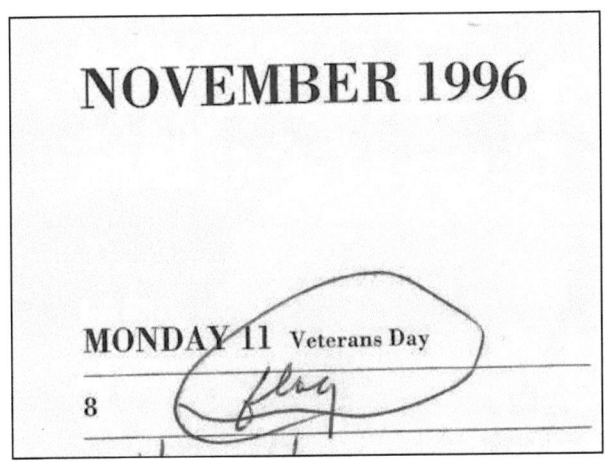

Part of a page from Larry's daily calendar book, November 11, 1996 and his flag flying proudly outside his home

Though he never talked about the war, Larry had a white flag pole in front of his modest Tudor-style home and flew the American flag every day, raising it in the morning and lowering, and properly folding it, each evening. However, the note on a plain white page in a pocket calendar found in a drawer made it clear that it was especially important to fly the flag on Veterans' Day.

Afterward

World War II was fought by 57 Allied and Axis countries with 15 million military personnel killed or missing in action during the conflicts. More than 292,000 Americans were killed, three of them classmates of Larry's at Purcell High School, and more than 1.7 million were physically affected by injuries. The nearly 671,000 wounded Americans was more than three times as many as in World War I.

Countless others experienced post traumatic stress disorder (PTSD), though this term did not come into use until the Vietnam War two decades later. An estimated 30 million civilian deaths were the result of bombings, starvation, and murder.

Despite the numerous casualties involved directly with retaking the Pacific islands, most were as a result of the harsh conditions experienced by members of all service groups. Accidents, breakdowns, disease, and various wounds caused the loss of about 50 percent of the original troops in the South Pacific.

One sailor recalled some years later that "...[being in the Navy during World War II] made me appreciate things a lot more. You didn't take everything for granted. You had to work for what you got. And I developed that in the Navy."

Printed by Libri Plureos GmbH in Hamburg, Germany